Cleveland Chapter of the
American Institute of Architects
1890–1990

GUIDE TO
CLEVELAND ARCHITECTURE

Published by The Cleveland Chapter
of the American Institute of Architects
Carpenter Reserve Printing,
Cleveland, Ohio.

Produced by Publishing Solutions, Inc.,
a pre-press technology firm of Akron,
Ohio. This book was produced on a
Macintosh IIci computer and output
to a Varityper 4300 imagesetter.

*Photographer Thomas
Eiben captures the
dynamic face of
change in downtown
Cleveland as the
massive Society Center
Building rises to
the left of the Terminal
Tower.*

Guide to
Cleveland Architecture

Cleveland Chapter, American Institute of Architects

Cleveland Chapter of the
American Institute of Architects

GUIDE TO
CLEVELAND ARCHITECTURE

Text by Members of the Cleveland Chapter of
the American Institute of Architects and distinguished guest authors.

Photographs by Thomas Eiben, Eric Hanson,
Jennie Jones, Bill Schuemann, Al Teufen and
David Thum.

Maps and drawings by Mark Gilles and Tony Hiti
assisted by Scott Wade and Gary Ogrocki.

General Supervision provided by The Commitee
on Historic Resources, chaired by Richard
VanPetten AIA, 1984-1988, Clyde A. Patterson,
Jr. AIA 1989-90.

Managing Editor, Art Direction, Robert Kalin.

Senior Editor, Robert C. Gaede FAIA.

Table of Contents

Introduction

Credit Lists

Original Task Force
Robert C. Gaede FAIA
William E. Samstag
Elizabeth Waters

AIA Committee on Historic Resources
Nino Arsena AIA
Stephen K. Birch AIA
Joseph Ceruti AIA
Amir H. Farzaneh
Robert C. Gaede FAIA
Robert A. Green AIA
Alfred W. Harris AIA
Robert M. McGaw AIA

Kevin M. Morand AIA
Clyde A. Patterson AIA
Edward A. Reich
Richard Van Petten AIA
Wallace G. Teare FAIA
William T. Wells AIA
Robert L. Weygandt

Authors
Stephen K. Birch AIA
Robert Bond
Melanie Boyd
Joseph Ceruti AIA
John D. Cimperman
Malcolm M. Cutting AIA
Robert C. Gaede FAIA
Victoria George
Kenneth Goldberg
Clay Herrick
James D. Herman AIA
Robert M. McGaw AIA
Steven McQuillin
Hunter Morrison

Holly Rarick Witchey
Edward A. Reich
Drew Rolik
Wilma Salisbury
William E. Samstag
David L. Sturgeon
Paul J. Volpe AIA
Elizabeth Waters
Robert L. Weygandt
Keith E. White AIA
Thomas Yablonsky
Pen M. Zimmerman
Richard L. Zimmerman

Advisors
Philip Heintzelman
Robert F. Bann
James T. Barbero
Tim Barrett
Robert Keiser

Funding Committee
William T. Wells AIA
Joseph Ceruti AIA
Jennie Jones
Robert C. Gaede FAIA

Researcher
Donald J. Petit

Typist
Tina M. Smith

Critics and Reviewers
Eric Johannesen
Holly Rarick Witchey
Steven McQuillin
Robert Keiser

Presidents of The Cleveland Chapter, AIA
Fred H. Holman, Jr. AIA 1988
Todd W. Schmidt AIA 1989
Keith E. White AIA 1990

Staff of The Cleveland Chapter, AIA
Dianne Hart, Executive Director

Acknowledgement

The *AIA Guide To Cleveland Architecture* would not have been possible without the support of a broad based group of Cleveland individuals and companies who answered our appeals from time to time. We of the *Guide* and Cleveland Chapter of the American Institute of Architects profoundly thank each contributor, making the preparation and publication of the Guide possible.

The following must be recognized:

Special Recognition
BP America
The George Gund Foundation

Major Donors
AIA College of Fellows
TRW Foundation
The Cyrus Eaton Foundation
Forest City Enterprises
Jones, Day, Reavis and Pogue
Squire, Sanders and Dempsey
City Blue Printing
Urban Design Center, Northeastern Ohio
Huntington National Bank
Jacobs, Visconsi & Jacobs Co.

Benefactors
Greater Cleveland Growth Association
Cleveland Restoration Society
East Ohio Gas Company
The Krill Company Inc.
Pekoc Hardware Co.
University Circle, Inc.
Construction Industry Service Program
Barber & Hoffman Inc.
Sam W. Emerson Company
The Thomas Brick Co.
Stouffer Corporation
Albert M. Higley Inc.
A.S.I.D., Cleveland Chapter
Central Cadillac

Supporters
Jennings and Churella
Charles E. McKnight
Northeast Ohio Masonry
The Brewer-Garrett Co.
Thomas A. Jorgensen
Western Reserve Architectural Historians

Acknowledgement – Cont'd

The AIA Guide to Cleveland Architecture is an amalgam of many authors, reviewers and participants. With such a diversity of contributors, the control of material, usage of sources and certainty of fact is all but impossible, even though attempted. Much information was gathered on site, via drawings or in conversations with owners and building managers.

Thus, no bibliography is offered. It is hoped that this fact will not materially diminish the reader's confidence in this document nor offend in any way a previous author whose product may be cited without direct credit. Authors were asked to develop their text in original language even if a strong dependency existed with one or more of the established sources on Cleveland's architecture.

There is not way to cite every resource used, but it is only proper to acknowledge the following as having frequently served so well in the assemblage of our material:

> Richard N. Campen, *Architecture of the Western Reserve,* 1800-1900 (Cleveland, 1971); and *Outdoor Sculpture in Ohio,* (Chagrin Falls, 1980)
>
> Clay Herrick, Jr., *Cleveland Landmarks* (Cleveland, 1986)
>
> Eric Johannesen, *Cleveland Architecture,* 1876-1976 (Cleveland, 1979)
>
> Mary-Peale Schofield, *Landmark Architecture of Cleveland* (Cleveland, 1976)
>
> David O. Van Tassel and John J. Grabowski, *The Encyclopedia of Cleveland History* (Cleveland, 1987)

Reference to any structure mentioned in this text does not constitute an invitation to visit. Permission, especially in the case of private residences, hospitals, institutions, fire stations, banking halls, etc., should be obtained before-hand from owners, occupants, operators, etc..

Request for permission to copy should be forwarded to:
The Cleveland Chapter of the
American Institute of Architects
410 The Arcade,
Cleveland, Ohio 44114.

AIA Guide to Cleveland Architects
First Edition, copyright 1991 by
The Cleveland Chapter of the
American Institute of Architects
Cleveland, Ohio

About the Guide

The concept of producing a new guide to Cleveland Architecture emerged in 1987. It was hailed as an excellent way to celebrate the 100th Anniversary of the Cleveland Chapter of the American Institute of Architects. The guide was to be the product of many people, all interested in Cleveland's architectural heritage, and it would recognize the contributions of the several hundred architects, past and present, whose efforts have graced the streets of this great city.

Although there have been many books covering Cleveland's growth and development, and of the notable buildings along the way, the story stops in the 1970's. Much has happened since, and it is appropriate that the gap from those years to the present, be closed.

A task force of the Chapter's Committee on Historical Resources, with the full Committee's help, sketched out the general outline of the Guide during the period 1987/1988. The work was detailed in 1989.

This guide varies from many by presenting the city's characteristic qualities by specific building types and historic districts and neighborhoods. A short biography of notable architects is included, as is a glossary of terms. Hopefully, the user of this quide will find it informative and uncomplicated, and will sense that more than a listing of architectural treasures is offered – that it captures the spirit, form and future of the city as well.

The task of finding funds to complete this work prevailed throughout. Special credit and thanks to supporters is presented elsewhere. Additionally, of special mention is the invaluable contribution of the professional photographers as well as the many authors, advisors and helpers who worked to make the Guide a reality. To them we offer boundless thanks, and sincerely hope that their work will serve to elevate our understanding, and our feelings for our city for years to come.

Robert Gaede, FAIA
Senior Editor

Dedication

Wallace G. Teare FAIA

The compilation of this guide was underway when, in the early spring of 1989, one of it's strongest supporters, Wally Teare, FAIA. passed away. A highly respected member of the Cleveland Chapter, and its president from 1948-1949. At the time of his death, Wally was serving as senior advisor to the chapter. He was also a member of the Committee on Historic Resources and of the task force at work on the guide.

In appreciation for his many years of dedication to the profession, a special fund was established with the proceeds provided for the preparation of this Guide. With thanks to those who contributed, and with a special expression of appreciation to Wally Teare, this Guide is dedicated to him and to the selfless image he provided throughout his many years of service to the chapter and the community.

Cleveland Chapter
American Institute of Architects

1890-1990

In Retrospect

Founded in 1890, the Cleveland branch of the A.I.A. was first
known as the Architectural Club of Cleveland. As the group
increased in size, the organization affiliated with the American
Institute of Architects. From its inception, its membership was
dedicated to the task of advancing the standards of architectural
education and practice. The organization was instrumental in
establishing a state law requiring all Ohio architects to pass a
registration test. The A.I.A. designation after an architect's name
symbolizes a high level of education, commitment, professional
competence and integrity.

Over the years the Cleveland Chapter of the A.I.A. broadened
its community and professional interests. As early as 1914 the
organization was active in the passage of a city ordinance
establishing a city planning department. In 1924 its architects
contributed to the establishment of the Cleveland School of
Architecture, an accredited organization empowered to grant
architectural degrees to students who met its academic requirements. The program was later absorbed by Case Western Reserve
University.

During the decade of the 30's, many worked for the federal
government's Historic American Building Survey and participated
in the recording of our national heritage. The effort is intact today
and largely employs architectural students.

In the 1940's the Cleveland Chapter helped develop new concepts
in housing for the underprivileged. In subsequent years, chapter
members have been involved in many aspects of community
service from architectural boards of review to landmark
designation.

Today the Cleveland Chapter, a city resource of dynamic quality,
maintains offices in the old arcade and has a membership of over
400 architects.

Dianne Hart
Executive Director
Cleveland Chapter of the A.I.A.

President's Letter

The Cleveland Chapter of the American Institute of Architects is proud to present this new *Guide to Cleveland Architecture*. The work was conceived by the Cleveland Chapter of the Historic Resources Committee in 1987, in anticipation of the chapter's Centennial year in 1990.

Not since 1958 has the considerable task of assembling such a compendium been undertaken by the profession. I sincerely wish to thank Robert C. Gaede, FAIA, for his considerable effort, enthusiasm and perserverance in overseeing the assembly of the material presented herein.

Additionally, I wish to thank the members of the original task force: William T. Wells, Richard Van Petten, Clyde A. Patterson, William E. Samstag and Elizabeth Waters, all of whom have provided invaluable assistance. Dianne Hart, the Cleveland Chapter's Executive Director, and a host of writers and photo-graphers, listed elsewhere in *the guide*, have made major contribu-tions to making the new *Guide to Cleveland Architecture* a reality.

And I wish to thank those corporations, groups, organizations and individuals who, as in so many worthwhile projects, contrib-uted funds toward the completion of this project. They are listed elsewhere in the text, but this letter would not be complete without an expression of the Chapter's gratitude for their support, without which, this guide would not have been possible.

Sincerely,

Keith E. White, AIA
President, Cleveland Chapter
American Institute of Architects
November 1990

Cleveland's skyline, dominated for decades by the Terminal Tower, changed considerably in the 80's with the addition of the BP America Building and the chisel-shaped silver tower of One Cleveland Center. In 1990 a new "tallest structure" emerged – the Society Center tower to attest to Cleveland's ongoing revitalization.

Built Cleveland

Introduction

Cleveland's architecture is better known for its reflection of changes in architectural fashion over the years rather than for innovative style. In a more conservative or cautious way architects of the day tended to adopt established, well accepted architectural designs. The result being that, at a given point in time, Cleveland's architecture tended to reflect the end of a stylistic period, rather than its beginning. The city's most prominent structure, the Terminal Tower, is a case in point. Constructed in 1930, it represents the culmination of Beaux Arts composition at the end of the 20's.

The Terminal Tower, located in the Southwest quadrant of Public Square, was the city's tallest building and remained its most familiar landmark for sixty years.

Cleveland's earliest surviving building, Dunham Tavern (1832-1842) is, likewise, a very late example of a Federalist house, its wood clapboard siding and modest, vernacular, classical trim echoing a style that had faded from the Eastern Seaboard years earlier. Unfortunately, time has not been kind, and much of Cleveland's early architecture has been lost. Many of the great houses that once graced Euclid Avenue were torn down in the first half of the 20th Century. And, in the post World War II era, urban renewal and highway construction did away with a large number of fine old structures.

Cleveland's buildings represent the full range of types required to sustain a major, modern industrial city: factories, shops, restaurants, theaters, churches, single and multi-family dwellings, public works, bridges and public transport structures. Overall, the mixture provides a richness of texture that gives Cleveland its own special quality of urban robustness and suburban grace.

In this guide you will find a summary of the best and most important architectural works of Cleveland's past and present. For future generations this guide, hopefully, will provide insight into a constantly evolving urban community in the America of the late 20th century.

Theodore Anton Sande

Cleveland Neighborhoods

The West Side and Lakewood

The architecture of Greater Cleveland's West Side neighborhoods, outside of the historic areas of Ohio City, is most notable near the Lake Erie shore.

Starting in the City of Cleveland to the west of Edgewater Park at West Boulevard and Lake Avenue, gracious homes mostly constructed from the turn of the century to the Depression (1900-1929) line Edgewater, Lake, and Clifton Boulevards.

Elements of Colonial Revival, Tudor, Mission, and Georgian are prevalent. A few homes were influenced by Frank Lloyd Wright with the use of stucco, banded windows, large overhangs and hipped roofs.

This expression of affluence and waterfront living extends from the Edgewater neighborhood of Cleveland through Lakewood, Rocky River, and Bay Village. Areas of note include historic Clifton Park and the Gold Coast (see the driving tour, Section 20F, of the guide).

Clifton Park, a district located at the eastern bluffs of the Rocky River with Lake Erie to the north, was the home of prominent early 20th century Cleveland families – Glidden, Case and Jennings. The Case house in the 17800 block of Lake Avenue is of Colonial Revival style and was designed in 1905 by Cleveland architect George Hammond who planned the original campus of Kent State University. The subdivision's oldest house still standing is the Jennings House (1899), of Victorian style with half-timbered gables and corner battlemented towers. Other notable homes are the Glidden's "Franklyn Villa" 17840 Lake, and "Inglewood" 17869 Lake.

The Gold Coast, developed on the sites of earlier Lakefront estates similar to Bratenahl (on Cleveland's east side), was initiated by the conversion of the Lake Shore Hotel (1929) to apartments in 1954. Notable are Winton Place (1961), the Carlyle (1968), the Meridian (1971), and the Waterford (1978). The tall apartment towers are set back from Lake Avenue, some with the stone and brick remnants of 19th century estate fences and gates still evident. Winton Place, designed by Chicago architects Loebl, Schlossman and Bennett, best reflects the earlier garden estate setting with a 500 foot setback and with the building occupying only 6% of the site.

The development of lake-side luxury has extended into Rocky River with conversion of the Westlake Hotel in the 1980's and into Bay Village with clustering of contemporary townhouses, designed by architect Robert Corna, around the 19th century Lawrence Mansion at Cashelmara.

In Lakewood, an historic urban ethnic village was developed at the turn of the Century near the National Carbon Company at W. 117th and Madison. Called the "Birds Nest" with five streets named after birds, the area predates the streetcar and contains eight churches with gold domes and brick and stone bell towers.

On the city's far west edge is the Riverside area clustering comfortable vernacular revivals along Riverside Avenue following the edge of the Rocky River Valley.

Cleveland West and Southwest

Reference to the Historic District section will reveal the characteristics of the Ohio City area, the Tremont area and the Brooklyn Centre area. Surrounding these are extensive urban areas dotted with significant structures and sites. Among these is the West Boulevard area beginning at Lake Erie and extending south to Clinton Road. At Detroit Avenue West Boulevard passes the unique Cudell Tower, built (1917) to honor Cleveland architect Frank Cudell. It was designed by Cudell but carried out by architects, Dercum & Beer. The Tower is in a restorative process. At Lorain Avenue the familiar feature of St. Ignatius Roman Catholic Church's minaret pierces the sky. Along the way are broad tree lawns fronting comfortable residences of the 1910-1930 era.

West of Ohio City, Franklin Blvd. and Detroit Avenue run parallel, the former a residential avenue, the latter commercial. Here houses, apartments, churches and store buildings of the turn-of-the-century describe a prosperous developing city of that era. Of special note is the Gordon Square Arcade, Detroit Avenue at W. 65th Street, a three-story multi-purpose structure which has enjoyed a remarkable regeneration after decades of gradual disuse.

South along Pearl Road (W. 25th St.) lies Old Brooklyn in the vicinity of Pearl and Broadview Roads. A cluster of churches and commercial buildings at that point reflect the early 20th Century's styles up to the Art Deco. Of special note is the Ameritrust branch (once Cleveland Trust) on the N.E. corner of Broadview and Pearl. Built (1924) its limestone exterior, in the manner of an Italian Pallazzo, and richly detailed interior was the product of Antonio DiNardo for the firm of Hubbell & Benes.

Close by, on Memphis Avenue at W. 35th Street, stands perhaps the oldest home in the city, the Federal-styled Gates House (1820). To the north lies the Cleveland Zoo featuring a variety of structures unique to its purposes. Neighbor to the Zoo is the natural bowl known as Brookside Field No. 1 where legendary baseball games were played before gatherings of as many as 100,000.

Cleveland's Near East Side

Between Downtown and University Circle is a large slice of the city extending some three miles in an east-west direction and two-and-a-half north to south. This once densely-populated area, developed over the period 1875-1915, has experienced the full gamut of urban pressures of the past century, socially and economically. Residences vary widely in scale and quality; some commingle with industry. Commerce marched out the radial avenues from Downtown – St. Clair, Superior. Wade Park, Hough, Euclid, Prospect, Cedar, Central, Quincy and Woodland. For a few decades East 40th and E. 55th were prominent avenues featuring major churches and noteworthy residences. In the East 80's the blocks north of Euclid Avenue were filled with grand city houses in late Victorian and turn-of-the-century finery. Institutions flourished, only to wither, and apartments with pre-zoning freedom, in-filled the neighborhoods randomly.

Today, after decades of diminishment, this large area we refer to as Central (west of E. 55th St. and south of Euclid), Hough (east of E. 55th St. and north of Euclid) and Fairfax (east of E. 55th St. and south of Euclid), still offers architectural islands and discoveries. Among the churches in the central area may be cited St. John's African Methodist Episcopal at 2761 E. 40th St. The congregation, founded in 1838, was the city's first black church. Shiloh Baptist Church, a congregation founded in 1849, acquired B'nai Jeshurun Synagogue (1906) at 5500 Scovill Avenue in 1925. The large, stone-faced structure was designed by Harry Cone.

A singular building at the corner of Cedar Avenue and E. 46th Street was erected in 1911 to house the Phillis Wheatley Association, organized by Jane Edna Hunter to serve young black women from the South. Hubbell and Benes were architects of the nine-story brick structure with flared cornice.

In the Fairfax area, a center of black culture, Karamu House, founded by Russell and Rowena Jelliffe in 1915, moved to its present location at Quincy and E. 89th Street in 1949. The then "modern" styling of the theatre structure and community service building of 1959 was the work of Small, Smith, Reeb and Draz. The Hough area was the scene of Cleveland's most serious rioting and fires in the late 60's. The aftermath left the district conspicuously marked by empty lots and abandoned buildings. Considerable reinvestment followed with such public structures as Giddings Elementary School (1970), 2250 E. 71st Street, by Don Hisaka & Associates; Martin Luther King Jr. Magnet School (1973), 1651 E. 71st Street, by Madison & Madison; Hough Multi-Service Center (1973), 8555 Hough Avenue, by Madison & Madison and Hough Norwood Family Center (1974), 8300 Hough Avenue, by Flynn, Dalton & van Dijk.

Lexington Village (see Section 14) at E. 79th Street and Hough initiated a large revitalization of the area's housing stock.

Broadway

One of Cleveland's distinctive districts, this neighborhood, originally home to immigrant families from Eastern Europe, especially Poland and Czechoslovakia, served the burgeoning steel mills of the industrial valley. It was centered along Broadway, particularly at E. 55th Street, and along Fleet Avenue. Largely constructed between 1890 and 1920, the area is typified by modest frame residences in the vernacular styles of that period.

However, several churches and institutional structures stand out. Among these are St. Stanislaus Roman Catholic Church (see Warszawa Historic District), still dominant even without the two soaring spires blown down in a windstorm in 1911. St. John Nepomucene (1918), by William Jansen, stands as an entry landmark to Fleet Avenue at its connection with I-77. Our Lady of Lourdes (1891), is the visual centerpiece of the Broadway, E. 55th Street commercial core, and is identified by its single soaring spire.

The Bohemian National Home (See Section 4, Theatres and Auditoria) is located at 4939 Broadway. A few blocks to the south is the Hruby Conservatory (1917), architects Steffens and Steffens, a delicately detailed terra cotta and brick structure. Nearby at 3289 East 55th is a small but noteworthy example of the Art Deco, the Jednota Building (1932) Walsh, Katonka and Miller, Architects, (originally First Catholic Slovak Union). Serving as a very visible sentinel to the area from the north is the old Republic Steel Works Office (now L.T.V.), (1917), architect Walker & Weeks, a brick and terra cotta office slab with repetitive windows and severely functional aspect.

Glenville

On Cleveland's northeast side a large residential quarter, constructed over the period 1890-1920, enjoyed a proximity to Rockefeller Park, Lake Erie and the City's Wade Park area, now University Circle. Split north-south by E. 105th Street, the district consisted of many blocks of streets with vernacular single-family housing, ample front yards and tree lawns. A notable variation was the lively 3-4 story apartments along the east side of East Boulevard,

the bounding edge of Rockefeller Park, between E. 105th Street and Superior Avenues. Now in a local historic district, these structures, with stacked balconies, produce a unique aspect.

The area's earlier social composition is reflected in the very large (1922) Cory United Methodist Church, 1117 E. 105th Street, designed to be Anshe Emeth Congregation and Cleveland Jewish Center, by Albert Janowitz. At 10932 St. Clair Avenue stands the two-towered, St. Aloysius (1925), William Jansen, Architect, a brick and stone church of Beaux Arts concepts. Nearby, at E. 106th Street and St. Clair Avenue stands the Glenville Masonic Temple, (1923), by the Carter-Richards-Griffith Co. This dignified limestone structure uses Renaissance motifs in a restrained manner.

Along East Boulevard north of Superior and above the Cultural Gardens is an area of private residences of more substantial size and character. A similar area exists in the Wade Park-Ashbury Avenue zone between E. 108th and E. 115th Streets. Overall Glenville expresses the ideals of the residential developer of the early years of the 20th century as well as can be found in the city anywhere.

Collinwood
The Collinwood district has a distinct focus – the Five Points corner of St. Clair Avenue, East 152nd and Ivanhoe Avenue. An area bounded or pierced by once-busy rail lines, including a major yard of the New York Central System, the residential quarter was inevitably close by industrial plants and its inhabitants dependent thereon. The huge rail yard has recently been reduced to a few of its service structures, its trackage removed. Here is where the electric engines of the passenger trains serving Cleveland's Union Terminal, were substituted for the steam engines of the main line. Five Points, mainly occupied by commercial structures, has as its physical centerpiece the tower of Collinwood High School (1907) (1926), Architect, Walter McCornack, a large, flat-topped Neo Georgian piece. It was in Collinwood that a fire with serious loss of life occurred on 4 March 1908 at Lakeview Elementary School. The fire resulted in stricter building codes across the country. The door swing controversy is, apparently, a myth as the outswinging requirement was already in place. Collinwood Memorial School, 410 E. 152nd Street, was built next to the ruins in 1910. It was designed by Frank S. Barnum; an addition of 1917 by Walter R. McCornack.

Bratenahl
This distinctive village extends in a narrow band along the Lake Erie shore with I-90 serving as its other boundary. Only 552 acres in area, Bratenahl resulted when its residents refused to be incorporated into Cleveland in 1903. In the years 1890-1930, the community's heralded estates took form with an ultimate array of showpiece mansions designed by leading architects for many of Cleveland's leading families.

Among the Tudor and Georgian Revival villas may be found Gwinn (1908), the estate of William G. Mather, designed by Charles A. Platt. As much was expended on the gardens as the residence and these were the work of Warren Manning. The Hanna mansion (1909), a grand Tudor piece by McKim, Mead and White and neighboring Shoreby (1890), by Charles F. Schweinfurth, the summer home of Samuel Mather, will be centerpieces in a large development of residences and marina altogether called Newport. Previously two 12-story apartment buildings and a cluster of eight townhouses together called Bratenahl Place (1967), by Nicholas Satterlee and John Terence Kelly, had given the community extra visibility.

East Cleveland

This densly-built inner-city suburb on Cleveland's east side, sits astride the topographic slope of the Heights as it descends toward the city. Bisected by rail and by Euclid Avenue, East Cleveland comprises blocks of solid houses of the vernacular revivals of the period of 1895-1925. Commercial structures mix with apartments and churches along Euclid. A portion of Forest Hills Park is within the city – a fragment of John D. Rockefeller's estate. Several high-rise apartments are sited along Terrace Road and Superior Road, including the 26-story Crystal Tower (1964), Bertram Koslen for design, Ruth, Huddle, White and Howe for construction, and the 27-story Windsor Park Place (1963), Weinberg and Teare, Architects. Nela Park described in Section 13 (Industrial Buildings), resides in East Cleveland's N.E. corner and a portion of Lake View Cemetery in the S.W. corner. Of note is the large, sandstone First Presbyterian Church (1893), 16200 Euclid Avenue, by William Warren Sabin, dominated by its Gothic-Romanesque revival tower. Additions (1923) and (1962), the latter by Ward and Schneider, expanded the facility. At 14410 Terrace Road is Kirk Middle School (1930), a thoughtful interpretation of Georgian styling, done by Warner, McCornack and Mitchell. At the junction of Superior Avenue and the railroad bridge was once the substantial New York Central and Nickel Plate RR Passenger Station (1930), where Cleveland's east-siders were able to entrain for New York City. The Station was demolished in 1966. Its architects were Graham, Anderson, Probst and White. To the east is the imposing red-stone Windermere United Methodist Church (1908), designed by the Austin Company, with its Austin Memorial Chapel (1962), architect Travis Gower Walsh.

Cleveland Heights/Shaker Heights

Visitors interested in surveying these two of several noteworthy suburbs making up the "Heights" area are directed to the Heights Driving Tour, Section 20E. By way of background the following comments, appropriately in the Neighborhood Section of the *Guide*, are offered.

As Cleveland's rapidly growing urban area expanded in the period of 1895-1940, the irresistible movement of the city's east side, white collar group led up the hill into the green acres occupied by the Euclid Golf Club and the once active Shaker North Union Settlement.

More than just a pair of comfortable, dormitory suburbs, Cleveland Heights and Shaker Heights are unique for the manner in which they were planned and the exceptional results of both plan and development. The latter was the site of the famed Van Sweringen brothers who tied the undeveloped lands of Shaker Heights to their daring and extraordinary Terminal group development at Public Square, today, the site of Tower City Center. The then enormous enterprise counted on the creation of a special living area as counterpoint to the downtown building projects. Shaker

Heights (and adjacent Shaker Square) were laid out on a grand scheme of boulevards and curvilinear side streets tied to a center city by rapid transit. A series of ponds and streams gave the

residential zone a natural greenway. Commerce was to be rigorously confined to a few selected sites. Public buildings and schools were pre-planned on spacious sites with monumental settings. Two country clubs would be embraced in the configuration. The grand plan of Shaker Heights survived even though the VanSweringen brothers passed away in the mid 1930's when the great depression had impacted their work.

In adjacent Cleveland Heights, development was also thoughtfully pre-determined with a street system recognizing natural stream beds and carefully controlled land use. Of special note are two distinct districts within the city: Forest Hills, once a portion of John D. Rockefeller's estate, and Chestnut Hills, an enclave atop the main entry slope, Cedar Road, up into the city. Forest Hills was initially laid out with strict architectural constraints. Architect Andrew J. Thomas of New York City designed the initial 81 residences of the development in the French-Norman Style; these are seen today as a neighborhood of uniquely consistent appearance. The failing economy of the 1930's precluded the fulfillment of the whole grand plan. The remaining sites were carried out in the Post WWII vernacular modes favoring the Ranch House style.

Chestnut Hills and adjacent North Park Blvd. and Fairmount Blvd. possess an unusual store of grand city houses in the favored revivals of the early 20th century. Well-maintained, these splendid houses and well-landscaped streets offer the epitome of an architecture of comfort and elaboration, of craftsmanship and variety.

Both Cleveland Heights and Shaker Heights are well provided with churches, schools and institutional buildings of interest. These are considerably referenced in the Driving Tour (20E).

The Flats – Shopping, Dining, Entertainment District
The "Flats" comprise the flat lands along the east and west banks of the Cuyahoga River, loosely bounded by West 9th Street on the east, Superior Avenue on the south, the shelf of land near West 25th Street on the west, and Lake Erie on the north.

The Flats primacy in Cleveland's history can be read from its street names: River, Center, Main, British, French, Canal, Washington, Elm. The flat and low-lying banks of the snake-like Cuyahoga River were the first areas explored by Moses Cleveland, and the starting point for the Western Reserve survey crews. As the City has grown, the "Flats" have been populated by the many river-oriented businesses essential to any thriving town. By the 1950s and '60s, the Flats' heavy (and, for the most part, "dirty") industrial character extended southward along the Cuyahoga as far as the city limits five miles away. However, in the past thirty years the Flats have changed dramatically. Many of the failed or failing industrial businesses have pared down operations, moved to sunbelt climes or disappeared. Increasingly, ecologically con-cerned citizens and businesses have cleaned up the Cuyahoga River and Lake Erie. The growing city has looked at the under-utilized real estate along the River with ever-hungrier eyes. And Clevelanders have sought more opportunities for dining, entertain-ment, recreation and night-life in the city's center.

Today, the popularly-redefined Flats area (limited roughly to the River banks and low land north of the I-71 bridge) is a bustling mix of restaurants, bars, nightclubs, boating and entertainment facilities. The River plays host to private craft, water taxis, cruise ships, a sculling league, canoe races and, most recently, high speed powerboat racing. Riverside restaurants feature boardwalks, decks, chaise lounges and pools. Bars and nightclubs feature comedy, live music, stage shows and major extravaganzas during home Brown's and Indian's games, summer festivals and holidays. The architectural character of the Flats befits its checkered history; it is an amalgam of historic and not-so-historic industrial buildings, a variety of bridge types, restored vintage structures, infill com-mercial buildings of the 19th and 20th Century (as along Old River Road on the Cuyahoga's east bank near the Lake), and trendier new commercial properties such as Riverbend Condominiums, (1984), by Anthony Paskevich and Associates and Shooters on the Water (1987), Robert Corna & Associates (exterior) and Voinovich-Sgro Architects interior. The many ambitious plans for the Flats and its environs are sure to enhance and modify its architectural appeal in the years to come.

These include Tower City (See Section 8), the projected Rock and Roll Hall of Fame, I.M. Pei, Architect, additional retail and office facilities, marinas, restaurants, clubs and bars, reuse of the U.S. Coast Guard station at the mouth of the Cuyahoga, and a number of housing developments.

Most dramatic among the water-side rehabilitations is the Power-house (1892), originally the Woodland Avenue and West Side Street Railroad Powerhouse, restored and adaptively re-used (1987-1989) under the direction of Robert Corna & Associates and Samuel V. Diaquila Architect. The original building was designed by John N. Richardson who continued with the 1901 additions including the 240 ft. high chimneys.

Thomas Yablonsky
Joseph Ceruti
Robert Bond

"The Flats – Shopping, Dining, Entertainment District"
Richard L. Zimmerman
Pen M. Zimmerman

Historic Districts

In 1971, the council of the city of Cleveland adopted an ordinance that permits the designation of sites and areas as Landmarks or Historic Districts. The ordinance establishes an overlay zoning that requires design review for any construction at the designated site or within the designated areas. The design review is undertaken by the Landmarks Commission through the City's permit process. The action by the Landmark's Commission may result in a Certificate of Appropriateness.

The public is often confused by National Register listing and local landmark designation. The National Register was established by the United States Congress in 1966 and is administered by the National Park Service under the Department of Interior. Reviews for National Register listing are undertaken by the Ohio Historic Preservation Office for listing by the National Park Service. Historic sites and districts are often on the National Register as well as locally designated.

The designated districts of the city are an assortment of very diverse areas and neighborhoods. The districts differ in scale, form, style and time of development. The diversity exemplifies the cosmopolitan nature of the city of Cleveland. The following is a brief description of National Register and Cleveland designated districts. (L.D. Landmarks Designation) (N.R. National Register)

Hessler Road and Hessler Court Historic District
The Hessler Road and Hessler Court District was the first area designated as a Historic District of the city of Cleveland. At the time of its designation, its area was under threat of demolition. As part of the University Circle development plan, the district represents a compact middle-class subdivision within a neighborhood characterized by large, individually designed, single-family houses with spacious lots. The prevalent architectural styles of the Hessler District are Neo-classical and Bungaloid, with a trace of Norman, Tudor and Swiss Chalet styles. Hessler Court has the only surviving exposed wooden block pavement in the city. Wooden block was extensively used for street pavement in the city during the 1870's. The Hessler District is located within the University Circle area of the city. (N.R.) (L.D.)

Wade Park Historic District

The Wade Park Historic District contains about sixty-five acres which forms the core of what is called University Circle. The district is a collection of some of the most significant cultural, religious and institutional buildings of the nation. The assembly combines works of architects of national and local importance, sculpture by internationally known artists Auguste Rodin and Augustus Saint-Gaudens, and landscape design by Frederick Law Olmsted, Jr. and Associates. The focal point of the district is a lagoon and fine arts garden. Jeptha Wade, a founder of Western Union Telegraph, donated the land comprising Wade Park to the City in 1883 and made an additional gift in 1892 of acreage reserved for the Art Museum. Many of the fine homes of what was the Wade Park allotment can be found adjacent to the institutional buildings. (N.R.)

Mather College Historic District (University Circle)

Five buildings, their green facing Bellflower Road, are considered the most architecturally and historically unified section of the Case Western Reserve University campus. These are the original buildings of the College for Women of Western Reserve University, opened in 1888, the fifth separate college for women in the United States. Clark Hall (1891-1892), a three story classroom building of sandstone and brick in a variant of the Queen Anne style, is the only Cleveland work of Richard M. Hunt. Cleveland architects Coburn and Barnum designed Guilford Hall (1891-1892), a four story brick Queen Anne dormitory. The next two buildings, constructed in 1901-1902, were both the work of Charles F. Schweinfurth: the Late Gothic Revival stone Harkness Memorial Chapel and three-story red brick and sandstone Jacobethan Revival Haydn Hall. The final building, Flora Stone Mather Memorial (1910-1912) was also designed by Schweinfurth. A 60 foot tower is the focal point of this stone and brick Jacobethan and Late Gothic Revival building. (N.R.)

Ohio City, Franklin Circle and Market Square

Ohio City is an ever expanding Historic District listed on the National Register as well as having Cleveland Landmark listing. Ohio City, or as it was incorporated, The City of Ohio, was an independent community from 1836 until 1854 when it was annexed to the City of Cleveland. The Market Square Historic District of Ohio City is the commercial area near the West Side Market and Franklin Circle is primarily a residential community that contains examples of styles popular in the mid and late 19th Century. The area continues to experience extensive restoration and renovation actively. The National Register Ohio City District centers around Franklin Circle. (N.R.)(L.D.)

The Tremont Historic District

The center of the Tremont Historic District can be considered West 14th Street. It is located on a plateau west of the Cuyahoga River. The first settlers of the area arrived in 1818 from New England. The area became known as University Heights because of the development of a short-lived university in 1851. Pelton Park (now known as Lincoln Park) was established as part of the campus. University Heights developed into an exclusive residential area by the time of the Civil War. By 1869 the "Connecticut Colony" arrived in the area, including some who were to become local industrial leaders. The growth of industry caused profound changes in the community. The original residents moved to out-lying areas and were replaced by Central and Eastern Europeans who came to Cleveland to join the industrial work force. Today in Tremont we can find many Victorian style homes of those early residents as well as the homes built to accommodate the new immigrants who came after the turn of the century. The Tremont area contains a myriad of historic church buildings. (L.D.)

The Brooklyn Centre Historic District

The Brooklyn Centre, later known as Brooklyn Village, was laid out in 1830 at the intersection of Columbus Road (Pearl Road) and Newburgh Roads (Denison Avenue). Brooklyn Centre developed as an agricultural community between 1852 and 1894. Brooklyn Centre was incorporated as Brooklyn Village in 1867, annexed to the city of Cleveland in 1890. A number of Italianate style houses of the period remain. The major growth period for the neighbor-hood was first and second decades of the 20th century. (N.R.)(L.D.)

Terminal Tower Group Historic District

The Terminal Tower was constructed as the tallest building of the City of Cleveland and remained the city's most familiar landmark for sixty years. It is located in the most prominent location of the City, the Southwest Quadrant of Public Square. The District is a complex of interconnected buildings, arranged in a triangular area of 15 acres. The architects Graham, Anderson, Probst and White incorporated the 12-story Hotel Cleveland (now Stouffer Tower City Plaza) that was designed by their predecessor firm, Graham, Burnham and Company. It is matched in scale and classical design by the Higbee Company Department Store. Between these two wings is the Union Station entrance, a 5-arch colossal Roman arcade. The sub-concourse was the Union Terminal during the railroad passenger era. Included in the group is the old Post Office Building and the recently renovated Landmark Office Towers. (N.R.)

Public Square Historic District

The Square was laid out as part of the town plan of Cleveland in 1796, the year Moses Cleveland landed at the mouth of the Cuyahoga River as leader of the survey party of the Connecticut Land Company. Today there are four quadrants, each containing about one acre of land. From 1852-1867 the two streets crossing the Square were closed by fences erected by residents opposed to commercial development. In 1860 a monument to Commodore Oliver Hazard Perry was erected at the center of the Square, it remained until 1892. The bronze statue of Moses Cleveland, unveiled in 1888, was designed by J.C. Hamilton. The statue of Mayor Tom L. Johnson (1901-1909) was erected in 1915, the work of Herman N. Matzen. Dominating the Square is the Soldiers and Sailors Monument, designed by Cleveland architect Levi T. Scofield and dedicated in 1894. See the section on Monuments for a detailed description of this quadrant. (N.R.)

The Mall Historic District

The district of public buildings adjoining a formal mall area was developed according to the directives of the Group Plan Commission composed of architects Daniel Burnham, John Carrere, and Arnold Brunner. First proposed in 1903, the plan was developed over the next 30 years becoming one of the most elaborate civic center complexes in the United States. The Mall, approximately 1,500 feet long and 500 feet wide, has seven structures adjoining it. The buildings, designed by a number of architects, stress similar massing, height, and Beaux Arts and Second Renaissance Revival architectural styles, all executed in stone. Many of the buildings contain impressive interior spaces. The Federal Court House and Custom House, includes sculptures by Daniel Chester French. In the early 1960's the excavation of the Mall between St. Clair and Lakeside Avenues provided an underground convention center. The Hanna Fountains were then installed in a long pool on the Mall. At the same time, the World War II Memorial Fountain with its bronze allegorical sculpture was completed at the south end of the Mall. It was commissioned in 1946, the work of sculptor Marshall Fredericks. The southern part of The Mall is being extensively reconstructed to accommodate a large underground garage. The World War II "Victory" Fountain will be restored as the centerpiece. (N.R.)

The Playhouse Square Historic District

This group of structures is a rare surviving collection of post-World War I legitimate, vaudeville, and motion picture theatres. Their significance derives from the ornate architecture, the unusual connected plan of four of the five theatres, and links with civic leaders and architects of local and national reputation. Playhouse Square, built 1920-1922, was the result of a collaboration between realtor Joseph Laronge and theatre owner Marcus Loew to develop upper Euclid Avenue into a theatre, office, and shopping district. Loew's Ohio and Loew's State theatres, designed by Thomas W. Lamb, opened in February 1921. Both auditoriums were placed at the rear of the Ohio Building, with long promenades to the street. Both theatre lobbies have elaborately coffered ceilings, and the State's Italian Renaissance style lobby is the largest in the world.

Next to open were the Hanna Building, the Hanna Building Annex and the Hanna Theatre, financed by the Cleveland News publisher Dan Hanna, Sr. in honor of his father Marcus Hanna. Designed by Charles Platt, a Renaissance Revival design was executed for both the exterior and interior. The Bulkley Building, with its Allen Theatre, followed. The developer, politician Robert Bulkley, hired architect C. Howard Crane. The Pompeiian style theatre has an ornate lobby rotunds and was designed specifically for movies. The final structure, the Keith Building and Palace Theatre, opened in November 1922. Edward F. Albee dedicated the building to his partner B.F. Keith, co-founder of the Keith Vaudeville circuit. Architects Rapp & Rapp's Neo-classical design combined a 21-story tower, the tallest in Cleveland at the time, with a lavish theatre containing a 3-story lobby emphasizing marble and metalwork. (N.R.)(L.D.)

The East 4th Street District

East 4th Street, first known as Sheriff Street, runs between Euclid and Prospect Avenues. By 1881 the Street was lined with masonry buildings two to five stories tall. In addition there were three wood-frame laundries and the famous Euclid Avenue Opera House that opened in 1875. The stage entrance faced Sheriff Street. Destroyed by fire in 1892, but rebuilt in 1893, it continued to operate until the 1920's. During the 1930's, East 4th Street was the home to milliners, tailors, insurance and real estate companies, furniture dealers, and violin makers. While East 4th Street declined in the 1960's and 70's, it still echoes its past. Two restaurant cafes opened before the turn of the century are still in business today. The Rathskellar was once Cleveland's most popular diner restaurant. Otto Moser's established in 1892 continues in operation. A visit to Moser's will provide you with an opportunity to see a multitude of autographed pictures spanning 50 years of American theater history. East 4th Street's density and activity provides the visitor with a feeling of the crowded urban setting common to American cities of the past. (N.R.)(L.D.)

Historic Warehouse District

This district, northwest of Public Square, served as the commercial center of Cleveland through the 19th century. The area illustrates the evolution of construction techniques, ranging from load-bearing walls, to cast iron facades, and finally the steel frame. By the 1840's warehouses, business blocks, clothiers, and dry goods stores lined the streets. The Hilliard Block and Johnson Block date from this period. After the Civil War, ornate examples of Italianate, Romanesque, and Eastlake influenced architecture appeared. The district was also the location of several important early skyscrapers in Cleveland: the Perry-Payne Building (1888), designed by Cudell & Richardson, with its interior light court; the 1891 Western Reserve Building by Daniel Burnham; and the 1903-1911 Rockefeller Building, financed by J.D. Rockefeller and designed by Cleveland architects Knox & Elliot, which demonstrates a strong influence by Louis Sullivan. Other structures of this period include the Commercial Style Bradley Building and Bingham Co. Warehouse, along with the Crown (now Courthouse Square) Building (1915). The district is experiencing a substantial renovation and adaptive re-use. (N.R.)(L.D.)

Upper Prospect Avenue Historic District

This prominent Cleveland street has experienced several phases of development, gaining significance from its architecture, residents and institutions. The street originally developed, in the years following the Civil War, as an exclusive residential district of single-family houses, mostly in the Italianate style. The growing population of the city, combined with the convenient transportation afforded by the streetcar line on the avenue, contributed to the trend of higher density development. Rowhouse complexes such as Six Chimneys and Nos. 3645-57 appeared in the late 1870's and 1880's. At the turn of the 20th century the first apartment buildings, such as The Plaza and Dixon Hall, designed in Gothic and Tudor styles, respectively, reflected the stately character of the street. Through this period Prospect Avenue remained the residence of notable families involved in commerce, industry and politics. The area was also complemented by fine examples of church architecture, including First Methodist Church (1905), by architect J. Milton Dyer, St. Paul's Episcopal Church, now St. Paul's Shrine (1874-1876), Gordon Lloyd; Trinity Cathedral (1901-1907), C.F. Schweinfurth; and Zion Lutheran Church (1902), Paul Matzinger, Architect. Prominent social and literary organizations also located in the area, such as the Rowfant Club in 1895, The Tavern Club, (1905) J. Milton Dyer, and the Central YMCA (1913), Hubbell & Benes. By the 1920's the character of Prospect Avenue began to change. New buildings were less elaborate and commercial uses were often in the form of additions to the residential structures. The new buildings emphasized terra-cotta exteriors, and several excellent, ornate, colorful, Neo-classical examples remain, including the Cook Building, now The Prospect Park Building (1918), Lehman & Schmitt and Filmlab Services Building (1919), W.A. Borch, Architect. Today Prospect is a mixture of these phases of residential and commercial development, along with more recent commercial structures. (N.R.)(L.D.)

Warszawa Neighborhood Historic District

This small district is the core of the primary Polish neighborhood in Cleveland at the turn of the 20th century and was named by the inhabitants after the Polish capital. The buildings are a mixture of 2-story residential and commercial structures built between 1880 and 1920. Architecturally, the majority utilize Queen Anne elements. Diversity in facade treatment includes dormers, oriel windows, and recessed porches. A visual focal point and center of ethnic community life is the St. Stanislaus Church compound (1868 and later), by William Dunn, dominated by the elaborate High Victorian Gothic church, and also containing a rectory, convent, 2 schools, and a power plant. Opposite Chambers Street is the Kniola Travel Bureau, located in a 2-1/2 story Queen Anne house. Originally this was the residence and office of Michael Kniola, who acted as a liaison between the community, government, and prospective immigrants, assuring their stable settlement. (N.R.)

Cultural Gardens Historic District

Cleveland's Cultural Gardens are a unique outdoor historical museum of ethnic heritage, landscape architecture and fine sculpture. The gardens are located in Rockefeller Park from Superior Avenue to St. Clair Avenue along Martin Luther King Blvd. The first garden was initiated by the Daughters of the British Empire in 1916. The chain of gardens was conceived by Leo Weidenthal with the dedication of the Hebrew Gardens in 1926. The number has grown to 24 gardens representing various nationality groups. (L.D.)

East Boulevard Historic District

The district owes its significance as a residential neighborhood to the presence of the adjacent Rockefeller Park and the Cultural Gardens. The district features a three-block row of apartment buildings of superimposed porches between E. 105th and Superior dating from 1905 to 1918. Between Superior and St. Clair, the boulevard is lined with large, two-story single and double-family homes. These houses display a mixture of early 20th century residential revival styles, including Dutch Colonial, Colonial Revival, Spanish Revival, and Federal Revival styles, dating from 1909 to 1936. (L.D.)

Newton Avenue Historic District

Located in Cleveland's Hough community in proximity to University Circle, the Newton Avenue Historic District is very compact and composed of 22 single family houses and 2 apartment buildings. The houses along the street were built in 1910 and 1911 and include such house types as Bungalows, Homesteads and Four Squares. The houses show elements of the Colonial Revival and Dutch Colonial Revival styles. The houses were developed by Philip Marquard, a noted early twentieth century residential developer. One of the more notable features of the street is the intimate feeling achieved by houses with little or no setback from the street. (L.D.)(N.R.)

Shaker Square Historic District

The district consists of approximately 275 buildings, the core of a much larger area developed by O.P. and M.J. Van Sweringen. It is one of the few historic districts in the nation to cross municipal boundaries, with an adjacent area in Shaker Heights having also been designated. At the center of the district is Shaker Square (1927-1929), a village green setting consisting of an open space enclosed by buildings in an octagonal formation, with roadways entering at mid-side. Each of the four quadrants contains a two-story central block flanked by one-story wings and square corner pavilions. The Georgian ornament combines with the red brick walls and slate roofs to create a harmonious design. The Square, designed by Small & Rowley, is one of the earliest planned suburban shopping centers in the United States and the first in Ohio. The Van Sweringen's integrated it into an innovative rapid system linking their developments, the Terminal Tower Group on Public Square and the suburb of Shaker Heights.

Surrounding this commercial node the Van Sweringen's developed a high-density residential district and neighborhoods of single-family houses. Although taking several decades to reach completion, deed restrictions enforced by the Van Sweringen Co. produced a unified district. Items governed included lot and building sizes, setback, cost, plans, materials, architectural styles, and color schemes. (N.R.)(L.D.)

Ludlow Historic District
The Ludlow neighborhood, part of the original Shaker Heights development plan of the Van Sweringen brothers, is located to the southeast of Shaker Square and straddles the municipal boundary lines of Cleveland and Shaker Heights. The neighborhood streets are laid out as ovals-within-ovals, creating an individual identity for the area within the larger development, as well as making it distinct from Cleveland neighborhoods to the south and west laid out in a grid plan. In contrast to the high-density residential development of the Shaker Square area, Ludlow was designated solely for single-family houses. Each neighborhood in the development had its own school on a specifically designated parcel. The elementary school in Ludlow, a two-story Colonial Revival structure, was designed in 1926 by Cleveland architect Charles Schneider. Deed restrictions imposed by the Van Sweringens throughout their development permitted only three broad categories of architectural designs, identified as American Colonial, English and French. The standard wall material, brick, has been combined with stone and wood detailing to create the ornamentation appropriate for each style. (L.D.)

Little Italy Historic District
This district of about 375 structures, located on the east side of Cleveland, includes residential, commercial, and industrial buildings, two churches, and a former elementary school. Dense development on small lots, along with a location on the side of a steep hill, has created a unique character for this neighborhood.

In the mid-1870's Little Italy was farmland. Growth began in the 1880's after installation of the New York, Chicago & St. Louis railroad line. By the mid-1890's residential development north of Mayfield Road was essentially complete. Development of the area south of Mayfield Road occurred mostly between 1905 and 1915.

Building materials varied, with the housing stock north of Mayfield primarily frame construction, while south of Mayfield the structures were generally brick. In 1911 Little Italy had a population that was 96% Italian born, with another 2% of Italian parentage. Significant institutions established to serve the neighborhood include Holy Rosary Church (1908), William P. Ginther, Architect and Alta House named for John D. Rockefeller's daughter. Another important influence in the area was the Lakeview Marble Works, which employed craftsmen who designed and executed monuments for placement in Lakeview Cemetery, Cleveland's most architecturally significant cemetery. Joseph Carabelli, a stone cutter, was one of the founding fathers of Little Italy. In the early 20th century, Little Italy was the second largest Italian neighborhood in Cleveland. Big Italy, centered around Woodland Avenue and East 22nd Street, had the largest concentration of Italians. That neighborhood began to decline however, in the 1920's. Efforts by the residents of Little Italy to preserve their heritage are highlighted by the Feast of the Assumption, celeb-rated annually on August 15 since 1895.

A significant adaptive re-use within the district is that of Murray Hill School (1895, addition 1909, 1916), Architect, Frank S. Barnum. Closed in 1978, the transformation to offices, studios and condo-miniums is under the direction of Stephen Bucchieri, Architect. Today, Little Italy has become a center for art stores and studios. (L.D.)

Miles Park Historic District
This district consists of an open space and small group of buildings dating from the 19th century and retains its character within a heavily urbanized area. The park, originally the Newburgh town square, was laid out in 1850. The First Congregational Church of Newburgh was organized in 1832 and became Presbyterian in 1840. The present brick and stone building (1872) is an example of the Romanesque Revival style, with the original pews intact. The Miles Park United Methodist Church was established in 1832. The visually imposing red brick building (1872-1883) is designed in High Victorian Gothic style. Newburgh was annexed to Cleveland in 1873. In 1877 the green was named Miles Park, after Theodore Miles, the donor of the land. The Miles Park Library (1904-1906), Neo-classical in design by Edward Tilton, is constructed of sandstone and yellow brick. The reading room is a domed octagonal space containing 8 wooden Ionic columns. (N.R.)(L.D.)

John D. Cimperman

Singular Buildings and Notable Architects

The architectural scene in Cleveland, as with many great cities across the land, is in a constant state of change.

Society National Bank, a monumental expression of 19th-century values, will become the Old World cornerstone of the New World Society Center. The Cleveland Public Library, one of the most gracious structures in the Group Plan of civic buildings around the Mall, will undergo modification to meet the needs of the library in the age of technology.

The Arcade, (below) Cleveland's most magnificent space, has been adapted to accommodate the public's need for fast food. The Powerhouse in the Flats, built to generate electricity for Cleveland's streetcar system, has been recycled as part of the Nautica entertainment complex. The Hanna mansion in Bratenahl, one of the grandest private estates in a city of fine homes, will be the centerpiece of Newport, a luxurious residential development on the shores of Lake Erie.

Society National Bank (formerly the Society for Savings Bank), with its dramatic red-stone restored in 1990, prevails as one of Cleveland's treasured heirlooms.

Despite changes that reshape the profile and alter the fabric of the city, the architecture of quality stands firm. Integral to the history of Cleveland, the great old buildings anchor the community to the past and provide a solid foundation for the future.

When the Arcade was built in 1889, they said it couldn't be done. So daring was the iron, steel and glass roof structure designed by Cleveland architects John Eisenmann and George H. Smith that no local firm would bid on it, and bridge builders had to be imported from Detroit. An interior shopping street of soaring heights, grand marble staircases, rich materials and finely wrought details, the Arcade creates an environment of elegance that cannot be matched by contemporary shopping malls.

Terminal Tower, by contrast, was regarded as old-fashioned when it was completed in 1930. The conservative design by Chicago architects Graham, Anderson, Probst and White was Influenced by the Beaux-Arts image of Hotel Cleveland (now Stouffer Tower City Plaza Hotel), which was built on Public Square in 1918. An incredibly complicated group of buildings culminating in the graceful tower that has long been the city's symbol, the vast complex built over a grand railway station documents the daring and vision of railroad magnates Mantis J. and Oris P. Van Sweringen.

The Cleveland Public Library, the work of Cleveland architects Walker and Weeks, was supposed to be the twin of the old Federal Courthouse, the first neoclassical building in the Group Plan. The 1925 library matches its older neighbor in size and scale. But its white marble skin, symbolic stone carvings and grand main entrance give it a sense of nobility appropriate to a pristine temple honoring the book.

Society National Bank, John Wellborn Root's red sandstone skyscraper on Public Square, expresses the indestructible quality of a fortress built to protect life savings. Although the heaviness of the 1890 steel-and-stone structure seems to weigh down the squat granite pillars at the base, the high arched windows, fanciful sculptures and ornate wrought iron lamp at the corner create a feeling of lightness that continues inside the main banking hall,

The Powerhouse in the "Flats" came close to being a ruin before it got a new lease on life in 1988-1989 to become, adaptively, an entertainment palace, with its familiar chimneys intact.

a gorgeous room topped with a floral stained-glass ceiling and decorated with moralistic murals in a medieval style.

The Powerhouse in the Flats symbolizes industrial Cleveland. Designed in 1892 by Cleveland architect J. N. Richardson, the sturdy brick building has a strong profile of tall smokestacks and immense arches that harmonize with the remarkable variety of bridge forms spanning the Cuyahoga River.

The industrialists who shaped the city in the late 19th century lived grandly in Victorian mansions along Millionaires' Row (as Euclid Avenue was once known) or in wealthy suburbs such as Bratenahl and Shaker Heights. The Hanna mansion, built in 1910 by McKim, Mead and White of New York, speaks eloquently of classical proportion, symmetry and architectural detail. The spacious Jacobethan Revival house with its splendid central hall, Hollywood swimming pool and stone terrace overlooking Lake Erie is guarded at the gate by a massive brick carriage house designed by J. Milton Dyer.

Known as "the prince of Cleveland architects," Dyer showed his individuality in such dramatically different buildings as the Renaissance-style Tavern Club, the Beaux-Arts City Hall and the Art Moderne Coast Guard Station at the mouth of the Cuyahoga River.

Walker and Weeks, Cleveland's premiere classical architects, got their start in Dyer's office, then designed a long list of landmark buildings, including National City Bank, Severance Hall, the Allen Memorial Medical Library at Case Western Reserve University and the Federal Reserve Bank, their pink marble masterpiece.

Charles Schweinfurth was admired primarily for his campus architecture, churches and residences, including his own home, a baronial stone castle that still stands with dignity in a deteriorated inner-city neighborhood. Among his other lasting contributions are the beautiful stone bridges in Rockefeller Park and Trinity Cathedral, his magnum opus in the English gothic style.

These masters did some of the finest work between 1890 and 1930, the golden age of Cleveland architecture. Gifted with an eye for quality and a feeling for the timelessness of good design, they helped mold the city into a special place where singular buildings stand proudly beside the river, the lake, the square and the mall.

Wilma Salisbury, Architectural Writer
The Cleveland Plain Dealer

Lost Cleveland

Buildings Gone But Not Forgotten

In a city as large as Cleveland it was inevitable that the pressures of growth would take a number of once-admired structures. And, if development was not responsible for the losses, there was always fire and abandonment. Urban renewal, with its capacity to devour whole neighborhoods, was not as damaging to Cleveland's fabric as to that of some cities. Even now, The Gateway Stadium and Arena program of land acquisition has cleared a twenty acre area adjacent to the southern edge of downtown and has caused a number of buildings of familiar, if not notable character, to vanish.

Citing lost favorites is a sad recounting and never quite complete. But, for example, the following are offered: The Central Armory (1893) and Egyptian-styled City Morgue (1894) were leveled to provide for the new Federal Office Tower. On the same block, the Hotel Auditorium (1927) preceded the present Bond Court Hotel.

One of Cleveland's first tall buildings to be demolished was the Old Central National Bank Building at 308 Euclid Avenue in the late 1940's to be replaced by the Woolworth Co. store.

Across the street from this has risen the massive BP America Tower and Garage. The site for this development contained several buildings, most notably The Burnham & Root Cuyahoga Building (1893) and The Williamson Building, once Cleveland's tallest (1900). The well-photographed implosion of these two structures was a dramatic instant in 1981.

The Society Center project at Public Square combined demolition and preservation. Most serious was the loss of the splendid terra cotta Engineers Building (1910) to accommodate the Marriott Hotel. The Society Tower rises from the one-time Cleveland Chamber of Commerce Building (1898), later Cleveland College. Happily, the original Society for Savings Bank by Burnham & Root (1890) has survived.

The Central Armory was a dominant element of the Mall area during its early assemblage. Eventually, most of the Mall gave way to a redeveloped block featuring the new Federal Building.

The Engineers Building, one of Cleveland's major losses, was destroyed in late 1989. The crisp lines of the terra cotta-faced building, which housed the headquarters of the Brotherhood of Locomotive Engineers, graced the approach to Public Square from the north for decades.

In the Warehouse District a streetscape of empty lots, now used for parking, attests to the serious losses of original 19th century structures. Perhaps the greatest of these was the Blackstone and Power Block Building (1881), a structure featuring a central atrium and elaborate Victorian detailing. Located at W. 3rd and Rockwell Avenue, it was neighbor to two structures of historic interest: The Hawley House Hotel at W. 3rd and St. Clair (lost to fire) and the Old Cuyahoga County Court House (1875) located where today's 55 Public Square rises.

At the northwest corner of Euclid Avenue and E. 9th Street, two noteworthy buildings preceded the present National City Center: the 1890 Hickox Building, featuring a slender turret at the corner, which came down in the 1930's for the short-lived Art Moderne Bond Store (1947).

Downtown Cleveland was once the locale of a number of now-vanished churches. The most significant of which may have been the enormous Euclid Avenue Baptist Church (1927) along E. 18th Street, North of Euclid Avenue a Byzantine Revival structure supported, in part, by John D. Rockefeller.

While the city's Playhouse Square Theater group is a preserved model for the nation, there were a number of motion picture and stage performance theaters lost. Most recently (1975) the Hippodrome, the city's largest, came down for a parking garage. All of the city's 19th century opera houses and vaudeville theaters have vanished.

Perhaps the best-loved retail emporium, The Sterling & Welch Co. store, a very large furnishings store featuring a five-story central light well, came down for a project never constructed. Clevelanders remember the 60-foot Christmas tree within the atrium as a regular holiday event.

This account hardly reveals the considerable list of admired structures here confined to a downtown review. In the older neighborhoods there were many structures such as church, school or commercial buildings, worth reporting in a larger volume. Suffice it to say that Cleveland's architectural heritage, considerable as it remains, was once even more extensive.

Clay Herrick

Cleveland Renewed

The decade of the 1980's was for Cleveland a Great Awakening. The city completed projects such as Playhouse Square Theater Centre and the Erieview Urban Renewal Program, constructed major new projects such as the BP America Building and the Galleria, and commenced ambitious mixed use developments such as Tower City Center and the North Coast Harbor. Not since the heady days of the late 1920's had Cleveland seen such a scale or diversity of development. A brief tour of downtown Cleveland's major development districts will reveal the range of Cleveland's recent accomplishments and suggest the future direction of downtown development.

Public Square is the physical and symbolic heart of Cleveland. Beginning in the late 1970's, the city, county, and state began a collaborative effort to completely renovate this important public open space. The public commitment was soon followed by major private investment. To the east, BP America built its headquarters, a 1.5 million square foot office and retail development. This project was soon followed by the renovation of the May Company Department Store, and the commencement of the Tower City Center project, a mixed use project which includes the renovation of the Terminal Tower, long the symbol of Cleveland; the conversion of the former railroad station to a 400,000 square foot retail center; the conversion of the abandoned U.S. Post Office to an office building; the renovation and reconfiguration of the RTA station; and the development of a new Ritz Carlton Hotel and additional office space. Subsequent phases of this project include new office and retail development, the construction of the Rock and Roll Hall of Fame and Museum (I.M. Pei Associates), and the

The BP America Building, occupying space on Public Square previously filled by both the Cuyahoga Building and the Williamson Building, soars to a height of 658 feet.

development of new housing on land across the Cuyahoga River on Collision Bend. Properties adjacent to Tower City Center, including the Landmark Office Tower, the Higbee Company Department Store, and the Stouffer Tower City Center hotel have all undergone extensive renovation in recent years.

To the north of Public Square, the Society Center project (Cesar Pelli, Architect) is under construction. This mixed use project includes a 55 story office tower, a 424 room Marriott Hotel, the renovation of the Society for Savings Building (van Dijk, Johnson & Partners), and the complete restoration of Mall A and the "Fountain of Eternal Life", a major sculpture by Marshall Fredericks. To the west of the Square, an equally significant project, the Ameritrust Center, is proposed. This 60 story office tower by Kohn, Pedersen & Fox will include a 480 room Hyatt Hotel and will complete the redevelopment of the Public Square District.

Silver in color and angular in shape, One Cleveland Center has been situated at a 45 degree angle to the major intersecting streets leaving a considerable plaza area both inside and out.

The Warehouse District is Cleveland's original retail center. The 1980's saw the rediscovery of this unique collection of 19th Century, loft, retail and warehouse buildings and their conversion to office, residential and retail uses. Among the most significant projects to be completed during the 1980's were the Hoyt Block, the Bradley Building, the Hat Factory, the Burgess Building, the Hilliard Block, the Johnson/Jobbers/ Chamberlain Block, and the 820 Superior Building. On the drawing boards or under construction are mixed use projects including Crittenden Court and the National Terminals Building; residential projects including the Worthington Building; and office projects such as the Western Reserve Building Annex, the L. N. Gross Building, and the Courthouse Square Building.

East Ninth Street/Erieview, located east of Public Square, is the city's major urban renewal project and most significant office concentration. Master planned in the early 1960's by I. M. Pei, the district developed gradually and was substantially completed in the mid-1980's. This decade saw the construction of the One Cleveland Center Building, Eaton Center, North Point Phase I, First Federal Savings and Loan, the Ohio Bell Building, and the Galleria, a 150,000 square foot retail center built upon the ill-conceived Erieview Plaza. In recent years, the district has witnessed the construction of North Point Phase II and the commencement of the Bank One Building on the site of the Hollenden Hotel, as well as the renovation of Bond Court Office building and the Lakeside Holiday Inn and the conversion of the Bond Court Hotel to the Sheraton City Centre Hotel. Future

The unique, Ohio Bell Erieview Tower has its main window-wall angled so that the street scene below (including the neighboring Galleria Plaza and St. Clair Avenue) is reflected in ever-changing mirrored images.

development in the district is likely to be on infill sites and on underdeveloped land east of East 12th Street.

North Coast Harbor is located at the foot of East Ninth Street as it meets the Inner Harbor. Planned as a major attraction for both Greater Clevelanders and visitors to the region, the North Coast project is proposed to include an aquarium and maritime center; retail, hotel, and office development; and public open space centered on the 7.5 acre harbor. This project will not only be the northern terminus of the East Ninth Street office corridor, it will compliment the recently renovated Cleveland Convention Center and become a popular gathering place for all Greater Clevelanders.

Playhouse Square is the city's theater district. At the center of the district are three magnificently restored theaters, the State, the Ohio, and the Palace which together constitute a 7,000 seat performing arts center. The renovation of these three theaters, completed in the mid-1980's spurred the conversion of abandoned retail buildings in the district to office use and has led to new development on underutilized sites in the surrounding area. The Rennaisance Building, a 300,000 square foot office building, and the 200 room Playhouse Square Hotel are currently under development in the Playhouse Square district. Future development in the district is likely to occur east of the Hanna Building and north of the Playhouse Square theaters.

These reflections capture activity in Cleveland's Downtown exclusively, but parallel activity is to be observed in the city's sub-centers, especially University Circle the rapidly developing areas around I-90 Westlake, I-77 Rockside and I-271 Chagrin. Altogether the physical development of Cleveland has peaked in this centennial year of the founding of the Cleveland Chapter, American Institute of Architects. After several decades of population shrinkage and physical stagnation, the city is on a new rise, one, which is fundamental to Cleveland's positioning for the future as a significant city expressed in a significant architectural language.

Hunter Morrison

Section 1

Libraries and Museums

The Cleveland Public Library (1925)
325 Superior Avenue
Architects: Walker & Weeks

The Cleveland Public Library, built at the site of the old City Hall, was the result of a 1916 design competition. An integral part of the Group Plan scheme, the Library is paired with the Federal Building and completes the original intent of providing a terminating south edge to the Mall.

A five story marble structure, the Library, adhering to strict Group Plan guidelines, is uniform in height, width, and massing to the adjacent Federal Building. A rusticated arcaded base, balustraded roof line and three story Corinthian colonnade typify its classic Beaux-Arts design.

One of the largest in the country, having 47 miles of shelving, it boasts a pair of grand staircases which rise with dignity through a well composed interior of Italian marble. The painted, vaulted lobby and vaulted and coffered ceiling of the three-story reading (now reference) room are reminiscent of a Roman bath. Although classical in design, the Library quickly gained national recognition with many functional innovations in library planning.

In 1960 the adjacent Plain Dealer Publishing Co. building was acquired to expand the library. This building, and the intervening Eastman Reading Garden, were the center of preservationist attention in 1989 when a plan to upgrade the Library was initiated with an architectural competition.

Western Reserve Historical Society Museum Complex
10825 East Blvd.

> **John Hay House** (1908)
> *Architect: Abram Garfield*
>
> **Mrs. Leonard C. Hanna House** (1918)
> *Architects: Walker & Gillette*
>
> **Central Addition** (1959)
> *Architects: Charles Bacon Rowley & Associates; Ernst Payer*
>
> **Frederick C. Crawford Auto-Aviation Museum** (1965)
> *Architects: Rowley, Payer, Huffman & Leithold*
>
> **Library** (1984)
> *Architects: Kaplan/Curtis*

The Western Reserve Historical Society housed in a complex of buildings one block long, is one of the largest private historical societies in the U.S. Visitors can view outstanding collections and displays relating to the history of Cleveland and the Western Reserve from the Revolution to the twentieth century. The complex consists of a pair of large residences in the Second Renaissance Revival style connected with museum wings intended to harmonize with the exterior of the two houses. The hardly discernible Rowley-Payer addition of an entrance hall, two exhibition rooms, and meeting room, join the Hanna and John Hay Houses, while preserving their individual character and the formal gardens of each.

The Mrs. Leonard C. Hanna House, a fine example of 16th century Florentine Renaissance architecture, was acquired by WRHS in 1940 to house its growing library. The downstairs rooms have been preserved, and still have all of their original intricate Italian decor. An impressive architectural feature in the Hanna House is a U-shaped staircase in the two-story entry hall, with a wide landing framed by large composite-order columns. Today this stately house is used primarily for exhibits and displays. The Frederick C. Crawford Auto-Aviation Museum, containing an extensive antique automobile collection, was added in 1965.

An integral part of the complex is the adjoining library (1984), housing the largest American history research center in northern Ohio. The arched terra cotta entrance of the Cuyahoga Building (1893) (now demolished) is the main architectural feature of this building.

The Cleveland Museum of Art (1916)
11150 East Blvd.
Architects: Hubbell & Benes
1st Addition: Hays & Ruth (1958)
2nd Addition: Marcel Breuer & Hamilton P. Smith (1970)
3rd addition: Dalton, van Dijk, Johnson & Partners (1982)

Following consultation with Edmund B. Wheelright of the Boston Museum of Fine Art and Henry W. Kent of the Metropolitan Museum of Art in New York, the Cleveland firm of Hubbell & Benes created a museum which was truly a model for its day in the planning of its working parts as well as a key element in the University Circle master plan. Upon completion, museum professionals from around the country observed, "nowhere had they seen a building more perfectly adapted to its requirements."

Overlooking the Wade Park lagoon, the 300-foot-long facade of white Georgian marble is broken only by a central Ionic portico separated from the main entablature by a wide attic frieze in the Beaux-Arts manner. A simple, axial, Neo-Classical design, composed of a vestibule with two great light courts on either side, established the basic plan. Various sized galleries surround these including atmospheric controls and a light diffusing chamber between the upper and lower skylights.

With a site orientation such that the north and south ends are separate visually, the large addition to the north by Marcel Breuer boldly addressed the Wade Oval, with a finely crafted 115-foot concrete canopy, dramatizing the new main entrance. An outstanding structure of the 1970s in the University Circle area, Breuer's addition completely contained the elegant 1958 glass and metal addition by Hays and Ruth. The layout was determined by circulation patterns. Breuer uses a suspended ceiling grid, similar to that which he used in the Whitney Museum of American Art, permitting the use of modular partitions for flexible installations. A sculptural placement of massive blocks, clad in bands of light and dark Minnesota granite, allows a wonderful play of shadows amongst the elements. Unconcerned with directly relating to the original building, Breuer was said to, "rather enjoy the tensions created by these juxtapositions." Though appearing closed and heavy, the interior opens to light courts in several areas.

Dalton, van Dijk, Johnson & Partners designed a third wing in 1982 neatly concealed by landscaping and a change in grade, to provide additional library and gallery space.

Allen Memorial Medical Library (1926) (1975)
11000 Euclid Avenue (at Adelbert Road)
Architects: Walker & Weeks
Interior Renovation: Blunden – Barclay

This clean, refined library and museum of classic design is one of the finer examples of the work of Walker & Weeks. Simple and rectilinear in form, the decoration is derived from the way the building is put together, not applied ornament. It is symmetrical with a rusticated base, two-story windows and a cornice. Subtle detailing enhances the central entry pavilion. The interior is treated with equal attention to quality and detail. The main reading rooms and library are finished in the English university tradition with baroque pedimented doorways. A special climate-controlled room to house rare books was installed in 1975.

Dunham Tavern Museum (1832-1842) (1986-1988)
6709 Euclid Avenue
Architect: Unknown
Restoration: Gaede Serne Zofcin

This clapboard tavern/stagecoach stop was typical of those found along the Buffalo-Cleveland-Detroit road in the mid-19th century. Constructed of heavy hewn timbers joined by wooden pins and hand wrought spikes, it is one of the few remaining pre-Civil War structures surviving in Cleveland today.

A thriving business for 25 years, the tavern became a private residence in 1857. Only 3 miles east of the center of Cleveland, its existence was threatened by commercial growth along Euclid Avenue in the mid-1930s. At this time The Society of Collectors, Inc. began to restore and develop the Dunham as a museum of early American life.

Today the structure has been beautifully restored to how it might have appeared as a tavern between the years of 1824-1853 when it was owned and operated by Rufus and Jane Dunham. This resulted in the controversial removal of a classical revival porch which had been an integral part of the building since 1896.

Ralph M. Besse Library (1985)
Campus of Ursuline College
2550 Lander Road
Architects: van Dijk, Johnson & Partners

Ursuline College, Ohio's first chartered college for women, was founded in 1871 by the Ursuline Nuns of Cleveland. Today, the campus is situated on 115 acres in Pepper Pike. Located in a peaceful residential community, the newest addition to the picturesque campus is the $3.8 million Ralph M. Besse Library, designed by Peter van Dijk. Encompassing 36,000 square feet, the Library has a capacity for 130,000 volumes and seating for 250 people. The modern design of the Library integrates "Ursuline Blend" brick, buff Indiana limestone and black Canadian granite. Doors and fixtures are of rift cut red oak with bronze, while the floor coverings encompass terrazzo, ceramic tile, red oak, and carpeting. Stained glass panels from the chapel and amber glass sconces from Merici Hall are just two of the artifacts incorporated into the design from the College's former Cedar Hill campus. The Library is named after a longtime trustee and supporter of the college and a major organizer of its move to the present campus.

Cleveland Public Library Branch Development (1978-1990)
Listed below are nineteen of twenty-nine branch libraries of the Cleveland Public Library system either built or substantially renovated in the period 1978-1990. Under the direction of Director Ervin J. Gaines and Deputy Director, Marian A. Huttner. These neighborhood branches demonstrate both a strong commitment to restorative architecture and to progressive contemporary solutions.

West Side Branches

Brooklyn (1919) (1985)
3706 Pearl Road
Architects: Ora Coltman
Renovation: Robert C. Gaede

A dark brick structure featuring two glazed roof monitors. The interior was totally renewed, the exterior preserved.

Carnegie West (1910) (1979)
1900 Fulton Road
Architect: Edward L. Tilton
Renovation: Koster & Associates
(See Section 19C)

Most monumental of the branches, this large facility on its triangular park survived with a reduced interior area of both restored and modernized spaces.

Eastman (1980)
11602 Lorain Avenue
Architect: Joseph Ceruti

A two-story branch due to site constraints, this brick masonry structure features a life-sized, bronze sculpture by William McVey at its main entrance along the retail block.

Fulton (1983)
3545 Fulton Road
Architects:Teare & Herman

A new structure of cubic form and exterior tile walls in modular square patterns. Its soft green cast and airy interior are notable characteristics. A large, abstract, sculptural column by David Davis is placed by the entry.

Lorain (1912) (1985)
8216 Lorain Avenue
Architects: Knox & Elliot
Renovation: Blunden – Barclay

An old Carnegie Branch, its large interior was fully opened up to satisfy contemporary library expectations.

West Park (1928) (1978)
3805 W. 157th Street
Architects: Walker & Weeks
Renovation: Carlson, Englehorn

The first of the series, this delightful Tudor Revival building was subject to an addition as well as a general upgrading.

South Side Branches

Fleet (1981)
6224 Broadway
Architect: Robert C. Gaede

A new structure comprised of three functional wings abutting a central square. Each wing features a stainless steel clad roof of a gentle shed form.

Jefferson (1918) (1981)
850 Jefferson Avenue
Architect: Ora Coltman
Renovation: Blunden – Barclay

A limestone-clad structure, scaled to its old residential neighborhood, brought back to contemporary usage via reopening closed ceilings with clerestories. This project won an Award of Excellence for Library Architecture in 1983.

South Brooklyn (1979)
4303 Pearl Road
Architects: Fred Toguchi & Associates

A new structure on a small "V"-shaped site looking at the junction of Pearl and State Roads. Its interiors feature an exposure of the mechanical and structural systems in the new functionalist esthetic.

East Side Branches

Addison (1990)
6901 Superior Avenue
Architect: Stephen J. Bucchieri

A composition of a large cube and attached cylinder incorporating considerable glass block, is altogether configured to a rectilinear module.

Collinwood (1928) (1980)
856 E. 152nd Street
Architects: Walter & Weeks
Renovation: Lipaj, Woyar and Tomsik

The interior spaces were filled with partitions which were eliminated to provide an open plan with modern furnishings.

East 131st Street (1929) (1979)
3830 E. 131st Street
Architects: Walker & Weeks
Renovation: Lipaj, Woyar and Tomsik

This branch is almost identical to Collinwood. The architects preserved the terra-cotta, ornamented arched entrance as well as modernized the interiors.

Glenville (1980)
11900 St. Clair Avenue, NE
Architects: Thomas T.K. Zung

A grand entrance canopy leads to a light-filled interior highlighted by an elevated story-telling loft. The brass tonal sculpture is the final work by Harry Bertoia.

Harvard-Lee (1979)
16918 Harvard Avenue
Architects: Whitley & Whitley

Of dark brick masonry inside and out, its high-ceilinged interior features stained oak beams, ceilings and trim.

Hough (1984)
1566 Crawford Road
Architects: Saunders, Van Petten

An L-shaped plan is topped by an active roof line of a succession of sharp gables. The pale exterior brick extends inside. The children's storytelling area features a repeat of the exterior forms.

Mt. Pleasant (1925) (1981)
14000 Kinsman Avenue
Architect: L. Kent Moatz
Renovation: Ernst Payer

Once a branch bank, this renovation was the second at the site. Color was freely used to enliven the interior.

Rice (1927) (1981)
2820 E. 116th Street
Architect: Walker & Weeks
Renovation: Ernst Payer

A large, rectangular space was made exciting by way of color and furnishings including a wall sculpture featuring book characters springing from a book's pages, the work of William McVey.

Sterling (1913) (1985)
2200 E. 30th Street
Architect: Edward Tilton
Renovation: Joseph Ceruti

The architect created a new cathedral ceiling with central skylight to make a small volume dramatic.

Union (1982)
333463 E. 93rd Street
Architect: Collins and Rimer

This branch features a design which reflects the characteristics of a nearby church building. Its interior has a quality of repose assisted by clerestory lighting.

Paul J. Volpe AIA
Melanie Boyd

Section 2

Public Buildings

The Cuyahoga County Courthouse (1912)
1 Lakeside Avenue
Architects: Lehman & Schmitt

The first building to be designed of the Group Plan, though the second completed. Construction began in 1905 but the earliest stages of planning were slow. The award-winning Beaux-Arts submittal was by Lehman & Schmitt, with chief designer Charles Morris an alumni of the Ecole des Beaux-Arts. Large and costly, it would create difficulty in obtaining design continuity throughout the Group Plan. Before construction began in 1905, three bays were removed from the north and south ends and two from the east and west, with the full fourth floor proposal reduced to a partial fourth floor, behind the portico.

The site, chosen in 1900, helped dictate the size and scope of the 1903 Group Plan scheme. Terminating Ontario Street the Court-house, with City Hall, anchors the north end of the Mall. It is a well-composed building of typical Beaux-Arts elements including a two-story Corinthian colonnade with balustraded roof line, arcaded rusticated base and end pavilions and central portico running the full four stories. A series of marble sculptures above the cornice, decorating the granite facade, trace the evolution of the English and American legal systems.

The grand interior, partly the design of Charles Schweinfurth, is incredibly rich in its use of marble, with patterned inlaid floors and thick balustrades. The central staircase, rising in easy stages with an almost musical lilt, encounters a large Tiffany stained glass window, strategically placed to catch the rising sun. Entitled Justice, and personifying Law and Justice, it was designed in 1913 (restored 1986-1988) by Frederick Wilson and Charles Schweinfurth. The Main Hall, the epitome of classic elegance, is vaulted with massive piers continuing to the floor, unbroken by the entablature which along with the columns about the perimeter, are set back. Courtrooms are done in English oak, chestnut and other fine woods. The Probate Court Room is especially ornate.

Frank J. Lausche State Office Building (1979)
615 Superior Avenue, N.W.
Architects: Ohio Building Authority; Fred Toguchi Associates;
Madison-Madison International; Ireland & Associates

An elegant, black glass building occupying an odd, triangular site, acts to contain the western edge of the city's business district. It is best experienced upon crossing the Detroit-Superior Bridge. The steel and glass office block seems to float upon a sturdy precast concrete base. Drastic ground level changes are resolved by use of terracing and ramps. The horizontal element is echoed by the main public lobby, a highly compressed space with dim recessed lighting, which contains a two-story sculpture, *Cloud Series IV*, by Lenore Tawney. This floor, pulled away from the exterior glass at the south west edge, provides an opportunity to visually connect downtown with the Flats. Two exterior sculptures of note are described in the section on Monuments.

Joseph L. Stamps District Service Center (1987)
4150 S. Marginal Road
Architects: City of Cleveland Division of Architecture,
Paul J. Volpe Commissioner; Gould Associates

Heavily insulated to shield against the winds off Lake Erie, this simple yet elegant building is prominently situated along the East Shoreway. Programmed and constructed to address the needs of the city's service vehicles, it consolidates several service departments into one functional municipal complex. The classically organized main facade is in keeping with the industrial vocabulary of the neighborhood yet relates to the graceful design of other public buildings. Constructed in multi-colored, layered, glazed block, the building makes a strong architectural statement, particularly at night as the result of the intricate facade lighting scheme. The highly functional, high-tech interior uses the significant change in grade to accommodate program functions and enhance the work spaces, which enjoy spectacular panoramic views of Lake Erie.

Old Federal Building (1911)
201 Superior Avenue, N.E.
Architect: Arnold W. Brunner

The cornerstone reads 1905. Expected to be completed in no more than two years, problems in funding and design changes delayed the public opening to 1910. With great excitement, the first building of the Group Plan was officially dedicated in early 1911, initially containing the U.S. Post Office, Custom House and Courthouse. Today it serves principally as a courthouse.

The five-story granite structure, a prime example of Beaux-Arts classicism, occupies the entire block bounded by Superior, East 3rd St., Rockwell and Public Square. A full-scale mock-up of a portion of Brunner's design was constructed first in order that the final effect could be judged. Its rusticated base and colossal Corinthian colonnades make it notably monumental. The design, based on the Place de la Concorde in Paris, and paired with the Cleveland Public Library, provides an ideal southern terminating edge for the Group Plan.

On Superior Avenue the public is greeted by two freestanding figures, *Commerce* and *Jurisprudence*, executed by Daniel Chester French in 1912, which enhance the left-and right-end pavilions respectively. Not only were original visitors astounded by the rich use of marble, they also enjoyed a series of thirty-five panels depicting worldwide postal delivery routes executed by Francis D. Millett, an alumni of the World's Colombian Exposition. All of the panels have since been removed and are stored in Washington D.C. Court Room No. 2 with its breath-taking richness of ornamentation and craftsmanship, has few equals in Cleveland.

The Justice Center Complex (1976)
Lakeside and Ontario

Police Headquarters Building
Architects: Richard L. Bowen & Associates

Cuyahoga County & Cleveland Municipal Courts Tower
The Correction Center
Architects: Prindle, Patrick & Partners
Consultant: Pietro Belluschi

Wrapping the corners of Lakeside, West Third and Ontario, this three-building complex unifies three separate facilities. The strongly vertical 26-story Courts Tower occupies the corner of the "L" and contains 44 court and 9 hearing rooms. Similar in massing and horizontal emphasis, the Police Headquarters, serving a department of 2,000, and the Correction Center are placed to the south and west respectively.
Differing in configuration, the Correction Center allows 777 cells, arranged in pods of 23, to be flooded with daylight. The deeply recessed base of the Police and Correction facilities, regular spacing of bays and perimeter columns, as well as continuous horizontal elements act to cohere the grouping. Bronze tinted glass enhances the play of shadow upon the building's surface.

Ground level changes are resolved within by use of a dynamic multilevel light court. Circulation between the buildings occurs through the block by way of this light court which opens with suspended glass curtain walls to the north, south, and east. It directly links the heart of the complex with Ontario, Lakeside, and St. Clair Avenue. The complex makes extensive use of brick pavers, precast panels and granite surfacing throughout. On the east plaza sits "Portal," a powerful steel tubular sculpture by Isamu Noguchi (see Section 3, Monuments and Plazas).

Cleveland City Hall (1916)
601 Lakeside Avenue
Architect: J. Milton Dyer
Restoration: City of Cleveland Division of Architecture

As the third building in the Group Plan, the long-awaited new City Hall was dedicated with much pomp on July 4, 1916, sixteen years after the site was chosen and ten years after the designs were approved. The site, chosen in 1900, along with that of the Cuyahoga County Courthouse, helped to determine the size and scope of the Group Plan. Terminating East 6th Street, City Hall, paired with the Courthouse, anchors the north end of the Mall. A well-composed building of Neo-Classic and Beaux-Arts design, it is similar to the Courthouse in size and proportion, though done in the more somber Doric order. A balustraded roof line, two-story colonnade and arcaded rusticated base are typical of both. Statues for the cornice and beside the entrance, representing administrative departments of the city, were designed but never executed. The central pavilion of the front facade has three entrance bays which run four stories with a fifth story concealed by a balustraded roof line.

The vestibule gives way to a handsome two-story rotunda of Botticelli marble. An uplit vaulted and coffered ceiling, containing skylights, rests upon large Doric columns. The second floor Mayor's suite contains rich wood detailing, as does the three-story Council Chamber which, paneled in oak, rivals the rotunda as the most impressive space in City Hall.

The exterior of City Hall is basically unchanged from the day it was dedicated, with the exception of flagpoles and outdoor illumination which were added in the early 1970s. The addition of an underground garage completed in 1975 has been the only major change. The interior has undergone extensive renovation, beginning in 1972 with the Mayor's office. Since then virtually every department has been systematically updated to bring the building to modern standards for a municipal office facility. The deteriorated central roof has been carefully replaced with copper, restoring the dignity and elegance of the original material and details.

The Federal Building (1967)
1240 East 9th Street
Architects: Outcalt, Guenther, Rode & Bonebrake; Shafer Flynn & Associates; Dalton & Dalton Associates

Typical of modern, commercial office buildings of the 1960s, the Federal Building establishes strength in design through a purity and rich variety of materials as well as close attention to detail. As part of the Erieview Plan proposed for downtown Cleveland by I.M. Pei in the early 1960s, this tall, sleek 32-story tower originally was designated as a massive 8-story building.

The office block, wrapped in a skin of stainless steel and glass, is lifted by a base of four recessed rectilinear volumes, clad in highly polished marble, resting upon a field of rough cut granite and slate. Curtain walls of glass stretch taut between the two larger end volumes, creating an interior lobby and plazas to the east and west with the smaller volumes encasing the double-sided elevator shafts. Regularly spaced piers of textural aluminum bring this basic steel and glass structure to the ground.

The larger-than-life statue of the young George Washington, as a surveyor, by Cleveland sculptor William McVey, fronts the tower on the west.

The Federal Building replaced the Old Central Armory and the Cuyahoga County Morgue. The Armory was a late Victorian confection with a castellated Gothic exterior. Designed by Lehman and Schmitt and constructed in 1896, it had served as the site of exhibitions, boxing matches, conventions, floral shows and public events for sixty years. The Morgue (1894) was one of Cleveland's rare examples of the Egyptian Revival Style and was also a product of Lehman & Schmitt.

The Cleveland Board Of Education (1930)
1380 East 6th Street
Architects: Walker & Weeks

Completing the east side of the Mall, between Rockwell and St. Clair, this sandstone structure rests just north of the Cleveland Public Library. Ascribing to the general classical formula and requirements of Burnham for Group Plan buildings, this six-story, E-shaped structure, uniform in height with its neighbors, is rather restrained compared with other works designed at this time by the respected Cleveland firm of Walker & Weeks. Designed with the intent of being the main entry, the East 3rd St. facade faces the Mall with its arcaded entry and two-story lobby of marble, with blue/green marble pillars. The backside, the East 6th Street facade, is set back on line with the western edge of Public Auditorium, and creates a particularly pleasant open green space. This landscaped approach, which covers an underground garage, now acts as the main entrance.

Offices and assembly rooms are scattered throughout the building. An assembly room which seats 375 people is decorated with panels by Cleveland artist Rolf Stoll. The board room on the third floor is paneled in golden veined Formoso marble.

The Public Utilities Building (1971)

1201 Lakeside Avenue
Architect: Thomas T.K. Zung

The first new municipal office building in 30 years, this project came out of the Carl B. Stokes administration. Terminating the northeast end of E. 12th Street, it was an integral part of the newly proposed Mall Plan for E. 12th Street.

Attempting to counter the sterility of the glass box, the architect worked with a layered richness in design. A long, narrow, marble-clad structure, it narrow-ends on Lakeside with its main entry pavilion facing west. The rhythm of recessed window bays is broken by central end pavilions echoing the main entry. Having a recessed base, three-story window wall shaft, and heavy cantilevered top, this five story building has definite classical design overtones. An interior light court rises the full five stories to an aluminum framed skylight.

Old Main Post Office (1934)

401 Prospect Avenue, N.W.
Architects: Walker & Weeks; Philip L. Small & Associates;
James A. Wetmore, Architectural Supervisor of U.S. Treasury
Department

Adaptive Renovation into
M.K. Ferguson Plaza (1990)
Renovation: van Dijk, Johnson Partners

The Post Office, bearing the stamp of the official 1930s architectural style, was built on the air rights of the Cleveland Union Terminals Co. as the last building in The Terminal Group. It is a simple, modernistic building with Art Deco detailing with no intention of being monumental but achieving it nonetheless. Fluted piers create window bays. The original sandstone was never secured properly, and in the mid 1970s the exterior was re-clad using formed concrete panels.

The only public space of this building was a 228-foot-long lobby of postal windows. Using an innovative system of chutes and conveyors, the Postal Service took advantage of the site by creating a direct link with the railroad below. Today this building is being converted to a corporate headquarters office building as part of the massive Tower City Center development.

Fire Station No. 20 & EMS Unit No. 4 (1985)
3765 Pearl Road
Architects: Ovington & Glaser; City of Cleveland Division
of Architecture

Located in the Brooklyn Center Historic District, this station
replaced two obsolete 19th century firehouses. The architects
designed this new facility to harmonize with its neighborhood by
using elements reminiscent of local historic commercial buildings
and churches. Although the clock tower was built to serve the
practical function of drying hoses, it becomes a prominent and
distinguishing component of the composition. Constructed of brick
with limestone details, this carefully composed building emanates
a feeling of warmth and romanticism, creating a focal point in the
community. The highly efficient interior is light and airy with high
ceilings and large windows of various configurations.

Fire Station No. 21 (1940) (1987)
1821 Carter Road (at Collision Bend)
Architects: A.C. Wolf & F.M. Griffith
Restoration: Lipaj Tomsik; City of Cleveland Division of
Architecture

Built as a headquarters for city fireboats, this two-story Spanish
Revival style fire station is located in the Flats on the west side
of the Cuyahoga River. Architectural features include a tile roof,
wrought iron around the windows and a limestone door surround.
The station has been completely renovated to make the interior
spaces more efficient as a modern fire station.

Fire Station No. 26 (1898)
7818 Kinsman Road
Architect: William Watterson

An excellent example of the Romanesque Revival style, this
massive brick fire station features a corner tower, arched windows,
and two arched apparatus doors with large side buttresses. This
facility is unusual because it is not typical of the other stations
built throughout Cleveland at the turn of the century.

Fire Station No. 36 (1921) (1987)
3720 East 131st Street
Architect: J.H. MacDowell
Restoration: Kaplan/Curtis Architects; City of Cleveland Division
of Architecture

Two stately, round-arched apparatus doors trimmed with large
stone blocks that are continued in the corner quoins and a wide
dentilled cornice give this renovated fire station an air of importance. Considerable exterior restoration and interior modernization
have preserved the historic and functional integrity of this
beautiful building clad in a pale tan brick rather than the conven-
tional red.

Fire Station No. 41 (1945)
3090 East 116th Street
Architect: Herman Kregelius

This distinguished, classically-inspired station sits quietly and
gracefully among its residential neighbors. The apparatus room,
central to the design, is faced in stone and reminiscent of a temple
portico. Single-story, flat roofed, brick structures surrounding this
room supply support facilities.

Burke Lakefront Airport Terminal and Tower (1963-1970)
1501 North Marginal Road
Architects: Central, 2-story section, Outcalt, Guenther, Rode,
Toguchi & Bonebrake (1963)
Western Concourse, Fred Toguchi Associates (1969) Tower (1970)

Burke Lakefront Airport was initially proposed in 1936 but the
idea did not materialize until 1947. With increasing usage the need
for up-to-date passenger services culminated in the lean and clean
structures constituting the terminal. Most obvious is the undulating
roof of the 2-story section, topping a functionalist glass and steel
base with a form clearly suggestive of flight.

Cleveland Hopkins International Airport (1951)
Architects: Outcalt and Guenther
Renovation: Bowen and Associates

The original rather modest passenger terminal at Cleveland Hopkins Airport – "International" came later – was replaced in 1951 with the first "big city" modern terminal by Outcalt and Guenther, employing a central terminal with ground level fingers, or concourses, to the north and west. A south concourse was added in 1968 which introduced holding rooms at an upper level and jetway boarding ramps. A unique feature was the terminus of the RTA rapid transit allowing direct connection to downtown Cleveland by train.

Planning for the present day terminal began in the offices of Bowen and Associates in 1973. The Bowen team brought auto traffic to the terminal by separate roadways for arriving and departing passengers, greatly enlarged the terminal to accommodate upper level ticketing lobbies and lower level baggage claim facilities, and enlarged and double-decked the north (A) and west (B) concourses. The expanded terminal increased the passenger capacity by 150% and provided an International Arrivals facility with a capacity of 350 passengers per hour.

The south (C) concourse was later renovated, and remodelings have been more or less continuous to accommodate the many changes occurring since deregulation of the air travel industry. The new FAA control tower was added in 1986 to the design of Leo A. Daley Co. of Omaha in association with Fuller, Sadao and Zung, Architects.

Turner Construction Company was the construction manager for the expansion, which, combined with appropriate airside improvements, cost approximately $80,000,000. Major metal sculptures in the main lobby and at the deplaning roadway were created by Clarence E. van Duzer.

The West Side Market (1912) (1989)
1979 West 25th Street
Architects: Hubbell & Benes
Restoration: City of Cleveland Division of Architecture;
Paul J. Volpe, Commissioner; HWH Architects Engineers Planners

Built at a time when eclecticism was still predominant, symbolism being more important than any discernible architectural style, the Market is transitional in concept, exhibiting definite classical references. It was proposed in 1905 as part of a group including a flower market and public bath/ auditorium, but due to a fund controversy, the Public Market building alone was completed in 1912.

The form is basically an interpretation of a Roman basilica, with a 124 foot x 245 foot long central hall lit by clerestories above the two side aisles. The 44-foot ceiling is vaulted with steel arches faced with buff glazed brick. Guastavino tile spans the spaces between.

The building is hugged on the northeast by permanent outdoor stands. Acting as a focal point of interest for the near West Side, the 137-foot copper-domed clock tower, originally a water tower, contrasts with the long, low lines of the market. The large window on the western end of the building was restored in 1989 as part of the major restoration program. The exterior of the building has been totally revitalized ensuring the preservation of the architectural heritage of this vibrant public market.

The Cleveland Convention Center

1220 East 6th Street

Public Auditorium (1922)
Architects: Frederick H. Betz & J.H. MacDowell
Consultant: Frank R. Walker

Music Hall & North Lobby (1927)
Architect: Herman Kregelius

Convention Center Addition & Mall Entrance (1964)
Architects: Outcalt, Guenther, Rode & Bonebrake

Complete Rehabilitation (1988)
Architects: URS Consultants; City of Cleveland Division of Architecture

Public Auditorium, a classically inspired granite building, was completed in 1922 as the fourth building of the Group Plan scheme. The largest and finest in the U.S. at the time of opening, it held two national political conventions during the summer of 1924. It soon proved to be insufficient in size. The architects extended their design north to include a lobby, executive offices, three small halls, and a ballroom, and to the south with Music Hall, which opened in 1927.

All done in an Italian Renaissance style, vast stretches of smooth exterior wall were made architecturally comprehensible by use of a high rusticated podium, a cornice line conforming to Group Plan recommendations, and careful placement of the arcaded windows. An inscription on the frieze reads, "A Monument Conceived as a Tribute to the Ideals of Cleveland, Builded by Her Citizens and Dedicated to Social Progress, Industrial Achievement and Civic Interests."

The classical simplicity of the 300 foot x 215 foot x 80 foot interior is manifest by the wide arched ceiling which provides an unobstructed view from each of over 11,500 seats, as no columns are used for support. The acoustical properties of Public Auditorium are excellent in spite of its size. It is lit by indirect lighting diffused through glass panels in the ceiling. Below, an exhibition hall of over 28,500 square feet was created. A stage, accommodating both Public Auditorium and the smaller, 3,000 seat, Music Hall, measures 60 feet x 104 feet with a proscenium on the Public Auditorium side of 72 feet x 42 feet.

In 1964, tremendously enlarged display areas were created (over 207,000 square feet), with exhibit space running under Mall B and continuing under Mall C. A new Mall entrance was created of glass and metal in a modern vocabulary.

In the late 1970s the Convention Center had become outdated and unable to compete with newer facilities. A massive renovation project was begun in 1983. During this time a ballroom was added, major spaces were reworked to make them more functional, and the interior underwent a complete revitalization. When this restoration was completed in 1988 it put the Center back into competition with major convention centers nationwide.

Cleveland Municipal Stadium (1931)
Lakeshore between W. 3rd and E. 9th Sts.
Architects: Walker and Weeks
Engineers: Osborn Engineering Co.

One of the nation's largest and earliest municipal stadiums built on a giant scale. Baseball attendance records were set in 1948 and season-after-season capacity crowds of 78,000-plus enlivened the football season. The 7th National Eucharistic Congress in 1935 drew and audience of 125,000.

The oval polygon shaped stadium is 800 feet long, 720 feet wide and 116 feet tall. Its structure is steel with tan brick outer walls and terra cotta trim. The superstructure is an aluminum roof with massive louvered exterior facing. The playing field is four acres in area, while the overall structure occupies twelve acres. Loges were added around the upper grandstand in 1974.

The general exterior expression of the massive building reflects a quiet Art Deco feeling. Because of its location on landfill below the plane of downtown, the structure does not overwhelm, a commendable aspect further strengthened by its low-key architectrual expression. To the north of the Stadium are the A. Donald Gray Gardens, a remnant of the 1936 Great Lakes Exposition.

County of Cuyahoga Human Services/ Support Agencies Building (1991)
East 17th St. between Superior and Payne Avenues
Architect: Richard Fleischman
County Architect: Berj Shakarian

This block-long, six-story structure, housing two separate and unrelated agencies, encompasses 300,000 sq. ft. of space wholly embraced in a curtain wall of two types of glazing. The pattern of glazing supports and the variation in glass create visual interest on all sides. Vaulted skylights at the ends and center add interest to the building's mass. Three atriums extend vertically to the skylights.

Baldwin Reservoir, Filtration Plant and Grounds (1925)
11216 Fairhill Road
Architect: Herman Kregelius
Landscape Architect: Albert D. Taylor

The Baldwin Reservoir occupies a 50 acre site on a plateau above the city's east side. Commuters traveling up Fairhill Road view its commanding presence daily but see only the Administration Building and Filters, a grand Palladian concept atop balustraded terraces and the Reservoir below.

A 3-story central pavilion features a great Palladian arch. Flanking wings contain the filtering equipment. The stone and brick structure is topped by hipped roofs in slate.

The underground reservoir is an extraordinary concrete structure, 1,035 ft. by 551 ft. in area, 39 ft. in height, its groined roof supported by 1,196 columns and the whole providing storage for 135,800,000 gallons of water, the largest covered reservoir in the world.

Paul J. Volpe AIA
Melanie Boyd

Section 3

Monuments & Plazas

James A. Garfield Monument (1890)
(Modified 1900) (Restored 1984)
Lakeview Cemetery, 12316 Euclid Avenue
Architect: George W. Keller
Sculptors: Alexander Doyle, Casper Buberl (Exterior Relief Panels)

The massive cylindrical stone body of the Garfield Monument with its conical top overlooks much of Cleveland's East Side from its elevation in Lake View Cemetery.

The Garfield Monument was erected as a Memorial to President James Abram Garfield (1831-1881) who was shot by an assassin on July 2, 1881 and died September 19, 1881.

The Garfield Monument is 180 feet in height and 50 feet in diameter. Architect Keller, who won a competition with this design, may have taken ancient round towers of Ireland as his prototype to which he appended a rectangular porch.

The interior, a spectacular display of Victorian craft, is lavishly decorated with mosaic scenes illustrating the life of the President, with colorful stained glass windows and, in the dome soffit, with gilded mosaic angels holding the signs of the compass overhead.

In general the decorative elements of the Garfield Monument are derived from Romanesque sources. The large three-stage circular tower with a conical roof 50 feet in diameter, is flanked by two small octagonal towers and entered through a large rectangular vestibule.

The exterior of this vestibule is decorated in relief with five panels showing Garfield as teacher, statesman, soldier, president, and as martyred president lying in state in the Rotunda of the Capitol.

The monument was modified (1900) by Charles W. Hopkinson when the surrounding deck was hollowed out below creating the current surrounding basement level.

Two spacious chambers exist above the Memorial room which contains a large white Carrara marble statue of the President. These chambers after having been unseen by the public for many years, are now open to view by appointment. The monument was extensively restored and up-dated in 1984 by Gaede Serne Zofcin, Architects, Inc.

Soldiers and Sailors Monument (Dedicated July 4, 1894)
S.E. Quadrant, Public Square
Sculptor/Architect: Captain Levi T. Scofield

The monument was erected to commemorate the heroic deeds of the soldiers and sailors of Cuyahoga County who defended the Union in the Civil War. The names of 6,000 men are engraved in marble within the base chamber.

There was considerable controversy over its location and design before it was finally placed on the southeast quadrant of Public Square. The site was relinquished by a monument to Oliver Hazzard Perry, hero of the Battle of Lake Erie, which was relocated to Wade Park overlooking the Lagoon.

The Monument is basically a square building sitting atop a sandstone esplanade 100 feet square and crowned by a 125 foot granite shaft with a 15 foot statue of Liberty on top.

Bronze sculptures on each of the four sides represent the Infantry, Artillery, Cavalry and Naval branches of service. A bronze eagle stands over the north and south entrances.

The memorial room, entered through large bronze doors, contains relief panels depicting several wartime events.

President William McKinley was the principal speaker at the 1894 dedication ceremony. In 1989 a dramatic revision of the site surrounding the Monument was carried out as the final phase of the upgrading of the Public Square. Berj Shakarian, architect for the County, directed this work, initially conceived by Sasaki Associates, Inc.

Wade Park and University Circle (1896)
East 105th to Ford Dr., Liberty Blvd. to East Blvd.
Landscape Architect: E.W. Bowditch

Wade Park and University Circle are bequests to the City of Cleveland by wealthy, late 19th Century industrialists. Jeptha Wade planned a park around Doan Brook (where University Circle is located) and provided the impetus for its development. In 1872 he donated it to the City of Cleveland. In 1893 a large park of seven sections was so planned that each could be united by a broad boulevard. The drive (Liberty Blvd., now Martin Luther King Jr. Drive) connecting Gordon and Wade Parks was completed with the assistance of John D. Rockefeller, who gave the land in between and $300,000 to improve it.

The development of University Circle as a cultural center began to take shape at this time. Western Reserve University began building on the edge of the park on Euclid Avenue in 1882; Case Institute joined it in 1885.

The Circle area now contains Cleveland's major museums and institutions. A walking tour of the Circle area is offered in section 19D.

The Mall, Hanna Fountains and War Memorial Fountain

Rockwell Avenue to Lakeside Ave., Centered on East 3rd St.
Concept Architects: Daniel Burnham, Arnold Brunner
and John Carrere

Cleveland's Mall is noteworthy for its size, its central placement and its creation long after the city's original street layout by a team of notable architects acting as the Group Plan Commission. The Commission was created in 1902, through the encouragement of the American Institute of Architects and the Chamber of Commerce, in order to create a proper municipal setting for a number of intended public structures – all in the spirit of the City Beautiful movement. A three-block-long and 500-foot-wide area was to be flanked by civic structures in formal array and similarly styled in a Neo-Classical manner. The Federal Building of 1910 was the first of these, and as the warehouse structures occupying the space gradually were removed (the last in 1935) the Mall's surface took form. The form is still emerging, as the area defined as Mall "A" (nearest Rockwell) is under reconstruction for a 900-car underground parking garage to be topped by an elegant plaza, designed by Richard H. Kaplan Associates, upon which the War Memorial Fountain and Figure, by sculptor Marshall Fredericks, will be returned. The massive work of polished granite and bronze was first installed in 1964, then removed for restoration by Marshall Fredericks in 1989. Also named the Fountain of Eternal Life, it symbolizes humanity's reaching heavenward from the flames of conflict.

The central portion of the Mall, referred to as Mall B, was also dug out for an underground garage and convention space in 1964. Its elevated top surface features the Hanna Fountains and Pool, with extensive planting and promenade areas. The designer was Michael Rapuano.

Mall C, closest to the bluff overlooking the lake, is the scene of numerous public programs such as festivals and food-oriented events. Both Mall C and A have withstood occasions when plans to occupy the sites with major new buildings were proposed. The resulting openness of the Mall provides Clevelanders with a distinctive sense of "place," especially in conjunction with the adjacent Public Square. Yet to make the setting complete, is the west flanking side of the Mall, north of St. Clair Avenue, not yet carried out in the manner of the rest.

Wade Memorial Chapel (1900)
Lakeview Cemetery
Architects: Hubbell & Benes

Wade Memorial Chapel sits among the winding roadways of Lake View Cemetery. Its exterior, simulating a Roman temple, belies the extraordinary richness of its artful Tiffany Studios interior.

This funeral chapel was erected to the memory of Jeptha H. Wade and is widely considered the most important structure in Lakeview Cemetery after the Garfield Memorial. Built to resemble a Greek temple, the classical style was adapted to meet the requirements of its site.

The fine craftsmanship resulted from the sensitive collaboration between the architect and decorative artists. The interior, designed by Tiffany Studios, contains some of the finest examples of Tiffany's work. The walls and ceilings are pure white marble with two murals of glass tesserae, each eight feet high and thirty two feet long, depicting the "Voyage of Life".

A spectacular stained glass window is the room's centerpiece. Floor, pews, chancel rail and lighting are all part of the richly decorated concept.

Cleveland Cultural Gardens (1926) (1939)
East Blvd. between Superior & St. Clair
Landscape Architects: A. Donald Gray & Others
Sculptors: Frank Jirouch, William McVey & Others

Conceived in 1926 as a commemorative project to recognize the contributions of various nationality groups to Cleveland's life, a unique series of cultural gardens was established in Rockefeller Park. The project continued throughout the Depression years and was not completed until the eve of World War II. The Cultural Gardens display both the formality of European planned gardens in combination with the local interpretation of English informality. A unified plan was prepared, with walks connecting the various gardens in a continuous chain. In 1939 the series of eighteen nationality gardens was dedicated as a unit. Subsequently several additional gardens were added. The gardens are filled with paved terraces, commemorative sculpture and organic landscaping. In recent years the gardens have deteriorated but steps have been taken to restore them.

Woodland Cemetery, (organized 1853)
Block bounded by Woodland Avenue on the south,
Quincy Avenue on the north, from E. 66 to E. 71 Streets.
Landscape Architect: Howard Daniels

Occupying a large rectangular site, Woodland Cemetery was once
the city's pride. Surrounded by an iron fence with stone pillars, the
cemetery was formally entered from the south at a stone gate and
office structure done in a high Victorian style, the work of James
Ireland. This building is in a serious state of deterioration, and its
survival is uncertain.

The cemetery was laid out in a rural cemetery style, with a main
avenue flanked by lesser roadways following circular and diagonal
paths. Many prominent Clevelanders were buried here including
John Brough, last Civil War governor of Ohio. The combination of
site planning and surviving tombstones and burial vaults provides
one with an exceptional testament to the form and detail of a
major 19th Century cemetery.

Lake View Cemetery (organized 1869)
12316 Euclid Avenue
Landscape Architect: Adolph Strauch

Occupying 285 acres of hilly terrain rising from Euclid Avenue
up to the level of the "Heights", Lake View Cemetery has matured
into a noteworthy combination of landscape design, arboreal park,
history and architecture. The third of the great garden cemeteries
to be developed in America (after Boston and Cincinnati), Lake
View has maintained its reputation for unique and exotic plant
forms – five hundred trees are identified for visitors.

The spectacle of Lake View's remarkable collection of monuments
is a grand testimonial to the tastes of the decades and to the
craftsmanship of the stone masons of Cleveland. The great

memorials to President James
Garfield and to Jeptha Wade
are described separately while
the Mausoleum is noted in the
Heights driving tour (See
Section 20E). Since Lake View
became the favored locale for
the burial of Cleveland
notables after the 1880's, the
list of distinguished citizens is
substantial. Among these are
John D. Rockefeller (whose
obelisk is the highest on the
grounds), Newton D. Baker,
George Humphrey, William G.
Mather, Marcus Hanna,

Architect Frank Cudell, Charles Chesnutt, and members of the
Severance, Blossom, Bolton, Hay and Holden families. Among the
gravesites is that of the mass burial of the victims of the tragic
Collinwood School fire of 1908.

A remarkable concrete dam was erected at the cemetery's
eastern section in 1977 by the Northeast Ohio Regional Sewer
District. Well screened, the dam comes upon the unwary visitor
as a great surprise.

Erie Street Cemetery (1826) (Restored 1950)
East 9th St. to E. 14th St., South of Bolivar Rd.

Built on land purchased by the City of Cleveland for $1.00 from
Leonard Case Sr., the cemetery is noted as the burial place of
Joc-O-Sot or Walking Bear, a distinguished Sauk chief who had
become the darling of the English royal court. The cemetery is
now a close-in green space for the center city. Its fanciful, stone
gateway arch facing E. 9th Street is a familiar object of the city's
streetscape.

Riverside Cemetery Administration Building (1897)
Architect: Charles W. Hopkinson

This highly visible, dark (Massachusetts Brownstone) structure,
commanding the entry to Riverside Cemetery, is a spirited design
in the Romanesque Revival mode. Red roof tiles cover the turrets,
gables and porch. The building suffered a serious fire in 1987 but
has been faithfully restored.

Lorain-Carnegie (Hope Memorial) Bridge Pylons (1932)
Architect: Frank Walker.
Engineer: Wilbur J. Watson & Associates
Sculptor: Henry Hering

The two pairs of giant Art Deco figures serve as gateways to
Cleveland's East and West Sides. Hermes, holding a tank-truck
in one instance and a coal-hauler in the other symbolizes the
progress of transportation. The 43-foot-high pylons are
constructed of local Berea sandstone.

The Lorain-Carnegie Bridge (renamed the Hope Memorial Bridge) dramatically spans the industrial valley between its two pairs of entry pylons, sculptured sandstone statements of 1930s public art.

The United States Post Office, (1910)
Custom House and Court House
(Old Federal Building)
Architect: Arnold Brunner
Exterior Sculpture on South Elevation:
Commerce (east) and Jurisprudence (west)
Sculptor: Daniel Chester French
Materials: White marble with granite base

These two massive pieces flank the monumental facades of the Old Federal Building and contribute strongly to the sense of civic importance of Superior Avenue as it arrives at Public Square.

George Washington (1973)
New Federal Building
Washington Square, Lakeside Avenue at E. 6th Street
Sculptor: William McVey

Commissioned by Cleveland's Early Settlers' Association in celebration of the 1976 Bicentennial. The larger-than-life bronze figure depicts Washington as a young man on a pre-revolutionary campaign as a surveyor.

General Moses Cleaveland (1888)
S.W. Quadrant, Public Square
Sculptor: James G. C. Hamilton
Materials: Bronze on granite plinth

Moses Cleaveland (1754-1806), founder of the City in 1796 in behalf of the Connecticut Land Company, is portrayed with the tools of the surveyor in his hands. The standing figure has long been the locale of open-air speech-making, a continuing Public Square tradition.

"Triple L. Excentric Gyratory Gyratory III" (1980)
Plaza in front of the National City Center
E. 9th St. and Euclid Avenue
Sculptor: George Rickey
Material: Brush Stainless Steel

Standing thirty-eight feet in height, this mobile wind-activated sculpture entertains the pedestrians at Cleveland's busy E. Ninth and Euclid intersection. Weighing 1,400 lbs., the "L"-shaped arms have a twenty-seven foot radius of movement.

Portal (1976)
Cleveland Justice Center
Sculptor: Isamu Noguchi
Materials: Steel-painted black

"Portal", Noguchi's curving antidote to the stern judicial tower above, rests on the Justice Center Plaza along Ontario Street.

Controversial when first erected as a companion to the Justice Center, "Portal" has been cynically interpreted as "justice going down the drain", though some experts believe it is Noguchi's best work.

This 36 foot high conception by the famed Japanese-American sculptor is gradually winning its way into the hearts of Clevelanders. It is particularly interesting for the architectural backgrounds which it frames as one moves about it. It was a gift to the city by The George Gund Foundation.

Last (1979)
Ohio State Office Building (Northeast corner)
Sculptor: Tony Smith
Materials: Steel painted Orange.
Dimensions: 35 feet high x 75 feet long
Fabricator: Industrial Welding Co., Newark, N.J.

This monumental piece is a composite of six hollow, rhomboidal 6 foot by 7 foot sections, assembled in place and joined within. The title stems from the sculptor's proclamation that this is the last arch he would undertake having done others at MIT, University of Nebraska and elsewhere.

Terminal (1979)
Ohio State Office Building (Northwest corner)
Sculptor: Gene Kangas
Materials: Welded steel pipe and steel plate

Terminal was done to enhance the environment at the knife-edge, western end of Cleveland's State Office Building. Kangas family members modeled for the steel silhouettes which now permanently "inhabit" this corner.

Commodore Oliver Hazzard Perry Monument (1860)
Rededicated (1937)
Gordon Park
Designer: William Walcutt
Materials: Marble with granite base

Originally located on S.E. Quadrant of Public Square, the site now occupied by the Solders & Sailors Monument.

Abraham Lincoln (1931)
The Mall, east side
Sculptor: Max Kalish
Materials: Bronze on a granite base
Height: 12 Feet

Max Kalish's only outdoor sculpture, this gracious depiction of the president fronts The Board of Education Building and faces the new Mall "A" Plaza.

Marcus A. Hanna Monument (1908)
University Circle
Sculptor: Augustus St. Gaudens
Materials: Bronze on granite base
Height: 17-1/2 Feet

St. Gaudens died before Monument was unveiled. It celebrates State Senator Marcus Hanna (1837-1904), an industrial giant, who helped make Cleveland a leading city in the nation both industrially and politically.

David Berger Memorial Monument (1974)
Jewish Community Center, 3505 Mayfield Road
Sculptor: David E. Davis
Material: Corten Steel

This powerful abstraction memorializes the eleven Israeli athletes who died in Munich at the 1972 Olympic games. It is a Cleveland Heights landmark.

Standing Cornice Sculptures C (1912)
Location: Cuyahoga County Courthouse
Architects: Lehman & Schmitt

Six eight-to-ten-foot Tennessee marble statues adorn the south and four adorn the north cornices of the Courthouse. These statues were designed as a "visual representation of the development of English and American Law." Of specific interest is the south cornice where depicted are (from left to right): Magna Charta author Stephen Langton, Simon de Montfort (House of Commons), King Edward I (English judicial reform), John Lord Somers (Declaration of Rights), John Hampden (author of the Petition of Rights), and William Murray, Earl of Mansfield (Development of Commercial Law).

The four north cornice statues were designed to represent the Law in all its manifestations. Depicted are, (from left to right): Moses (for moral law), sixth-century Roman Emperor Justinian (for civil law), ninth-century King Alfred the Great (for English common law) and thirteenth-century Pope Gregory IX (for ecclesiastical or canon law). Sculptors were Daniel Chester French and Karl Bitter (south side) and Herman Matzen (north side).

Two bronze sculptures repose at the north street level entrance and sit atop Vermont granite bases. These depict Chief Justice John Marshall (for the doctrine of judicial interpretation of the law in the Federal system) and Ohio Chief Justice Rufus P. Ranney (for the same doctrine in Ohio Law).

Two bronze statues flank the south entrance to the Courthouse and depict Thomas Jefferson and Alexander Hamilton, representing the application for principles of English law to the American Commonwealth. Of particular interest is the six-foot- high portrayal of Jefferson, seated contemplatively, with papers of state in hand. Oddly, the sculptor chose to seat his figures in Greek Klismos chairs.

The many figures adorning the Courthouse were the product of several distinguished artists: Isadore Konti, Daniel Chester French, Herman Matzen, Karl Bitter and Herbert Adams.

Steven K. Birch, AIA, ASID

Section 4

Theaters and Auditoria

Playhouse Square
(See Section 19A, Downtown Walking Tour-East)

Cleveland is, perhaps, one of a hundred cities having accomplished major renovations of the legendary fantasy palaces-showplaces for movies mixed with live entertainment, frequently vaudeville – built principally in the years between 1915 and 1932. However, the city stands alone in possession of the Playhouse Square Center, a tightly-knit complex of five theaters, three fully restored with two of the longest lobbies in theaterdom and over 7,000 seats for live drama, opera, ballet, movies and touring troupes of entertainers. The Loew's Ohio and State Theatres (1921), designed by Thomas Lamb, and B.F. Keith's Palace Theatre (1922), by Chicago architects Rapp & Rapp, share the common history of so many great old vaudeville/movie houses: closed in the sixties for lack of business, subjected to threats of demolition, and redeemed from such a fate through the heroic efforts of an individual (in this case Ray Shepardson) or a preservation group (here read the Junior League of Cleveland and the Cuyahoga County Commissioners). In a few instances, the next chapters were written by dedicated sponsors and individuals with the vision to raise the funds and restore these monuments to their former eminence. And thus it has been here. The Playhouse Square Center, having devoted two decades to the effort, now operates an entertainment center which claims to rival Lincoln Center in New York.

The great proscenium arch of the Palace Theatre stage culminates a progression of richly decorated architectural spaces.

The Ohio Theatre, badly damaged by fire after a period when it served as the Mayfair Casino, was re-opened in 1982 with a more nearly contemporary styling and color suited to its principal resident company, the Great Lakes Theatre Festival. The State Theatre celebrated its rebirth in much more literal Italian Renaissance garb two years later, but with a new stagehouse sized and equipped to please its first performers, the Metropolitan Opera. It is now home to the Cleveland Opera and the Cleveland Ballet. The State Theatre lobby is notable for its enormous murals by James Daugherty, now fully restored. The Palace Theatre, whose restoration most closely follows the original "fantasy", was re-opened in 1988. It's neo-classic lobby alone is worth the price of admission. The revival of all three theaters was shepherded by van Dijk, Johnson and Partners with Peter van Dijk and consultant Roger Morgan playing the principal roles.

The Pompeiian style Allen Theatre (1922), architect C. Howard Crane, with nearly 4,000 seats, was designed for moving picture audiences only. After closing in the sixties, its elaborately colonnaded lobby and rotunda have served a succession of restaurants, but the auditorium is slated for demolition.

The Hanna Theatre (1922), designed by architect Charles Platt as part of the Hanna Building complex, was built by the Shubert Syndicate for its road show circuit, eclipsing the legendary Euclid Avenue Opera House. Seating about 1,500, it is long and narrow with Corinthian capped pilasters, fresco paintings and coffered ceilings.

The Colony Theatre at Shaker Square (1937)
Architect: John Eberson

Built as a part of the Georgian-style Shaker Square shopping center, the Colony Theatre's interior is noteworthy. It was designed by John Eberson (architect of Akron's Civic Theatre, an atmospheric gem) and completed in 1937, in the Art Moderne style of that period, with grand flowing lines and a balcony, seemingly unsupported, a characteristic of Eberson's interiors. Designed for moving pictures only, the Colony boasts excellent sight lines and acoustics, even though both have been enhanced by a larger projection screen and more recent sound equipment. The interior has not yet been fully restored and the entrance was materially altered in the early 1980's.

The Bohemian National Hall (1897)
4939 Broadway
Architects: Andrew Mitermiler and John W. Hradek;
Steffens, Searles & Hirsh

This neighborhood house, whose presence on the Cleveland scene is testimony to the breadth and depth of the city's ethnic populations, was built in 1896-1897 by an amalgam of 40 Czechoslovakian social groups, a number which soon grew to 73 as the Hall took its place at the center of Czech society here. Only Chicago exceeded Cleveland in the number of Czechs. Of brick and stone, in a Romanesque style, the three-story edifice contains meeting and social rooms along with an Italian Renaissance style main auditorium with an ample backstage area and seating for 1,000.

Cleveland's Public Auditorium (1922)
Music Hall (1927)
Architects: J. H. MacDowell and Frank R. Walker
Music Hall: Herman Kregelius

This enormous limestone-faced block was built in 1922 along the east side of the mall in accordance with the 1903 Burnham Plan. Its principal auditorium carries a 215' x 300' ground plan to a height of 80 feet, and shares its 6,200 square foot stage with the 2,800 seat Music Hall located behind and south. Architects J.H. MacDowell and Frank R. Walker also included a relatively intimate theater for 700 elsewhere in the plan. The original building has been much enhanced by underground extensions to the west and north and new main entrances from the Mall, all to form the needed inventory of facilities for the Cleveland Convention Center. The earliest additions were completed under the architects Outcalt and Guenther in the late fifties. More recent work has been accomplished by URS Consultants with the City Architect Paul Volpe.

Grays' Armory (1894)
Bolivar at Prospect
Architect: Fenimore C. Bate

This building was erected as a headquarters for the Cleveland Grays, a military/social organization now enjoying its second century of participation in the pageantry of Cleveland. Designed in the Richardsonian Romanesque style with the familiar rusticated stone and brick, the armory is notable for its drill hall, located in the rear of the building.

The Cleveland Play House Group (1926)
(Brooks and Drury Theatres)
Bolton Theater (1983)
Architects: Small and Rowley
Renovation and Extension: Philip Johnson in Association with Collins, Rimer and Gordon

The Cleveland Playhouse group reads on the skyline like a 14th century Romanesque village, a whimsy of its designer, Philip Johnson. Whimsy or not, the complex skillfully weaves entry, the historic Brooks and Drury Theaters, the Bolton Theater, lobbies, exhibition galleries, and a former 5-story department store, into a functional and visually pleasing home for the Cleveland Play House, founded in 1915. The 160-seat Brooks Theater, is an intimate brick house connected to the larger Drury Theater. The 644-seat Bolton Theater is reminiscent of Mr. Johnson's work at Lincoln Center. Altogether the ensemble is exciting architecture and promotes first-rate theater.

Severance Hall (1931)
Architects: Walker & Weeks

At the entry to University Circle is the home of the world-renowned Cleveland Orchestra built as a gift to the city by John L. Severance in memory of his wife. The safely Neo-Renaissance exterior of the great hall surprisingly encloses the city's finest Art Deco interior, culminating in a unique auditorium ceiling of gently curved abstracted foliage forms. The marble and brass details throughout are of special quality. In 1958, under the direction of acoustics consultant Heinrich Keilholz, the firm of Garfield, Harris, Schafer, Flynn and Williams designed substantial modifications to the interior, particularly the stage.

Masonic Temple Auditorium (1919-1921)
East 36th between Euclid and Chester Avenues
Architects: Hubbell & Benes
Chief Designer: Francis Wyman Crosby

Third major home of the Cleveland Lodge of the Scottish Rite Masons, this massive "L"-shaped building encompasses a 2,250-seat auditorium in addition to all the necessary meeting rooms associated with such a structure. The dark red brick building uses spare ornament and detail over its two rectangular elements. A proposed 25-story tower at Euclid Avenue was never constructed. The large auditorium was second only to the Hippodrome Theater (1908, demolished 1981) when completed. It served as the home of the newly founded Cleveland Orchestra from 1921-1931.

Keith E. White, AIA

Section 5

Arcades/Passages/Lobbies

The Galleria, one of Cleveland's new arcades, commands the corner of E. 9th and St. Clair with its great glass vault.

The arcade concept must have been born long ago in the casbahs of ancient cities. It flowered again in the 19th century, especially in London, when developers rightly employed them to provide unique solutions to extend the street front and to allow connecting links between urban blocks and places. Cleveland's swiftly expanding downtown turned to the arcade as a repeated architectural solution and added to it a variety of passages and lavish lobbies for new office buildings altogether making up an outstanding array of linkages. The concept continues afresh with the Galleria of 1987, the BP America Atrium and the new concourses (1990) at the Tower City Center adding conspicuously to the tradition.

Most remembered and publicized has been *The Arcade*, an 1890 extravaganza consisting of two 9-story office towers connected by a 5-story, glass-roofed atrium. The delightful ironwork details dominate a functional, even playful, interior while the building's two separated facades are stolid, stone and brick expressions of Romanesque Revival form. George Smith combined with John Eisenmann as architect and engineer for this spectacular piece enjoying its centennial in 1990.

Close by The Arcade and connecting Prospect Avenue to Euclid Avenue are a pair of parallel arcades. *The Colonial* (1898) and *The Euclid* (1911). Located in adjacent buildings these 440 foot long arcades are very different in appearance, the former with a fully-revealed glass roof and second floor balcony, the latter with an all-terra cotta interior surfacing a great barrel-vaulted ceiling. Architect for The Colonial was George H. Smith and for the Euclid, Franz Warner.

The Landmark Office Towers encompasses the Van Sweringen Arcade and other public ways.

Within the giant office cluster now known as Landmark Office Towers, is a major space labeled the *Van Sweringen Arcade*, actually restored and renovated from the one-time main banking room of the Midland Bank and constructed in 1930 in a richly-detailed art deco mode. The original building was part of the huge Terminal Tower group designed by Graham, Anderson, Probst and White while the renewal was done by Teare, Herman and Gibans.

Grand lobbies are additional demonstrations of the city's developers' and architects' desire for impressive spaces. In the instance of the *Huntington Building*, constructed in 1924 as the Union Trust Building to the design of Graham, Anderson, Probst and White and the *National City Bank Building*, 623 Euclid Avenue, the building lobbies stretch into arcades and into connections with other buildings. The coffered ceiling and pink marble surfacing of the latter is especially worthy of note.

The 1986 *B.P. America Tower*, H.O.K. Architects, provides a multilevel atrium and lobby with several upper floors opening on to the wedge-shaped space. Exhibit areas and fountains permeate this complex people-place faced in polished red granite. Notable lobbies are to be found at the *Bulkley Building* (1921), C. Howard Crane, Architect, and the *Leader Building* (1912), Charles A. Platt, Architect. Of recent vintage is the glass-roofed atrium of *North Point Office Building* (1987) along with a companion space connecting to the later North Point Tower (1989), by Jerry Payto Architects.

Robert C. Gaede, FAIA

Great Banking Halls

National City Bank (1895) (1914)
623 Euclid Avenue
Architects: Shepley, Rutan and Coolidge
Renovation: Walker and Weeks

This extraordinary product of the Beaux Arts period was retrofitted into an earlier commercial space in a truly grand manner. Parallel to the building's elongated lobby in a more subdued classical mode, the banking room is carried out in pink marble and features a double colonnade of giant fluted columns carrying an exceptionally rich coffered ceiling. The banking screen, check desks and other room elements have been preserved to the present. The terminal vista upon entry is a grand staircase to a mezzanine level.

Society National Bank (1889-1890)
(Originally Society for Savings Building)
127 Public Square
Architects: Burnham and Root

The steel frame skeleton of this bank building is covered in a fanciful overlay of past architectural styles. John Wellborn Root designed the exterior of this structure, a combination of Romanesque, Gothic, and Renaissance stylistic features, to resemble a medieval fortress tower. The short, robust, granite pillars on the ground story are a melding of Romanesque and Gothic in style. Inside the great banking hall twelve marble-faced columns support a twenty-six foot high ceiling with a central stained-glass skylight. The interior was designed by Chicago decorator William Pretyman, and the murals by Walter Crane, an English painter and illustrator, an associate of English designer William Morris. Crane completed the "Gothic" intent of the decorator. The building as originally constructed included a nine-story light court which has since been covered over, so that the skylight is artificially illuminated today. The upper floors have been re-structured to permit full-floor office loadings as part of the combined restoration-renovation of this preserved landmark.

The banking room of the Society National Bank, preserved in the reconstruction of 1989-1991 is remarkable for its overlay of the decorative arts reflecting late Victorian ideals.

AmeriTrust Building (1905-1908)
(Originally Cleveland Trust Company)
Euclid and East 9th Street
Architects: George B. Post & Sons

"Progress with Caution" was the motto of The Cleveland Trust Company, when they hired the New York architectural firm of George B. Post & Sons to design a three-story, white granite office tower around a central grand banking hall on a trapezium-shaped site. The central pediment displays sculptures by Karl Bitter which depict, allegorically, the primary sources of wealth in the United States, Land and Water, with their concomitant occupations-Industrial Labor, Agriculture, Mining, Commerce, Naviagation and Fishery. The interior of the rotunda features a dome, eighty-five feet high, with Tiffany-style stained glass panels sixty-one feet in diameter. Thirteen bays support the three-story office building circling the rotunda. The fluted columns, Corinthian pilasters, bronze doorways and grilles, marble floors and walls are reminiscent of the Italian Renaissance. Also found decorating the upper levels of the banking hall are thirteen mural paintings illustrating the development of civilization in the Midwest by Francis D. Millet (who later lost his life on the Titanic). The interior was modernized to a degree during the course of a renovation carried out in the 1970's.

The rotunda of Ameritrust's main banking room is an astounding space rising to an immense stained glass dome. The heavy bronze railings of the balconied floors are a notable achievement.

Huntington Bank Building (1924) (1975)
(Originally Union Trust Building, later Union Commerce Bank)
917 Euclid Avenue
Architects: Graham, Anderson, Probst & White
Renovation: Dalton, van Dijk, Johnson & Partners

Built for the Union Trust Company in 1924, the "L"-shaped banking room of today's Huntington Bank still stuns the visitor with its enormous scale and dramatic classical detailing.

When this twenty-two story office building was completed in 1924 it was the second largest office building in the world. Its proportions, for 1920s standards, are remarkable. It measures 146 feet on Euclid Avenue, 258 feet on East 9th Street, and 513 feet on Chester. In 1923, when the building was under construction, 2,500 bankers in town for the American Institute of Banking Convention toured the site of the lobby in 250 automobiles. The interior is designed to resemble the great basilicas of Rome and has over thirty acres
of floor space. The L-shaped banking hall was the largest in the United States; the main lobby is fifty feet wide. It stands three-stories tall with barrel-vaulted ceilings, double skylights, monumental Corinthian columns made of Italian marble, side aisles with coffered ceilings, and murals painted by Jules Guerin of New York. In 1930 the Cleveland Stock Exchange established its headquarters in the building. Graham, Anderson, Probst & White were also the architects of the Union Terminal which was under construction at the same time as this structure. The banking hall was substantially restored in 1975 by removing drop ceilings and restoring the railings of the mezzanines.

The Federal Reserve Bank (1923)
Superior Avenue at East 6th Street
Architects: Walker & Weeks

One of the finest structures in Cleveland, this building was conceived by Cleveland bankers, designed by Cleveland architects, and completed by a Cleveland contractor. After Cleveland was named as one of the districts of the Federal Reserve in 1913 twenty-five prominent Clevelanders were approached for ideas on the appropriate design for a bank. Afterwards four specialists in bank design worked for thirteen months creating over 1,000 sketches and 1,924 working drawings used in construction. The twelve-story, foursquare building is modeled after Michelozzo's Medici-Riccardi palace in Florence, the fortress/home of the Medici, the great bankers of the early Renaissance. Like the Medici palace, the ground floor is heavily rusticated with higher stories more decorative – as the Medici wanted their palace to seem impenetrable, the architects of The Federal Reserve Bank, Walker & Weeks, wanted their bank to seem impenetrable. The base of the building is pink granite, and the upper stories are faced with a pinkish Georgia marble. Elaborate iron grilles accent the windows and form a decorative motif on the interior. These were fabricated by the Rose Iron Works of Cleveland. The interior of the great banking hall is also decorated in a magnificent interpretation of the Italian Renaissance with marble floors and gold, Sienna marble-faced walls and pillars. The vaulted ceilings are coffered and ornamented with gold gilt. This building, Frank Walker's and Harry Weeks's masterpiece in terms of bank construction, cost over $8 million dollars at the time of construction.

Dr. Holly Rarick Witchey

Section 7

Clubs and Societies

Of all of the manifestations of industrial civilization edifices for social clubs are the final symbols of wealth – of having "arrived." Compared to the need for places to live, learn, worship and work the club seems to be a frivolous excess; but as a measure of success it is perhaps as important as a fine house, church or office. It is a place where the like minded, "the right kind of people", can assemble and congratulate each other.

Like other older American cities, Cleveland flourished in the unprecedented industrial expansion of the late 19th century. There are enough remnants of this period reflected in the few residential, religious and commercial buildings remaining to show how exuberant and optimistic this time was.

The University Club (1863)
3813 Euclid Avenue
Architect: Joseph Ireland

The University Club was originally the Stager-Beckwith house, built about 1863. It is on the north side of Euclid Avenue between East 36th and East 40th Streets and is the only remaining 19th century mansion from the days when Euclid was known as "Millionaire's Row." It is a three story brick structure with a four story tower over the front entry. Its style can be called Second Empire with Italianate overtones.

The building has served as a town club since 1913, and a large dining room and ancillary meeting rooms were added by J. Milton Dyer, architect. After a period of decline the club was refurbished in 1980 by HWH Architects and Engineers, and the mansion portion has been restored making it one of the most successful and long-lived adaptive reuse efforts in Cleveland.

The Tavern Club (1905)
Architect: J. Milton Dyer

The Tavern Club on the southwest corner of Prospect Avenue and East 36th Street is a somewhat romantic expression of its time. Architect J. Milton Dyer used a lofty late medieval or "Northern Renaissance" style, as Eric Johannesen called it in his *Cleveland Architecture 1876-1976*. Its decorations of Flemish bond brick and wood half timbering are solid and substantial and make no attempts for academic purity. The window openings and their types reflect the internal needs of the building and display an ordered playfulness that is more in keeping with residential architecture of this period. Perhaps the most distinctive feature of this building is its massive, two story, hipped roof that is punctuated with different sizes of dormers and two half-timbered and windowed gables. One of these is centered over the entrance on East 36th, and the other faces Prospect. This part of the building houses squash courts. Perhaps an appropriate style label of Burgher Gothic could be applied to the Tavern Club.

The Cleveland Athletic Club (1911)
Architect: J. Milton Dyer

The Cleveland Athletic Club is on the south side of Euclid Avenue opposite the end of East 12th Street. At first glance it looks like a typical frame and curtain wall office building of the period. But to give it an appearance of greater height the windows diminish in size to the seventh floor, and above that they divide into twos and finally threes by the time that fourteen stories are reached. In fact the building is an office building to the seventh floor. Above that there are ample dining rooms, physical training rooms, a swimming pool and sleeping rooms.

The ground floor shop fronts are a mix of post World War II remodelings, but the original off-white terra cotta skin suggests perpendicular gothic derivation especially at the top three stories. The spandrels below have stylized linen-fold ornament which is a motif found on medieval gothic furniture and wall panels.

The Hermit Club (1928)
Architect: Frank B. Meade

The Hermit Club is on the north side of Dodge Court just east of East 15th Street. Frank B. Meade designed this second home for the organization, Meade also having designed the first one. The Hermit is a men's club dedicated to the enjoyment of music and the theatre; and is remarkable for its longevity and presence in the edifice built for it. This is a distinction shared only with the Tavern, Union and Cleveland Athletic Clubs. What is the most remarkable is the scale and informality of this three story medieval, half-timbered public house in the

midst of the masonry formality of downtown Cleveland. It is completely expressive of the suburban ideal and of the academically correct style-borrowing of the late twenties. There are intimate dining and tap rooms on the ground floor and a large dining room above with a stage.

The Rowfant Club (1838) (1858)
Renovation: Charles Heard

The Rowfant Club, on the south side of Prospect Avenue just east of East 30th Street, was originally the Merwin residence and was remodeled by Charles Heard in 1858. This brick building was first constructed in 1838 probably in the Greek Revival style which is suggested in the five bay front with central entrance. Renaissance Italianate decoration is evident in the pediments over the entry porch and over the central bay at the roof. That style is also apparent in the paired brackets and dentils of the cornice and also in the brackets with either pediments or individual cornices at the window heads.

The club has occupied this building since 1895 and is dedicated to the appreciation of literature. The house itself has been changed very little but two additions are the rear include a Richardsonian Romanesque dining room with brick fireplace by Charles F. Schweinfurth, architect, and another meeting room.

The Cleveland Club (1931)
(Tudor Arms)
Architect: Frank B. Meade

The Job Corps building on the southwest corner of Carnegie Avenue and East 107th Street was built in 1931 to the design of Frank B. Meade, architect, as the Cleveland Club which subsequently became the Tudor Arms Hotel and then the Graduate House. It is an 11-story brick structure surmounted by a three story tower at the 107th Street corner and with a three-story block facing Carnegie on its west side.

The building is decorated with limestone trim around and in some of the large grouped perpendicular gothic style windows that light the major interior spaces. Stone thistle medallions occur in a row below the castellated cornices on the principal street facades and there are stone traceries in the tower. This Tudor Gothic style building with Art Deco suggestions on its vertical elements has served as a local landmark because it commands major commuting routes to the eastern suburbs.

The Union Club (1905)
Architect: Charles F. Schweinfurth

The Union Club, at the northeast corner of Euclid Avenue and East 12th Street, is Cleveland's quintessential town club. Charles F. Schweinfurth designed an Italian Renaissance palace that dominates its corner despite the taller buildings that have gone up across the streets from it. Until recently its sandstone fronts and terra cotta cornices were black with the grime of Cleveland's industrial activity. A cleaning (1988) exposed its beige and cream colors (no one was consciously aware of the presence of the terra cotta cornice under the dirt) but that in no way had diminished the power of its overhanging cornice, the moldings around its windows or of the main entry on 12th Street. As if to suggest its exclusivity, the Union Club is set back from its property line to expose areaway windows and allow room for street trees on the Euclid side. All this is protected by an elegant and substantial iron fence.

Thwing Hall (1908)
Architects: Lehman and Schmitt

Thwing Hall, 11111 Euclid
Avenue, was originally built as
the Excelsior Club. It is a three-
story brick building with
limestone accents and gabled
slate roofs. It contains a large
dining room on the ground
floor, an elegant ball room on
the third and meeting room and
a bowling alley. It has been
known as Thwing Hall since
1929 when Western Reserve
University established a library
within.

For many years Thwing has been Case Western Reserve's student
union; and from a recent addition and restoration by Don M.
Hisaka, architect, it has become an important example as an
adaptive reuse for old buildings.

Fenn Tower (1930)
Architects: George B. Post & Sons

The National Town and Country
Club was built on the northeast
corner of Euclid Avenue and
East 24th Street. Now called
Fenn Tower, it is part of
Cleveland State University.
The architect employed a
set-back style with vertical
emphasis and Art Deco
detailing. At 19 stories high
it has been used for academic
purposes since 1937, first by
Fenn College, now by the
University.

Edward A. Reich

Section 8

High Rise Commercial Buildings

The Terminal Tower Complex (1930) (1990)
(Now Tower City Center)
Public Square
Architects: Graham, Anderson, Probst and White
Tower City Center: RTKL (1990)

The Terminal Tower is *the* Landmark of the City of Cleveland.
For the last sixty years it has remained the greatest single visual
symbol of the City to its residents and to visitors. Situated at the
southwest corner of Public Square, Cleveland's finest public
"room", it serves as the anchor for and the heart of the City.
From the Tower's upper-floor observation deck, generations of
Clevelanders have gained a new perspective on their native town.
At the time of the Terminal Tower Complex's completion in 1930,
the Tower was the second tallest building in the world, exceeded
only by New York's Woolworth Building. For the next four
decades, the Tower, at 708 feet, was to remain the tallest building
outside of New York City.

The Terminal Complex was noteworthy for other reasons: it was
one of the first, and certainly most significant, developments of
air-rights over a rail terminal in the U.S.; the Tower piers were the
deepest in history, bearing on bedrock 250 feet below street level;

the structural design of the Complex was unique in the number of streets relocated, bridges built, rail lines and approaches relocated, and varied support and framing conditions encountered; the electrification of steam trains passing beneath the complex was one of the first such installations in the U.S. The Builder's Exchange contained a nine-story parking garage, an innovation at the time. The Terminal Complex embraces Cleveland's Public Square as its landscaped entry plaza, and provides a thriving layering of transportation, retail, hotel and office uses within its classic lines. On the basis of such unique features, the Terminal Complex deserves a rightful place among such major urban mixed-use structures as Rockefeller Center and Grand Central Station. Its graceful and distinctive central tower, reflective of McKim Mead and White's New York City Municipal Building, created for Cleveland a powerful symbol which stood unchallenged until 1985 when the BP America tower rose close by.

The Terminal Complex, originally referred to as Cleveland's Union Terminal, was planned, developed and constructed from 1922 through 1930 by the Van Sweringen Brothers, Oris Paxton and Mantis James. The Van Sweringens had entered the real estate business decades earlier and by 1906 had acquired control of the land surrounding the Shaker Lakes, on which in 1911 they had begun to create the Village of Shaker Heights. By 1916 the Brothers had added the acquisition of the Nickel Plate Railroad to obtain a right-of-way for their proposed Shaker Rail Line, and a four-acre parcel on Public Square for a downtown terminus of the line. In 1918 negotiations began on forming a combined terminal at Public Square for a number of rail lines, and in 1920 the Shaker lines began operation. A plan for the Terminal Complex was approved by Cleveland voters in 1919. Over the following several years related development negotiations continued and ground was broken late in 1923. The Terminal Tower Complex at Public Square originally included Cleveland's Union Terminal (the City's main train station and central light rail hub), the Tower, the Hotel Cleveland, Higbee's Department Store, and three adjacent buildings to the south of Higbee's: The Builder's Exchange (Guildhall), the Medical Arts (Republic) Building, and the Midland Building. These latter three structures have since been renamed Landmark Office Towers, the Hotel Cleveland has since become Stouffer's Tower City Plaza hotel, and the central complex has been renamed Tower City Center. Expansion of the Tower City Center has taken place (1988-1990), a Ritz-Carlton Hotel, a new grand concourse space and mall and an additional office structure. As Cleveland moves into the 1990s, its landmark Tower will lose its "tallest" status to Society Center and Ameritrust Center.

The BP America Building (1985)
(Formerly Sohio)
200 Public Square
Architects: Hellmuth, Obata & Kassabaum

In November of 1981, the Standard Oil Co. (Sohio) strengthened
its commitment to Cleveland with the announcement of plans to
build what would become the largest and most expensive office
structure in the City. In the process, two aging landmarks of
Cleveland would be lost: Daniel H. Burnham's fine Cuyahoga
Building (1892) and George B. Post & Sons' Williamson Building
(1900), at sixteen stories. Completed as the BP America Tower,

the structure became the second most prominent structure in the City's skyline. In distant views of the City it is paired with the Terminal Tower as a twin emblem of the town. The building's 1.2 million square feet of office space dwarfed the next largest private office structure (the Huntington Building: 879,000 square feet), and exceeded even the largest public office structure in town, the Federal Office Building. The building rises 45 stories and 650 feet above the street, yet offers a sensitive gesture to the pedestrian environment of Public Square in the form of its eight-story landscaped atrium housing public, retail and commercial spaces. Its stair-stepped profile reduces its apparent bulk in the skyline, and enables it to harmonize with many of the older structures of the City. Its main mass is split into two slightly flared halves oriented to its two frontages on Superior and Euclid Avenues.

Like the Terminal Tower across the Square, the BP America Building lays rightful claim to many superlatives. Its caisson foundations were the deepest in North America; its 4,100 slabs of granite cladding hide 20,000 tons of structural steel; it contains 36 elevators, 10 escalators, 3 fountains, 1 waterfall and 1,500 plants. At its completion, the building consolidated Sohio employees from eight different office structures around town, and gave Clevelanders a dramatic new presence on the skyline. And by that presence The BP America Building has enabled citizens, planners and builders alike to reassess their vision of Public Square and its place in a growing City of the 90s.

The atrium of the BP America Building rises seven levels around a trapezoidal space which has its west wall completely glazed and facing Public Square. An elaborate water cascade on the east acts as the divider between the land-scaped floor and the building's lobbies.

National City Center (1980)
1900 East Ninth Street
Architects: Skidmore, Owings & Merrill (Chicago)

The latest arrival at downtown Cleveland's "banking intersection" of East 9th Street and Euclid Avenue was the National City Center complex constructed in 1980 on the northwest quadrant. The main tower became the seventh-tallest structure in the City, at 35 floors, 410 feet, with 750,000 square feet of office area. The reinforced concrete tower was built on a "floating pad" foundation of 7-foot thick concrete, and clad in whitish beige travertine. Linked to the tower by a four-story annex and atrium is the earlier National City Bank Building at East 6th Street and Euclid Avenue. This earlier structure is actually the combination of two much older and architecturally

noteworthy precedents: Henry Ives Cobb's Garfield Building of 1893-1894 at the corner of East 6th, and Shepley, Rutan & Coolidge's New England Building of 1896 (later modified by Walker & Weeks in 1915) immediately east. Much of their classical detailing and appeal has been preserved and enhanced, particularly in the main banking lobbies. Other structures that had occupied the site of the complex were the Hickox Building of 1890, designed by George H. Smith (who had a hand in The Arcade, The Colonial Arcade and The Rose Building); Walker & Weeks' deco-modern classic, The Bond Clothing Store of 1947; and the Roxy burlesque theater. National City Center is one of the few developments in the denser stretches of the financial and office district to embody open public spaces. The tower's setback creates a large triangular entry plaza at the East 9th Street-Euclid Avenue intersection, punctuated by the stainless steel mobile, George Rickey's "Triple-L Excentric Gyratory Gyratory III". North of the tower is the lowered corner plaza along Vincent Avenue which serves as a dining terrace for the ground-floor restaurant.

The Diamond Building (1972)
(Formerly The Diamond Shamrock Building)
1100 Superior Avenue
Architects: Skidmore, Owings & Merrill (Chicago)

One of the latter-day Erieview urban renewal area sites to be developed was that of The Diamond Shamrock Building, begun in early 1971 as home for the company of the same name. This 22-story, 285-foot office tower occupies the southwest corner of East 12th Street and Superior Avenue; it is a dark bronze block of sheer aluminum and tinted glass. The building is arcaded slightly at the lower floor to enable pedestrian activity along its retail/ commercial spaces, a feature only recently utilized as the surrounding parcels have been occupied by other office buildings, in-town apartment towers and the adjacent Chester Commons park. By the mid-'80s, The Diamond Shamrock Corporation had deserted Cleveland for the Sunbelt, and the tower reverted to market office tenancies, renamed The Diamond Building.

AmeriTrust Tower (1971)
(Formerly Cleveland Trust)
900 Euclid Avenue
Architects: Marcel Breuer and Hamilton Smith; Flynn, Dalton, van Dijk & Partners

Since 1908 the Cleveland Trust Co. served the banking needs of Clevelanders from its distinctive Italian Renaissance Revivalist headquarters bank on the southeast corner of East 9th Street and Euclid Avenue. Designed by George B. Post & Sons, this classical "temple" structure housed banking offices in a three-story ring around a 61-foot diameter, 85-foot high rotunda, topped by a stained glass dome. By the late '60s the Cleveland Trust Co. (soon to be renamed AmeriTrust Co.) felt the need for expansion of its facilities and for consolidation of its downtown office space. The company enlisted Marcel Breuer and Hamilton Smith to design the firm's new headquarters. The resulting design called for demolition of an existing annex to the immediate south of the "temple" and the construction of two 29-story, 383-foot high office towers, flanking the Revivalist bank on the south and east. Ground was broken in 1968 and construction completed in 1971 on the first of the two towers, along East 9th Street south of the bank. The new structure provided 427,000 square feet of office space; a 750-car parking garage was built across Prospect Avenue and is connected by one of the city's few over-street pedestrian bridges.

The Ameritrust Tower is composed of bold gray precast panels, molded and curved to form window openings, and darker granite panels. The strength and solidity of the design provides an effective backdrop for the restored classical bank. Unique features of the tower's design include the sculptural "mouse-hole" high in the south parapet wall visible from East 9th Street-Prospect Avenue-Huron Road intersection linking the Ameritrust complex to its parking garage, the first such bridge in Cleveland.

Eaton Center (1983)
1111 Superior Avenue
Architects: Skidmore, Owings & Merrill (Chicago)

One of the components of the early '80s building "boom" in
Cleveland that expanded the City's central business district
eastward was the Eaton Center at the northwest corner of East
12th Street and Superior Avenue. Though Eaton Center is no
farther east than 100 Erieview, it had taken the downtown
business district almost 20 years to resume its eastward thrust
to East 12th Street.

Eaton Center began as a decision by the Catholic Diocese of
Cleveland to lease land east of St. John's Cathedral to Oliver
Tyrone Corporation for an office building. Once the Eaton
Corporation made a lease commitment for over a third of the
28-story, 614,000 square foot structure's office space, the building
was christened Eaton Center. The first all-reflective glass building
in Cleveland, Eaton Center consists of one 25-story black octagonal tower embedded almost completely in another 28-story black
octagonal tower. The resulting building has many varied perimeter
window-office conditions, a three-floor Eaton corporate headquarters executive office suite, and a first floor of retail/
commercial space.

The Society Building (1969)
(Formerly The Central National Bank Building)
800 Superior Avenue NE
Architects: Charles Luckman Associates; The Austin Company

Another early bank headquarters to appear along the financial
district's spine of East 9th Street was The Central National Bank
Building on the southwest corner of East 9th Street and Superior
Avenue. The Central National Bank had served Clevelanders for
nearly a century before being acquired by Society National Bank.
It had maintained headquarters banking offices in such historic
structures as The Perry-Payne Building and the Rockefeller
Building in the Warehouse District, 308 Euclid Avenue in the
Shopping District, and in the Midland Building of the Terminal
Tower Complex before deciding to erect its own structure. In
preparing its site, Central National was forced to raze several local
landmarks: Pat Joyce's Tavern, Kornman's Restaurant and the
Ellington Apartments. The 23-story, 305-foot tall, brick-veneered
steel frame was begun in the latter part of 1967 and was completed just over 2 years later. Like the later National City Center to
the south, the Central National Bank complex sat on a "floating"
foundation pad of concrete. Over 1.8 million bricks were used
to clad the office tower and adjacent parking garage. The
development's distinctive red color and strong vertical emphasis
make it unique among high-rise office buildings in the central
business district. Other unusual features include its raised-
"podium" or platform base, the retail/commercial space on the
ground floor of the garage providing pedestrian activity along East
9th Street and Vincent Avenue, and the semi-enclosed plaza along
East 9th Street.

The Huntington Building (1924)
(Formerly the Union Trust Building)
925 Euclid Avenue
Architects: Graham, Anderson, Probst & White

In 1920 The Union Trust
Company was incorporated
in Cleveland to create a local
source of financing for major
industrial and construction
ventures in the area. It began
business as the fifth-largest trust
company in the U.S., having
been formed by the merger
of 29 financial institutions,
including three major local
banks. By 1923 The Union
Trust Company had begun erecting what was to be one of the
most impressive banking structures anywhere. The bank's new
high-rise headquarters was located at what was then considered
the limit of the central city the northeast corner of East 9th Street
and Euclid Avenue. When completed in 1924 it was one of the
largest office buildings in the nation, containing 30 acres of floor
space.

It featured the largest banking lobby in the country, a three-story L-shaped space that is overpowering even today.

The bank's most striking features include its colonnades of immense Corinthian marble columns flanking the fifty-foot wide lobbies, the grand scale and hierarchy of its spaces, its double-skylight barrel-vaulted ceilings, muraled lunettes, coffered ceilings and sumptuous detailing. The public spaces underwent a sensitive restoration from 1973-1975 by Dalton, van Dijk, Johnson & Partners. A decade later, The Union Trust Company, which had since become The Union Commerce Bank, was acquired by Huntington Bancshares, Inc., and the grand structure was renamed The Huntington Building. Today an upper floor private club, the Mid-Day Club, continues to host the Cleveland business and banking community in the spirit of the original Union Trust Company formation.

The Ohio Bell Building (1983)
45 Erieview Plaza
Architects: Dalton, Dalton, Newport;
Madison-Madison International

The Ohio Bell Telephone Company was the last of Cleveland's major utility companies to seek a newer expanded facility for its corporate headquarters offices. The site Ohio Bell chose was one of the few "missing teeth" ringing Erieview Plaza at the base of 100 Erieview. The 16-story, 253-foot, pale gray granite and green glass structure rose at the northern corner of Erieview Plaza between East 9th Street and Lakeside Avenue. With its window detailing varied by solar orientation, and its curved northwesterly facade viewing Lake Erie, the building forms a distinctive silhouette in the downtown skyline. The design is also a good example of architecture that both complements the existing fabric of the City and points in new interesting directions. The 405,000 square foot headquarters consolidated most of Ohio Bell's employees from eight other office locations throughout town, leaving mostly equipment at its previous headquarters building at 750 Huron Road.

The Hanna Building (1921)
1422 Euclid Avenue
Architect: Charles A. Platt

The 16-story Hanna Building was erected at Playhouse Square by Dan R. Hanna, Sr., in memory of his father, Marcus A. Hanna. The building has much in common with the Leader Building; both are solid and severe blocks visually subdivided into layers and relieved only by arched entries and a textured skin with minimal Renaissance detailing. Housed in the buildings' annex is the 1535-seat Hanna Theater, which was originally a legitimate theater graced with lavish materials and polychrome Pompeiian decoration. The Hanna was one of the five theaters (the others: State, Ohio, Allen and Palace) to establish Cleveland's Playhouse Square entertainment hub.

One Erieview Plaza (1965)
One Erieview Plaza
Architects: Schafer, Flynn & Associates

One Erieview Plaza is noteworthy for several reasons. It was the first financial institution office headquarters to locate along Cleveland's "banker's row", East 9th Street, since The Union Trust Co. over 40 years earlier. It was the third sizable structure erected in the Erieview urban renewal area, and some felt the best to date. It was a fairly clear stylistic break with the more uniformly textured International Style high-rises in town, such as The

Illuminating Building, 100 Erieview, and The Federal Office Building. One Erieview Plaza instead, utilized a white precast frame with inset bronze glazing to define a balanced horizontal-vertical aesthetic. Columns were deleted from the building corners for greater corner visibility. Colonnades along the north and east facades broadened sidewalk areas for the pedestrian. One Erieview Plaza offered yet another viable alternative for urban office design.

The Standard Building (1925)
(*Formerly The Brotherhood of Locomotive Engineers Cooperative National Bank Building*)
1370 Ontario Street
Architects: Knox & Elliot

Its 21 stories clad in ornate panels of cream-colored terra cotta, The Standard Building has held a commanding presence just off Cleveland's Public Square since its construction in the "Roaring Twenties". Originally built to house the cooperative banking venture of the Brotherhood of Locomotive Engineers (a powerful local union then headquartered across Ontario Street in the recently demolished Engineers Building), it has since housed numerous banks, law firms, City and County offices, the Marshall Law School, and even the Prohibition-days office of Elliot Ness. After more than 60 years, The Standard Building still houses offices of various railway organizations, and also still sports many doorknobs, plaques and accessories containing railway scenes and memorabilia. The original mezzanine, bank lobby and grand staircase are preserved, as is the original crystal dome ceiling.

The East Ohio Building (1959)
1717 East Ninth Street
Architects: Emery Roth and Sons

The second "modern skyscraper" to be built after Cleveland's post-War construction lull, shortly after the Illuminating Building, was The East Ohio Building on the southeast corner of East 9th Street and Superior Avenue. On the site that had earlier held The Oriental Theatre burlesque house in the '20s and the Greyhound Lines in the '30s and '40s rose this 21-story, 280-foot black-glass-and-aluminum curtain-wall structure. And it rose quickly; construction proceeded at the rate of a new floor every four days. Work was completed and the building was occupied in just 14 months. The building has served as home for The East Ohio Gas Company for the last 30 years. Prior to that, the utility company, which was incorporated as a subsidiary of the

Standard Oil Co. in 1898 and divested in 1943, had occupied its former building at East 6th Street and Rockwell Avenue (now occupied by NBC affiliate WKYC). The East Ohio Building, termed a "spaceframe" by its architect and developer, became one of the first in a long line of major office facades to form today's high-rise canyon along East 9th Street.

Tower East (1968)
20600 Chagrin Boulevard at Northfield Road
Architects: Walter Gropius, The Architects Collaborative

This structure, one of the last of Gropius' designs, embodies the "floating" separateness of two-story base from the office tower and equipment penthouse. The bracketed open corners defy the structural "logic" of Miesian International Style detailing, but add definition to the tower massing. The interior spaces, particularly the lower level public areas, are noteworthy for their finesse and variety. Belying its name, Tower East today serves as the western terminus of the burgeoning Chagrin Boulevard executive office corridor.

North Point I and II (1985) (1990)
901 Lakeside Avenue
Architects I: Dalton, Dalton, Newport (Jerry Payto, designer)
Architects II: Payto Architects

North Point I is a uniquely eccentric office structure. Its seven levels are placed five above grade and two below, atop the foundations of the former Cleveland Press building. Its large triangular floor plans are split by an angled atrium that sights on the City's waterfront and Inner Harbor. Its articulated skin of tile and glass is a refreshing change of pace from its more monolithic neighbors. Recent additions to the building include the linking of a new 1,000 car parking garage to the north, and the construction of its big brother, North Point II, more properly called North Point Tower, to the east.

North Point Tower is a 20-story 587,000 square foot office structure clad in colorful tile panels and a composition of black, silver, and deep green glasses. Its triangular bulk is terraced at the top three floors. North Point Tower is joined to its earlier sibling by a new nine-story glass-roofed atrium linked to the Tower's three-story lobby. It also shares the original building's landscaped entry plaza on Lakeside Avenue.

The Keith Building (1922)
1621 Euclid Avenue
Architects: George L. and C. W. Rapp

The Keith building and its Keith Palace Theater was erected in memory of Edward F. Albee's theater partner, B.F. Keith. The theater was billed as a "The Most Beautiful Playhouse" in the World. Rising above the Palace was the 22-story classical skyscraper in white terra cotta, then the tallest building in Cleveland. Capping the structure was a distinctive addition to the skyline, a 3-story electric sign advertising the vaudeville troupe based at the Palace. Extensive terra cotta restoration has been underway (1988-1990) maintaining the tower's elegant skin.

Renaissance at Playhouse Square
and Garage (1990)
1350 Euclid Avenue (Euclid Avenue at East 14th and Huron)
Architects: Richard L. Bowen & Associates, Inc.
Architects for Garage: Kaczmar Associates, Inc.

Truly intended as a Renaissance for Cleveland's historic Playhouse Square area, this 15-story office structure represents the first new construction at Playhouse Square in 67 years. The building's 293,000 square foot of office and retail spaces begins in a broad 3-story granite clad base flanking East 14th Street. Housed within this base are two floors of restaurant and retail facilities lining a grand lobby, connected to the adjacent 417 car parking garage by a pedes-trian bridge. The building then terraces upward through a variety of steps and setbacks, with granite giving way to broadened areas of glass. At its top, Renaissance sports a skyline profile punctuated by three glazed octagonal turrets. The proposed Playhouse Square Plaza to be constructed at what is now the intersection of Huron Road and Euclid Avenue would become an effective "front door" to the Renaissance.

100 Erieview (Tower at Erieview) (1964) (1987)
1801 East Ninth Street
Architects: Harrison & Abramovitz
Renovation: Kober/Belluschi

The BP America Building's place as a visual counterpoint to the Terminal Tower in the downtown skyline was for years held by the dark tower at East 12th Street and Superior Avenue. 100 Erieview, also known as the Erieview Tower, was the first and most significant structure erected as part of the Erieview urban renewal plan made public in late 1960. The Erieview project was originally conceived as a 163-acre urban renewal area ranging from East 6th to East 17th Streets between Chester Avenue and Lake Erie. I.M. Pei & Associates prepared a master plan calling for extensive parks and greens subdivided by lengthy low-rise buildings and punctuated occasionally by stark high-rise struc-tures. The hub of the Pei plan would become a 40 story tower located at East 12th and St. Clair.

By early 1963, developers John Galbreath and Peter Ruffin broke ground on Harrison & Abramovitz' modern (and starkly institutional-looking) office tower, 40 stories and 529 feet in height. Construction moved quickly on the 703,000 square foot, dark-green-and-black curtain wall structure and its related improvements: a massive tree-lined plaza with combined fountain/reflecting pool/ice rink linking the structure to East 9th Street, and an underground 450-car parking garage. The tower's top-floor restaurant and private club, Top of the Town and The Clevelander

Club, both provide dramatic day or night views of the entire downtown, Lake Erie and Burke Lakefront Airport.

The remainder of the Erieview urban renewal area did not fare quite so well, however. Additional structures were slow to arrive, the original master plan was either modified or ignored, and thus into the late '70s Erieview Plaza was a somewhat cold and forbidding place most of the year. The East 9th Street corridor seemed to mark an effective limit to the downtown's growth, particularly near the Lake. All this changed with the construction in the early '80s of a number of structures flanking East 9th Street, and in 1987 of The Galleria at Erieview, a two-level high-fashion shopping mall that occupies the former Erieview Plaza. The mall begins at 100 Erieview's lobby and stretches to the monumental arched entrance at East 9th Street. Along the way it provides a festive skylit pedestrian concourse. The Galleria has become a premier shopping destination in downtown Cleveland – an airy and glittering cluster of many of the finest retail shops and restaurants in the heart of Cleveland's financial/office district.

The Illuminating Building (1958)
(55 Public Square)
55 Public Square
Architects: Carson & Lundin

From just after the Depression until well after World War II there was virtually no new construction in downtown Cleveland. The City core was actually shrinking, with the demolition of the 308 Euclid Avenue Building and two buildings facing Public Square: the Cleveland College Building and the Old County Courthouse. Skepticism greeted the periodic announcements of proposed buildings throughout the '40s and '50s. By the time of its ground-breaking in the early 1956, the Illuminating Building at 55 Public Square was the first new sizable construction project in the City's core in almost 25 years. The building was also the City's first example of modern high-rise architecture and its first glass-and-aluminum curtain-wall structure.

The Illuminating Company had long enjoyed a Public Square location. Incorporated in 1892 by merger of The Brush Electric Light and Power Co. and the Cleveland Electric Light Co., The Cleveland Electric Illuminating Company erected its original headquarters building at 75 Public Square in 1915. This 15-story Italianate building by Hubbell & Benes, with its wide overhanging eaves, flat brackets and strict "columnar" order of base-shaft-and-capital, still stands at the northwest corner of Public Square. On a one acre site just west of this older "skyscraper" rose the new skyscraper – a structure of 12 floors of reinforced concrete atop 10 floors of steel framing, all bearing on a "floating" concrete pad two stories below street level. The 22-story, 300 foot tall office tower entered the skyline simultaneously with Manhattan's noted Seagram Building by Mies van der Rohe and Philip Johnson.

**The Bond Court Office Building and
Sheraton City Centre** (1971)
The Bond Court Hotel (1971)
Fromerly Bond Court Hotel)
1300 East 9th Street and 777 St. Clair Avenue NE
Architects, Office Building & Garage: Skidmore, Owings & Merrill
Architects, Hotel & Garage: Bialosky & Manders

The Bond Court complex of an office tower, hotel and parking
garage was named for old Bond Court, a narrow east-west street
bisecting the block bounded by East 6th and 9th Streets and St.
Clair and Lakeside Avenues. On the northern half of the bisected
block stood the recently completed Federal Office Building, when
in the late '60s, the Erieview urban renewal area was expanded to
include all of the southern half. On this site was to rise the 20-
story, 270-foot Bond Court Office Building, connected by an
atrium mall to a six-story, 620-car parking garage. George E.
Ebeling's Hotel Auditorium, built in 1927 to serve conventioneers
and visitors to Public Auditorium, was razed in 1969 to clear the
site. Construction began in 1970 on the bronze office block of
aluminum and glass, with the first tenants occupying space in
early 1972.

Construction of the 22-story, 526-room Bond Court Hotel followed
in early 1973, and moved rapidly along at the rate of one floor
poured every three days. Though a major fire and partial building
collapse delayed construction, the Hotel opened in 1975. The
hotel exterior cladding is brick, secured in the same fashion as that
of The Central National Bank Tower, and so in the second half of
1984, the Hotel underwent a similar construction suit, settlement
and brick veneer repairs.

Ohio Bell Telephone (1927)
750 Huron Avenue
Architects: Hubbell & Benes

The Ohio Bell Telephone Building is one of the few Cleveland
structures to mirror the Manhattan "setback" towers evolving
under New York City's 1926 zoning laws. It also reflects the
influence of Eliel Sarrinen's "Modern" skyscraper style of the '20s.
This 24-story structure rises to 365 feet in several tiered masses,
with the vertical emphasis maintained by thin exterior wall piers
framing ribbons of windows, recessed spandrels and blunted
massive corner piers. Based on a concrete pad reputed to be the
most massive continuous pour of its day, the building originally
housed offices, switchboards, equipment, service and employee
areas and a restaurant. Upon construction of the newer Ohio
Bell headquarters at Erieview the older structure was converted
primarily to the housing of equipment.

One Cleveland Center (1983)
1375 East Ninth Street
Architects: Hugh Stubbins & Associates

In the early 1980's, as development activity along East 9th
Street and eastward began to
heat up, Cleveland acquired its
"silver chisel", One Cleveland
Center. Designed by Hugh
Stubbins & Associates, and
bearing a kinship with the
massive Citicorp Center in
Manhattan, this faceted metallic
prism became, at 31 stories and
450 feet, the fourth-tallest
building in Cleveland. Though
the building's site had been
slated for high-rise apartments
in the I. M. Pei Erieview urban
renewal area master plan almost
20 years earlier, Medical Mutual
of Cleveland acquired the land
from John Galbreath in 1979 to
develop a "people-oriented"
office development.

One Cleveland Center's people-
orientation is easy to see. The structure's base is sculpted into a
five-story glass garden atrium, inviting pedestrian traffic from the
corner of East 9th Street and St. Clair Avenue. Its fitness center,
operated by the YMCA is directly connected and surmounts the
building's parking structure. Its angled orientation to the City's
street grid and its prismatic shape make it an attractive counterpoint to other architecture throughout town. Its reflective metal
and glass skin gives it a sheen and a lightness lacking among its
more somber neighbors.

Ameritrust Center
(Proposed construction date 1993-1996)
Public Square
Architects: Kohn Pedersen Fox

Soon after the title of tallest structure in Cleveland goes to the
Jacobs Brothers' Society Center, it will most likely be assumed
by another Jacobs Brothers development: Ameritrust Center. At
a proposed height of 900 feet in 60 stories, Ameritrust Center will
include a 484-room Hyatt Hotel with a soaring 12-story atrium,
over 1 million square feet of office space, as well as several
restaurants and meeting facilities. Like Society Center, Ameritrust
Center will derive its name from its prime tenant, a major regional
banking institution. Unlike Society Center's historicist aesthetic, the
proposed Ameritrust Center will be decidedly Post-Modern.

It will rise from a twelve-story buff-colored granite base, extending upward in two "shear wall" masses to the west and north. The
western "wall" (plans call for 26-stories in height) will terminate
the composition as an edge to the perceived Public Square

"room." The much higher "wall" along the northern edge of the complex will terminate in a decorative cap that will override the curved bloc glass wall of the office tower shaft. This decorative peak will become one of four very distinctive building tops ringing Public Square and defining Cleveland's skyline for years to come.

Society Center (1989-1991)
Public Square
Architects:
Tower: Cesar Pelli & Associates; Kendall/Heaton & Associates
Society for Savings: van Dijk, Johnson & Partners
Hotel: Cesar Pelli & Associates; Glover, Smith, Bode Inc.

The Society Center complex, under construction on the northern edge of Public Square is a product of Richard E. Jacobs and David A. Jacobs, developers of the Galleria and of the Ameritrust Center. Renovating and incorporating the historic Society for Savings Building (1889) into its base, the complex will include a 57-story 1.25 million square foot office tower, a 424-room Marriott hotel, a multi-level underground garage, and the redevelopment of a portion of Cleveland's mall to the east. Designed by Cesar Pelli, the composition counterpoints the red historic bank structure with a lighter-toned, vertically-emphasized granite office tower capped by a reflective metal pyramid and spire. At a height of 888 feet, the Society Center will displace the Terminal Tower as Cleveland's (and Ohio's) tallest building.

Cleveland's Memorial Plaza immediately east of the new office tower, site of the War Memorial fountains and statue, will be completely refurbished and will serve as forecourt to both the Marriott and the Tower.

The Rockefeller Building (1905) (1911)
614 Superior Avenue NW
Architects: Knox & Elliot

The Rockefeller Building is the second historic structure to occupy its site; it was preceded by Cleveland's famed Weddell House of 1847 at which then-President-elect Lincoln addressed the citizenry in 1861. Situated at the southerly boundary of the Warehouse District, the Rockefeller Building stands in tribute to the architectural work of Louis Sullivan and other Chicago skyscraper stylists. Knox and Elliot created a clearly expressed high-rise structure veneered with textural ornamentation. Oil magnate John D. Rockefeller erected the building in 1905 to house shipping, coal and iron offices for Cleveland's growing river-related businesses. After the building was expanded, then purchased and renamed by Josiah Kirby in 1920, Mr. Rockefeller repurchased the building in a fit of pique, restoring his name to it in 1923.

Crown Centre (1990)
5005 Rockside Road, Independence (at I-77)
Architects: Kaczmar Architects, Inc.

The rapidly developing south-side office area astride I-77 at Rockside Road features numerous new hotels and office structures. By far the tallest and most visible is Crown Centre, a 14-story, "V"-shaped tower clad in granite and reflecting pink glass. The building announces the arrival of the commuter to the urban sprawl of Cleveland. Its mutually reflective wings create ever-changing visual images. The pyramidal tops, accented in neon and a six-story atrium with water feature are distinctive aspects.

Richard L. Zimmerman
Pen M. Zimmerman

Section 9

Low Rise Commercial and Institutional Buildings

The Galleria at Erieview (1987)
1301 E. 9th Street
Architect: Kober/Belluschi Associates

In late 1987 The Galleria at Erieview became one of Cleveland's shining lights, then, its only *new* downtown shopping mall. Built at the base of the former 100 Erieview office tower on what was previously an immense tree-lined open plaza (a component of I. M. Pei's urban renewal plan of 1960), the Galleria connects the renamed Tower at Erieview with the pedestrian activity of East Ninth Street. The Galleria's two levels contain 200,000 square fee of retail space, with a food court, art gallery and several restaurants. Designed in the high-fashion Post-Modern style of a "boutique" mall, The Galleria's architectural signature is its three-segment barrel-vaulted skylight spanning virtually the entire public area of the mall and punching through the East Ninth Street facade in a grand glass-and-granite arch. The Galleria's quality merchant mix, active food court and plaza, and the renovated Tower's well-appointed office floors have added a note of excitement and vibrancy to the East Ninth corridor.

Severance Town Center (1963)
(Formerly Severance Shopping Center)
Mayfield Road at Taylor Road, Cleveland Heights
Architects: The Austin Co.

Severance Center was one of the first enclosed shopping malls in the country, following the leader by only seven years. Severance Center embodied the most basic of mall plans: two anchor department stores occupying opposite ends of one long "double-loaded corridor" of shop fronts, punctuated at midpoint by a clerestoried, fountained entrance court. The Center's architecture was suited to the plan: it too was clear-cut, simple and comprehensible. The mall was sited to make use of several floor levels through grade changes, and to incorporate below-grade truck service for anchor stores. The site planning has also preserved large peripheral development tracts which have over the years become populated by institutions, public buildings, office buildings and apartment structures. The mall has undergone several renovation/expansions and now boasts a food/entertainment court and the new name of Severance Town Center.

The Arcade (1890)
401 Euclid Avenue
Architect: George H. Smith
Engineer: John Eisenmann

The Arcade consists of two 9-story office buildings linked by the central 5-story commercial arcade of iron and glass. This arcade rises from two "street" levels (since Euclid and Superior Avenues are at different elevations) through four levels of stepped balconies to the glass roof 100-feet above. The main facades are load-bearing, while other walls and the arcade roof are carried on a skeleton of iron, oak and steel. Innovative for its time, the roof is supported on triple-hinged trusses erected by a bridge company. The many glittering glass storefronts of office and retail spaces are lit by a dramatic 300-foot long light court of striking verticality, lightness and interest. It was one of the nation's earliest forerunners of today's modern shopping mall. The stone and brick exterior exemplifies the Richardsonian Romanesque style except for the Euclid Avenue entrance, remodeled in the 1930s in the Art Deco mode.

The Colonial Arcade (1898)
530 Euclid Avenue
Architect: George H. Smith

This two-story passage
was designed by one of the
architects of The Arcade although it is on a smaller scale.
It served as a link from the
Colonial Hotel on Prospect
Avenue to the shopping district
corridor along Euclid Avenue.
The original upper balconied
level surmounts a lower floor
subject to an art-deco renovation at an earlier time.

The May Company Building (1914)
158 Euclid Avenue
Architects: Daniel Burnham & Company

Originally built as a 6-story structure in 1914 to reestablish the
May Department Stores Co. as Cleveland's preeminent retailer,
the structure received two additional floors in 1931 in response
to continuing competition. The building, with its finely detailed,
Neo-classical terra cotta facade decoration and clearly expressed
skeletal structure, has much in common with Henry Bacon's Halle
Building at Playhouse Square of 1910/1914. The store's 17 plus
acres of floor space bolstered The May Company's claim as "Ohio's
Largest Store". Of note are the windows which express the Chicago
School esthetic of narrow end lights flanking a wide center panel.

The Perry-Payne Building (1889)
740 Superior Avenue, NW
Architects: Cudell and Richardson

The Perry-Payne Building was rightly viewed as a commercial
architectural masterpiece in its day and for some time thereafter.
Built by prominent lawyer and railroad executive Henry Payne and
named for himself and his wife (maiden name Perry), the building
advanced the clear design intent of the architect's earlier works,
the Worthington and Root & McBride (Bradley) Buildings. Here
a great inner light court was ringed by office floors of tile and
concrete on iron posts. The eight-story load-bearing exterior walls
were punctuated by large areas of glass and the building's mass is
softened by both a ninth-floor central gallery and twin balconies
projected over the heavily-columned main entrance. The original
windows were bricked in for smaller openings and the light court
has been filled in. The building, abandoned for years, awaits a
renewal.

Joseph M. Bruening Red Cross Center (1990)
American Red Cross, Greater Cleveland Chapter
3747 Euclid Avenue
Architects: HWH Architects Engineers Planners

A three-story structure with one-story wing consolidates two previous facilities into one building, clad in red brick with mirrored glass openings. The 90,000 square foot building provides program and administrative services as well as a fully-equipped blood center serving northern Ohio. A glass atrium highlights the building and projects forward into an extensive plaza.

The Rose Building (1900) (1988)
(Now Blue Cross/Blue Shield)
2060 East 9th Street
Architect: George H. Smith
Renovation: Voinovich, Sgro

Ten stories high, the Rose Building was one of Cleveland's first steel frame structures. The beams are rolled steel and the columns steel angles secured by steel bands. The building was fireproofed with clay tile and floors reinforced with tile arch construction. At the time of its construction, skeptics doubted the commercial feasibility of an office building so far from the financial core of the city (only as far as the corner of Prospect Avenue and East Ninth Street) but the building soon proved successful. Since 1908, its earnings have gone to the Benjamin Rose Institute, a philanthropic organization dedicated to care for the elderly. Of special note is the splendid terra cotta skin of the building.

The Halle Building (1910) (1914) (1948) (1983-1985)
(Formerly The Halle Brothers Company)
1228 Euclid Avenue
Architect: Henry Bacon
Renovation: Cope Linder Associates

Designed as a speculative office block at the fringe of downtown just after the turn of the century, this terra cotta clad building is notable for its exquisitely decorated skin. Occupied by the Halle Co. continuously from 1910 through the late '70s, the building has since been restored and renovated as an office structure by Forest City Enterprises, and has become a prestige address at Playhouse Square. The building serves as an important example of adaptive re-use. Much of the original detail of the main floor has been preserved as well as the elevator enclosures and column capitals in upper floors.

The Bradley Building (1884) (1985)
(Formerly The Root & McBride Warehouse)
West 6th Street at Lakeside Avenue
Architects: Cudell & Richardson
Renovation: Schmidt Copeland Parker Stevens

The Root & McBride Warehouse was designed and constructed
as a utilitarian commercial building of sturdy masonry piers
framing multi-story window clusters in a simple, yet elegant,
composition. The verticality of the window arrangements and
the delicacy of their fanlights create a surprisingly light architecture among the building's more traditional Warehouse District
neighbors. Acquired and renamed by the prominent Bradley
family, the building underwent a major renovation in time for its
centennial and now serves as an office and commercial structure.

The Western Reserve Building (1891) (1902) (1990)
West 9th Street at Superior Avenue NW
Architects: Burnham & Root
Addition: Keeva J. Kekst

Built by industrialist Samuel
Mather to house offices of his
company, the Western Reserve
Building bears resemblances to
both the Society for Savings
Building and Root's Monadnock
Building in Chicago completed
the following year. The building
incorporates load-bearing
masonry walls, interior iron
columns floors of tile arch and
cement, as does the Society
structure. The relatively plain
wall surfaces punctuated with
oriel bays and terminating in a
flared cornice hearken to the
Monadnock. The Western
Reserve Building is further
articulated to suit its steeply-sloped irregularly triangular site.
Renovated in the early '70s and now with an addition on its north
flank, the Western Reserve serves as a handsome gateway
structure for Cleveland's resurging Warehouse District and Flats.

Shaker Square Shopping District (1927-1929)
Shaker Blvd. at North and South Moreland Blvds.
Architects: Philip L. Small and Charles Bacon Rowley

While not the first planned suburban shopping center in the U.S.,
and also not consciously styled as an English village green, Shaker
Square was a strikingly innovative development dependent on
European models. Greek agora, Roman fora, and Neo-Classical
town squares anchored by fountains and equestrian statuary
provided the inspiration for the Square's monumentally-scaled
space ringed by human-scaled structures. In keeping with the
consistent visual character of the evolving residential areas of
Shaker Heights, the Square's symmetrically massed structures

consist of red brick and slate roofs, accented by white trim and bearing the gamut of Georgian detailing: multi-pane windows with fanlights, panelled doors, fluted pilasters and broken pediments. The square has remained a pleasantly viable pedestrian commercial district to this day.

The First Federal Savings Bank Building (1987)
1215 Superior Avenue N.E.
Architects: Richard L. Bowen
and Associates, Inc.

The First Federal Savings Bank Building, erected on the northeast corner of East 12th Street and Superior Avenue in 1987, became one of the easternmost downtown office buildings thus expanding the City's financial district. This seven-story structure occupies a narrow north-south site, filling out the fourth quadrant of the intersection, flanked by Reserve Square, the Diamond Building and Eaton Center. Its reflective horizontal banding of blue glass mirrors its neighbors, tree-lined East 12th Street and the Cleveland sky, offering a constantly changing and visually intriguing image of the City. (The bank headquarters' use of blue glazing is the only such coloration in downtown.) The building base of white and gray marbles, its dramatic lobby, atrium and skylights, and the notches carved into the sheer glass prism for unique office plans add to its appeal as a quality office location. The First Federal Savings Bank moved into its new headquarters from its location in Reserve Square.

The Bulkley Building (1921)
1501 Euclid Avenue
Architect: C. Howard Crane

The Bulkley Building was constructed at the heart of the Playhouse Square district in 1921 by Robert J. Bulkley. After years of successful law practice in the City, Mr. Bulkley served as a Congressman in the 1920s, then joined the US Senate for almost the entire decade of the '30s. He was also influential in the formation of the Northern Ohio Opera Association, was a speaker at Cleveland's 1936 Great Lakes Exposition, and assisted in the opening of the Metropolitan Opera in Cleveland in 1942. The 8-story stone office building bearing his name housed not only his own firm's law offices, but also an arcaded lobby flanked by retail shops, the Allen Theater and various theater support areas. The Bulkley Building's future is linked to those of prominent neighboring structures like the Keith and Hanna Buildings, as the Playhouse Square Theater District continues to evolve into a vibrant office, retail and entertainment hub within the City. Major restoration of the lower two floors was carried out in 1990, Richard Trott & Associates, architects.

The Society National Bank Building (1889-1890)
(The Society for Savings Building)
Public Square
Architects: Burnham & Root
Renovation: van Dijk, Johnson & Partners

This medieval fortress of a bank was erected on Public Square to replace the earlier headquarters structure sited in the same block. Designed at a time when traditionally styled revival architecture buildings were slowly giving way to a newer expressions of steel-framed "skyscrapers", The Society for Savings Building was an effective transitional edifice. It embodied Renaissance, Romanesque and Gothic features within a steel-framed reddish stone castle. Its design incorporated both 5-foot thick stone ground floor walls (to reflect proper financial stability) and a nine-story skylit light court (to illumine the growing ranks of clerical workers and managers). The large and grandly decorated main banking lobby stands in awesome counterpoint to the brutally imposing exterior. Still attached to the building's south-eastern pier is one of Public Square's historic street lights.

The Society National Bank Building is being renovated (1990) and will be incorporated into the base of the new Society Center currently under construction on its north and east flanks.

Premier Industrial Corporation, Building No. 1 (1913)
4515 Euclid Avenue
Architect: J. Milton Dyer

Built for the Standard Manufacturing Corp. to wholesale plumbing fixtures, this five-story loft, office and one-time showroom facility is one of the city's citadels of terra cotta surfacing.

Premier headquartered itself here and ultimately fanned out over neighboring blocks. The stunning commercial-modern design by Dyer languished over the years until the owner decided to renew the structure. The exterior facades have been substantially restored (1990) by Gaede Serne Zofcin.

Edgell Communications (1981)
7500 Old Oak Boulevard, Middleburg Heights
Architects: Tufts & Wenzel
Landscape Architects: William Behnke Associates

Originally built for the Harvest Companies, this publishing headquarters is remarkable for its dynamic brick design, its many energy-efficient features and its skillful placement in a scenic landscape on a 43-acre site.

A pair of short brick silos (stairwell towers) surmount two broad sloping roofs flanking a central entranceway. The low profile of the exterior belies a high-ceilinged, spacious interior, a two-tiered space consisting of a mezzanine level overlooking an open modular workplace of 48,000 square feet.

Regional Transit Community Responsive Center (1985)
4601 Euclid Avenue
Architects: Lesko Associates

This sprawling, low-rise structure houses the maintenance and storage of vehicles and the dispatching of same for the Regional Transit Authority's specialized service. The building's Dri-vit exterior skin is configured to pick up nearby architectural forms and to screen the vehicles from the street.

TRW Inc. Headquarters Building (1985)
1900 Richmond Road
Exterior Architects: F.C.L. Associates
Interior Architects: Interspace, Inc.

The splendid estate of the Chester and Francis Bolton Family in Lyndhurst became the locale of the new headquarters of TRW Inc. providing a park-like setting which includes the Bolton House itself (1917), renovated and restored in (1985) by van Dijk, Johnson and Partners. The five- and six-level building spreads out in a four-spoke pattern which centers on an immense central atrium. The exterior is characterized by strip window walls with bronze-tone aluminum frames, spandels and trim. The building's functionalist expression retreats into the surrounding landscape. Significant contemporary sculpture is arranged throughout the grounds.

The building interiors are open and spacious with the giant center park dominating. Many key walls are replete with noted originals and reproductions of significant artist's work. The close alliance of exterior vistas of the surrounding park and the artistic interior spaces was a planned format to enhance both satisfaction and efficiency on the part of the building's users.

Stouffer Tower City Plaza (1918) (1962)
24 Public Square
Architects: Graham, Burnham & Co.
Additions: Perry, Shaw, Hepburn & Dean (Boston)

The present hotel, occupant of a site dedicated to a hostelry usage since 1815, is a charter member of Historic Hotels of America. The National Trust's program to recognize grand hotels in the nation. The 12-story building, once rated at 900 rooms, now has 500 at the scale and quality expected by modern travelers. Faced with white brick above a granite clad base, the hotel fully engages into the Terminal Tower group.

A one-time light well is now an internal atrium. The addition of 1962 expanded the hotel westward to include a 400-car parking garage and a 35,000 sq. ft. ballroom/exhibit space at which many of Cleveland's major events have been held since. In 1977-1978 a major renovation took place under the combined direction of Weinberg Teare & Herman, Bialosky & Manders and Lesko Associates. More recently the improvements have included enhanced public areas and suites.

Richard L. Zimmerman
Pen M. Zimmerman

Section 10

Educational Buildings

Case Western Reserve University

See also the University Circle Walking Tour,
Section (19D)

Thwing Center, Student Union (1980)
11111 Euclid Avenue
Architects: Don M. Hisaka & Associates

Thwing Center, a modern two-story glass and metal atrium
combines the Victorian past of Thwing Hall, a historic ballroom
and private social club and a mansion, Hitchcock Hall.

Hitchcock Hall, built in 1897 as a private residence was purchased
by Western Reserve in 1934 for use as a graduate school and
student organization center.

Thwing Hall, built in 1913, architects Lehman & Schmitt formerly
the Excelsior Club, a private men's club, was purchased by the
University and opened in 1934 for use as the Leonard Case
Library, the Graduate School, and the School of Library Science.
Also, Thwing Hall was made into the Student Union in 1957.

Thwing Center is the focal point of the Case Western Reserve University campus. The existing East building, Thwing Hall, has spacious, high-ceilinged rooms; wide, bright hallways; mosaic and hardwood floors; and marble stairways. Also, restored was a classic ballroom with a vaulted ceiling, presently used for concerts and other events. The existing West building, Hitchcock Hall is presently used as a lounge. A bookstore occupies the rear portion of the central connecting atrium.

Adelbert Hall (1881-1882)
2040 Adelbert Road
Architect: Joseph Ireland

Adelbert Hall, the work of Joseph Ireland, was commissioned in 1881 by Amasa Stone, a member of the building committee for another of Ireland's works, the National Bank Building (1867). Adelbert Hall was the last of Joseph Ireland's Cleveland buildings of which there is a record, before he returned to New York in 1885.

In 1881 Western Reserve College moved to Cleveland from its location in Hudson, Ohio, under auspices that its name be changed to Adelbert College in memorium of Amasa Stone's son, and that the citizens of Cleveland provide the site. The Liberty Holden homestead, across Euclid Avenue from Wade Park, was purchased in 1881. Stone commissioned the building (with $500,000) and supervised the construction himself.

Ireland's Adelbert Hall incorporated ornamental architectural details from one of his earlier works, the Daniel P. Eels House (1876). The building, an eclectic mixture of Gothic, Queen Anne and Romanesque styles, is a fireproof structure with stone exterior walls, brick partition walls, and floors of masonry arches on iron girders. Ireland had been responsible for the first fireproof structures in Cleveland (Society for Savings 1866-1867 and National Bank Building 1867). The red horizontal banding in the buff sandstone is characteristic of the polychromy of the 1880's.

The tower of Adelbert Hall was rebuilt in 1897 with money provided by Amasa Stone's dauther, Flora Stone Mather, and extensively remodeled in 1901. The building was used for classrooms until 1958, and presently houses the University Administrative offices. The rooms are arranged around an atrium space with a skylight, renovated in 1901 to provide a magnificent divided stairway. The upper floors at the east side housed both a large assembly hall and a small museum. In its early years it also housed the college library as well as the offices of the college president and treasurer.

Franklin T. Backus Law School (1896)
Adelbert Road
Architect: Charles F. Schweinfurth

The Franklin T. Backus Law School Building was the first academic building at the South end of the campus in 1896, forming a gateway to the University. It was the first professional school building erected on this campus. It is constructed of Ohio buff sandstone, laid in courses, and stands two stories in height. Each room is abundantly lighted with spacious windows and finished in dark quartered white oak. The portico includes a floor of Italian white marble, Pompeian brick walls, and oak paneled ceiling. The approach to the portico was formed by a broad flight of stone steps, flanked with buttresses on which stood candelabra. An inscription on the frieze from the works of Samuel Johnson reads: "The law is the last result of human wisdom acting upon human experience for the benefit of the public..." The building was renovated in 1983 to serve as the home of the University Health Service, after the school of law moved to its present location in Gund Hall.

John D. Rockefeller Physics Building (1905)
Main Campus   Case Western Reserve University   Architects: Watterson & Schneider

This 3-story, four-square masonry structure dominates the west edge of the central mall of the old Case campus. Constructed of semi-glazed red brick with deeply recessed joints, and decorated in terra cotta trim, often of elaborate configuration. The building offers a series of giant plaques featuring the names of 28 notables who have contributed to the advancement of physics through the centuries. The building contains the Robert S. Shankland Lecture Hall. Built from an $85,000 gift of John D. Rockefeller.

Clark Hall (1892)
Bellflower Road
Architect: Richard Morris Hunt

Clark Hall, the College for Women's first building and the oldest building on the Case Western Reserve University campus, was commissioned in 1892 by Mrs. Eliza Clark for the sum of $50,000, to house classrooms, a chapel, library, gymnasium, and offices. Mr. and Mrs. Jeptha H. Wade donated the land. Clark Hall, a variant of the Queen Anne style, is a three-story classroom building of sandstone and buff brick. Its gable projections and irregular mass produce an ingenious arrangement of interior rooms with varying sizes, shapes, and heights. Nearly all of the original rooms are intact down to the last detail of their golden oak woodwork.

The Chapel was originally in a large room on the second floor with a groined roof, high-pointed oaken arches, and large traceried window. This room next became the main reference room for the Library, before its present use as a lecture hall.

Cleveland State University

Several CSU buildings are described in a shorter version in the Downtown Walking Tour, Section 19A.

University Hall (1910)
(Originally Samuel Mather Mansion)
2605 Euclid Avenue
Architect: Charles F. Schweinfurth

University Hall, built from 1906-1910 by Samuel Mather at a cost of $1.2 million, was the last and most expensive mansion on Cleveland's one-time "millionaire's row". It now stands alone as a reminder of an earlier age of wealth.

Samuel Mather, a native Clevelander, born in 1851, followed his father in the iron ore industry founding the Pickand Mather Company in 1883. Mather saw the opportunity to integrate all the facets of the ore to mill process, extending his interests from mining and shipping iron ore into ships and furnaces.

Design of the 45-room mansion was entrusted to the Architect, Charles Schweinfurth, a perfectionist in workmanship and materials. The mansion is 189' deep, 91' wide, and 51' high and was built on a 150-foot by 700-foot lot.

University Hall is faced in dark, reddish-brown, handmade water-struck brick with Indiana limestone trim. All first floor ceilings are 12' high. The second floor had 7 bedrooms, fireplaces, spacious baths, and generous closets. The third floor contained 8 additional bedrooms and a 65' x 27' ballroom (with a capacity of 300) with a 16' arched ceiling and a balcony on the North wall for society orchestras performing at Mather soirees. Sixteen fireplaces, including a 14th Century hearth imported from Venice, grace the rooms along with ornate handcarved woodwork. The original, highly imaginative, light fixtures can still be seen in the main stair hall and other rooms. Some of the original artwork of the mansion still remains today, including an Albert Bierstadt painting entitled "Emigrants Crossing the Plain" painted in Paris in 1860; an I. Gudin painting entitled "Aurora Borealis and the Statue" (1865); and a classic marble figure sculpted by Antonio Rossi of Rome in 1870.

At one time an attached Italian-style sunken garden graced the rear of the home, beautifully landscaped and dotted with imported statuary. At the far end of the yard was the garage and squash court. An impressive iron fence along Euclid Avenue was lost to a WWII scrap iron drive.

The mansion has undergone many owners, but not many remodelings since the death of Samuel Mather in 1931. The Cleveland Institute of Music occupied the mansion until 1940. The Cleveland Automobile Club then occupied the property until Cleveland State University acquired the mansion in 1968, when it was renamed University Hall and renovated for use as a conference facility. In February 1973 University Hall became the first building in Cleveland to be placed in the National Register of Historic Places.

Physical Education Building (1973)
2451 Euclid Avenue
Architects: Dalton, van Dijk, Johnson and Partners

This dominating structure of semi-glazed jumbo brick units reflects a two-part plan expressing the two giant rooms within – the Natatorium and Gymnasium. Of distinction are the rounded corners and the strongly-sculptured concrete members of the glazed areas and entries on the south facade.

James A. Rhodes Tower (1971)
1860 East 22nd Street
Architects: Outcalt, Guenther, Rode & Bonebrake

The James A. Rhodes Tower is the only modern high-rise structure to appear on the campus of Cleveland State University. Situated at mid-block between Euclid and Chester Avenues, and between East 21st and 22nd Streets, the Tower is a 23-story, 363-foot high composition of monolithic white granite and vertical slot windows. The Tower was originally sited to visually pinpoint the center of the CSU campus within the City's skyline, and to establish the growing school's new focal point as is expanded westward toward the downtown core. Rhodes Tower has since been joined by a major parking structure and by a new Student Union Center, with still more structures on the way. The Tower began as one component of the CSU master plan made public in 1966. The Tower and related library and classroom buildings were completed and in use by late 1971. It houses several hundred faculty and department offices, five floors of library space, and computer and audio-visual facilities.

University Center (1974)
2121 Euclid Avenue
Architects: Don M. Hisaka & Associates
Architects and Engineers: Hoag-Wismar-Henderson
Landscape Architects: Sasaki Associates, Inc.

Making the strongest statement from the street is the concrete framed and surfaced building, with two sides of punctured planes expressing windowed activity areas surrounding two sides of glazing in a structural frame expressing a giant atrium. From the fortress-like street approach, the visitor emerges into the big room with dramatic visual references to taller neighbors and busy plazas.

Main Classroom Building (1970)
1899 East 22nd Street
Architects: Dalton, Dalton and Little

Of striking dimensions, this five-level classroom and auditoria building surmounts parking adjacent to the depressed East 22nd Street which allows a connecting plaza to flow overhead and free movement to and from this central facility. Concrete, brick infill and stone cladding give this contemporary structure a somewhat brutalist cast, yet embrace the 323,000 square feet within a skin made more lively by extensive glazing.

Convocation Center (1991)
2000 Prospect Avenue
Architects: URS Consultants
Associated Architects: C/A Architects, Richard L. Bowen &
Associates, Whitley & Whitley

Occupying the area bounded by Carnegie and Prospect Aves. and E. 18th and E. 21st Sts., this massive structure is comprised of an arena and a multi-story wing to the east serving support functions. The arena, seating 13,000, is elliptical in form with brick base and ribbed metal upper area. The wing is brick, topped by a barrel-vaulted atrium. Four cylinders at the corners of the ellipse serve vertical circulation. Sloping glazed roofs shield the entrance areas.

Baldwin-Wallace College

Marting Hall (1896) (1989)
(Originally Memorial Hall)
Seminary Street
Architects: Godfrey Fugman of C.S. Cramer
Renovation: van Dijk, Johnson & Partners

Baldwin University was founded in 1845 by John Baldwin as the Baldwin Institute. German Wallace College was founded in 1863 by Dr. William Nast and Jacob Rothweiler. The two institutions were united in 1913 to become Baldwin-Wallace College.

Memorial Hall was renamed Marting Hall in 1938 in honor of Dr. John C. Marting, financial agent of German Wallace College and trustee for nearly half a century. Marting Hall was built in 1895-1896 of Berea stone for the sum of $40,000.

The four-turreted tower with octagonal roof is the most distinctive feature of Marting Hall. Horizontal bands transversing the whole tower are borrowed from Henry Hobson Richardson's design for the tower at Trinity Church. The central facade of Marting Hall is easily related to the front gable of Richardson's Crane Memorial Library, in that they both possess a massive arched entrance, a great turret guarding the entrance, a large stone tablet set into the wall over the entrance, and a series of arched windows above.

Flooding closed Marting Hall in 1982. It has undergone renovation and has reopened in the Fall of 1989, once again serving as the center for the History, English, Philosophy, and Religion Departments.

Carnegie Hall (1882) (1905)
(*Originally Ladies Hall*)
59 East Bagley Road
Architect: Unknown

The Ladies Hall of Baldwin University (a dormitory) was dedicated in 1882 after $40,000 were spent during 10 years of construction. It was situated on the Southeast corner of Elm and S. Seminary Streets. Built of Berea sandstone, coursing of uniform thickness, and wall of irregular outline, it stands 3 stories in height and is 60-feet by 96-feet.

The roof is of Gothic style with windows in the upper story. The platform for the front of the building was constructed from the largest piece of prepared stone in the state, quarried in Berea, and measuring 14-feet in length by 10-feet in width and 9-feet thick, weighing 10-tons.

The land on which Ladies Hall was situated was sold to the Cleveland Sandstone Quarries Company, causing the structure to be moved almost 3/4 mile. 1905 marked the rededication of Ladies Hall, renamed Carnegie Hall, in honor of Mr. Andrew Carnegie. The Carnegie Foundation assured the $6,000 cost of moving the structure to its present location on East Bagley Road, provided the structure would be used as a science building. Mr. John Paul Baldwin, grandson of the founder of the college, supervised the removal and reconstruction of the building. The stones were marked so that the building could be reconstructed in its original form, with the exception of changing the entrance location from the end to the side.

John Carroll University

Grasselli Tower (1935)
20700 North Park Blvd., University Heights
Architects: Philip L. Small and Associates

The architectural flavor of John Carroll University was set by the dominating tower centered on the boulevard extending northeast from Fairmount Circle constituting the formal approach to the campus. Construction of the new campus began in 1931, and for a time after 1935 the tower surmounted a group of three buildings all built in the Collegiate Gothic style. The campus has subsequently expanded eastward to embrace numerous buildings, but with the exception of the Grasselli Library (1961) by Ernst Payer, the Gothic Revival mode has prevailed. Consequently, John Carroll University presents an unusually consistent design theme.

Cuyahoga Community College Group

District Office (1973) (1979)
700 Carnegie Avenue
Architects: Visnapuu & Gaede, Inc.
Landscape Architects : William A. Behnke Associates;
John E. Litten Associates

This structure is readily seen at the junction of the Innerbelt, East 9th Street and Broadway. Its two-story masonry block form with attached cylindrical stair is surmounted by a half-pyramid light-scoop favoring an atrium within.

Metro Campus (1966-1970)
2900 Community College Avenue
Architects: Outcalt, Guenther, Rode and Bonebrake
Landscape Architect: Ernest L. Dewald

A massive, condensed campus of similarly styled structures blend dark red masonry with sand-color precast panels. The varied building heights and several internal courtyards produce an urban campus of dramatic form. The whole is raised on a parking garage serving as a stylobate.

Unified Technologies Center (1986)
2415 Woodland Avenue
Architects: Richard L. Bowen & Associates, Voinovich-Sgro Inc.

Placed adjacent to the Metro Campus, this brick and glass structure reflects the hi-tech nature of its purpose.

Western Campus (1974-1976)
11000 W. Pleasant Valley Road, Parma
Architects: Master Plan, Caudill Rowlett Scott;
Individual Wings, Lipaj-Woyar-Tomsik, Madison-Madison
International, Richard L. Bowen & Associates
Landscape Architects: William A. Behnke Associates

A large structure with an auditorium loft serving as a focal point and a number of fully compatible wings extending northward, this strongly-stated masonry building with deeply recessed windows, commands a prairie-like setting in functionalist style and soft red color.

Eastern Campus (1971) (1981)
4250 Richmond Road
Architects: Richard Fleischman Associates
Main Building: VanAuken Bridges Inc.
Landscape Architects: John E. Litten Associates

The 1981 building is the dominant structure and is placed on a rise with a major approach from the east. An irregular mass in plan, it plays cascading glazed areas against solid brick planes. At the entries, structural and sculptural concrete beams, steps and wall planes create playful spatial forms.

St. Ignatius High School (1889) (1984)
1911 West 30th Street
Architect: Brother Frederick Wipfler, S.J.
Renovation: Don Hisaka and Associates

1889 marked the year of the first building housing living quarters for St. Ignatius High School at the corner of W. 30th and Carroll Avenue. In 1891, the North wing was added for classrooms. The windowless South facade suggests an unbuilt, but planned for, South wing (meant to house a chapel and an assembly hall).

The central building has been expanded several times through the years, but architectural interest centers on the main block due to its commanding size and strongly stated Victorian German Gothic detailing. The playful tower of St. Ignatius remains to this day a major skyline feature of the near west side.

Extensive alterations and additions were put in place in 1984-1985 including a new library and a 2-1/2 story high atrium.

Laurel School for Girls (1928-1981)
One Lyman Circle, Shaker Heights
Architect: J. Graham

The original plan, a reproduction of the English Tudor, Layer-Marney tower in Essex, England, provided for two separate buildings, one a dormitory accommodating up to 40 students, and the other containing classroom facilities for 500 students in grades K through 12.

Large, casement bay windows, crenelated tower and arched main doorway are just a few elements of the Tudor style of the facade. The first floor houses the Alumnae Room with oak wainscoting, beamed ceilings, and Caen stone fireplace. The Chapel, on the second floor, exhibits a high, patterned, oak-beamed ceiling which slopes gently to an apex. Lyman House, the residence for the Head of the school, was designed in 1931 by D. Dunn. The South end of the main structure is connected to the Margaret A. Ireland building (designed in 1963 by Little, Dalton & Associates) by a glass walkway and houses the early childhood program. Laurel School became a day school exclusively, causing the dormitory interior to be remodeled to house the Mabel Shields Andrew Science Center in 1968. The Middle School was designed in 1981 by Fred Toguchi. The dormitory was then connected to the main building by a glass enclosed bridge. A gym designed by Toguchi was also added in 1981.

All buildings curve to front Lyman Circle, named in honor of Headmistress Sarah E. Lyman, who was responsible for the school's move to Shaker Heights from its original Cleveland location.

Robert M. McGaw, AIA

Section 11

Religious Buildings

Epworth-Euclid United Methodist Church (1926-1928)
East 107th Street at Chester Avenue
Architects: Bertram Goodhue, and Walker and Weeks

At University Circle, surmounting the Lagoon, is Epworth-Euclid
Methodist Church, a familiar Cleveland landmark. In the early
1920s Bertram Grosvenor Goodhue was commissioned to draw
up the plans for this church. Goodhue died in 1924, and the plans
were completed by the local firm of Walker and Weeks, who also
supervised construction of the church. Epworth is one of
Cleveland's most architecturally distinctive buildings. Its shape,
massing, and tapering octagonal roof over the crossing are
outstanding features. Epworth is said to be reminiscent of Mont

St. Michel. Its style has also been labelled "highly stylized Gothic." The church is basically modified cruciform in plan and has a high central fleche. The exterior, faced in a golden Plymouth granite, is ornamented with figures by New York sculptor Leo Friedlander. On the interior, the tower is supported by four great arches. The most significant openings are the large rose window facing east, the arched transept windows, and the small lancet windows in the tower.

First Church of Christ, Scientist (1931)
2200 Overlook Road, Cleveland Heights
Architects: Walker and Weeks

Modeled after the Pantheon in Rome, this classical church is on a picturesque site overlooking the city. The octagonal, limestone- clad structure has an aluminum roof and seats 1190. It also features a 155-foot high bell tower which houses the church offices on its first floor. The bells within the tower are false ones, being halves of bells secured in place. Modern lighting has made the tower a dramatic night-time feature in the city's University Circle area.

First United Methodist Church (1905) (1966)
Euclid Avenue at East 30th Street
Architect: J. Milton Dyer

The First United Methodist parish, established in 1827, was the first of its denomination in the Cleveland area. First United Methodist Church was designed by J. Milton Dyer and was completed in 1905 at a cost of $250,000. It bears a strong resemblance to Trinity Cathedral at Euclid and East 22nd and, like it, is faced with Indiana limestone.

First United has a square crossing tower with lancets in threes and corner pinnacles. There are traceried windows and a tripartite main entrance. The interior body of the church is designed as a preaching auditorium. In 1966, a 3-story, Christian education wing was added to the back of the church by Travis Gower Walsh.

Trinity Cathedral (1901-1907)
Euclid Avenue at East 22nd Street
Architect: Charles Schweinfurth

Charles Schweinfurth began plans for this church in 1890, though the cornerstone was not laid until May 12, 1903. The cathedral was consecrated on September 24, 1907. Trinity Cathedral is considered Schweinfurth's masterpiece and one of the finest examples of the Perpendicular Gothic style in the United States. The parish, which dates back to 1816, built Cleveland's first church in 1829. Today, Trinity is the seat of the Bishop of the Episcopal Diocese of Ohio.

This cruciform-plan church has an exterior of Indiana limestone. The square central tower, situated over the crossing, is crested by a balustrade of vertical motifs. Buttresses, the strong use of finials, and window mullions also emphasize the vertical.

The interior is furnished to conform with the exterior design of the building; brick, stone and oak are used. Some of the wood carvings, such as the choir stalls, were done by artists from Oberammergau, Germany. Certain other furnishings were brought from the 1855 Trinity Cathedral, now demolished, on Superior Avenue. Overall, Trinity imparts a true feeling of a Medieval English Cathedral. Of note is the great Flentrop organ, installed in 1977, which is independently mounted at the rear of the nave. Also of distinction is the Chapter House wing with its exceptionally fine wood trusses and ceiling.

Park Synagogue (1947-1950)
3300 Mayfield Road, Cleveland Heights
Architect: Eric Mendelsohn

The unity of heaven and earth is symbolized in Park Synagogue, which departs from the traditional Near Eastern forms often used for synagogues. Constructed of reinforced concrete, the dome measures 100 feet in diameter and rests upon 10 supports. The dome's drum contains several large plate glass windows, and is copper clad on the exterior. Park Synagogue was built by the Anshe Emeth Congregation. It is the only structure in Ohio by the internationally respected Mendelsohn, remembered for his advanced modernist concepts.

Friendship Baptist Church (1893-1894)
(Temple Tifereth Israel)
East 55th Street and Central Avenue
Architects: Lehman and Schmitt

The cornerstone of this square, rugged stone structure was laid in July, 1893. The structure features a great square lantern and a huge dome. On the main (East 55th Street) facade there is an arcaded porch and two round towers. Originally, a stained glass rose window, now removed, adorned the facade. The entrance consists of tripartite Roman portals flanked by turreted towers.

The congregation which built this temple was organized in 1850. It was considered "one of the most influential Reformed Jewish Congregations in America." This was the first "Open Temple" in the world, where all were welcomed regardless of affiliation. In 1940 the temple was purchased by Friendship Baptist Church.

St. Mary's Romanian Orthodox Church (1958-1960)
3256 Warren Road, Cleveland
Architect: Haralamb Georgescu

This modern church, which seats 650, was dedicated on August 21, 1960. Los Angeles architect Haralamb Georgescu modeled the church after Transylvanian Carpathian churches in Europe. St. Mary's features a steep pitched roof on a white glazed brick structure. Upon completion, the structure featured the world's largest church enamel. It was designed by Edward and Thelma Frazier Winter and made by the Ferro Corporation of Cleveland.

11.4

Saints Constantine and Helen Greek Orthodox Cathedral
(1956-1957)
3352 Mayfield Road, Cleveland Heights
Architects: Carr & Cunningham

Officially consecrated on December 1, 1963, this modern church
was designated a cathedral on December 16, 1967. The contemporary interpretation of the traditional Byzantine church is especially
evident on the exterior. Though apparently rectangular in shape,
it is actually a subdued cruciform plan with only two small wings
indicating the transept. The brick facade is articulated by bands of
recessed brick, and there is a Spanish tile roof. The main entrance
is framed with sandstone and contains a multicolored mosaic of
the patron saints.

Calvary Presbyterian Church (1888-1890)
Euclid Avenue at East 79th Street
Architect: Charles F. Schweinfurth

Calvary Presbyterian Church is constructed of rusticated stone in
an ashlar pattern. There are two towers of unequal height which
flank the main Euclid Ave. entrance. The East 79th Street facade is
asymmetrical in design.

The interior is a traditional open plan with the nave divided by
three aisles. The main body of the nave is separated from the two
side aisles by narrow columns.

A wrought iron gate in the interior is complimented by mahogany
and golden oak. In the chancel, light reflects from a golden
mosaic. Perhaps the most notable feature of this church is the
Tiffany window to the left of the altar.

St. Ignatius Roman Catholic Church (1925-1930)
10205 Lorain Avenue at West Boulevard
Architects: Edward T. P. Graham and F. Stillman Fish

Designed by E. T. P. Graham and F. Stillman Fish, this church has
an Indiana limestone exterior and features a rose window on the
front (Lorain Avenue) facade. Below, an arched arcade defines the
entrance. Rich carvings representing popes and bishops decorate
the entrance. The monumental campanile rises 210-feet and
contains balconies, open belfries, and a cupola.

St. Joseph's Roman Catholic Church (1871-1873)
Woodland Avenue at East 23rd Street
Architects: Cudell and
Richardson

St. Joseph's was built 1871-1873 and designed by Cudell and Richardson, Cleveland's most prominent architects of the era; their name is indicated on a stone on the building. It is the most characteristically German of their churches and, in fact, was built for a German parish. This High Victorian Gothic church features a westwork, three entrances with Gothic arches and gables with traceried windows above, and a steep hipped roof. A number of stone carvings decorate the building.

On the interior is a three-aisled hall with aisle arcade, a blind triforium, and a clerestory. The three-sided apse has tall clerestory windows. This is a basilican plan church on the interior, with a narthex, six nave bays, and an apse. There was much wood trim, and numerous religious statues throughout, but this work was removed in late 1990.

Originally the area surrounding St. Joseph's was a densely populated residential neighborhood. Urban renewal and the construction of the nearby interstates destroyed the homes which surrounded the church. The dwindling number of parishioners resulted in the church being closed in 1987 and deconsecrated. While demolition threatens this structure, plans for adaptive reuse are now being sought.

St. Michael's Roman Catholic Church (1889-1892)
(Michael the Archangel)
3114 Scranton Road at Clark Avenue
Architect: Adolph Druiding

This church has rock-faced stone masonry bearing walls, timber roof framing, and plaster vaulting. The two towers rise to unequal heights, with the taller one to the north reaching 232 feet. There are three arched doorways between the towers. Above the doorway is a great pointed arch and a large rose window with elaborate stone mullions.

Inside, the side aisles are set apart by arcades. Tennessee pink marble wainscotting provides a contrast to the white marble floor with its blue insets. A profusion of statuary fills the church. For many years, St. Michael's was considered Cleveland's largest and most artistically notable church.

St. John's Cathedral (1848-1852) (1946-1948)
(The Cathedral of St. John the Evangelist)
East 9th Street at Superior
Architects: Patrick Charles Keely
Renovation: Stickle and Associates

The Cathedral of St. John the Evangelist is the spiritual head-quarters for Catholics in the Cleveland diocese. The original Ornamental Gothic cathedral on this site was built 1848-1852 and designed by Patrick Charles Keely, a prominent midwestern church architect.

As early as the 1910s, plans were made to relocate the cathedral. Finally, the original cathedral was instead expanded, modernized, and almost completely rebuilt from 1946-1948. The original center tower at the west end was removed, and a new one was constructed on the south side. The main entrance, however, remains at the west end of the cathedral. The cathedral was lengthened to the east, and the entire structure was refaced with Tennessee quartzite. Little remains of the original church, except for the stained glass windows and the general lines of the interior. Attached are other buildings, faced with the same material, which house operations of the Cleveland Catholic Diocese. In 1977, the sanctuary area was renovated to conform to the liturgical changes required by the Second Vatican Council.

Holy Family Catholic Church (1965)
7367 York Road, Parma
Architects: Conrad and Fleischman

The unusual design of this large structure makes it one of the Cleveland area's most distinctive modern churches. The basic plan is circular and features several in-curving and out-curving sections. This 164-foot diameter church was dedicated September 4, 1965. The walls are textured, poured concrete with a limestone aggregate. The floor is of concrete topped with terrazzo. Both stained and clear glass are used in the openings.

St. Stanislaus Roman Catholic Church (1885-1891)
6509 Forman Avenue at East 65th Street
Architect: William H. Dunn

Built by a Polish congregation, this church was dedicated in 1891 and is part of a complex of buildings at this site. The structure is brick with stone trim and was built after Eastern European prototypes. The original 232-foot spires, destroyed in an 1909 storm, were rebuilt as crowned belfries and now rise only 122 feet. The large stained glass windows reveal a complex iconography. Throughout the interior are many ornate wood carvings. The altarpiece is a 19th century wood carving of notable quality.

True Holiness Temple (1916)
(Second Church of Christ, Scientist)
Euclid Avenue at East 77th
Architect: Frederic W. Striebinger

The Second Church of Christ, Scientist, was designed by Frederic W. Striebinger and completed in 1916. It is Neo-classic Revival in design and has a pronounced Roman (Pantheon) influence. It is noted for its low central dome on a drum, its Euclid Avenue portico entrance with six columns, and its large, arched clerestory vaults. Remarkably, the entire exterior is terra cotta surfaced.

In 1948, the Play House, Cleveland's nationally-renowned resident theater company, purchased the vacant church. In the next year, alterations were made adapting the building to theater use, including the construction of a stage and balcony; afterwards a false ceiling was installed. Later a supper club and art gallery were located within the building. In 1982, the Play House vacated this building for its enlarged complex at East 86th and Euclid. The former theater then returned to ecclesiastical use.

Old Stone Church (1853-1855)
(First Presbyterian Church)
Ontario Street at Public Square
Architects: Charles Heard and Simeon Porter

Old Stone Church – officially First Presbyterian Church–is the second church to occupy this site. The original First Presbyterian Church was built 1831-1833 and demolished for the construction of the existing edifice.

This church, built of Berea sandstone, had its cornerstone laid on September 9, 1853. The church was completed and dedicated on August 12, 1855. In 1857, it was completely gutted by a fire though the exterior walls remained intact; it was then rebuilt. In 1884, another fire extensively damaged the interior of the church, though the exterior walls again remained. At this time the east spire was removed, and Charles Schweinfurth was hired to rebuild the interior.

Within, the roof is a semicircular arch with wooden tie beams at the base resting on a pair of arched braces. The painted and frescoed walls are by Julius Schweinfurth, the stained glass windows by John LaFarge and Louis Tiffany. Old Stone Church has had many notable Cleveland names on its roster and is now one of downtown's oldest structures. Its presence on the north side of Public Square is one of the city's most familiar architectural sights.

Church of the Covenant (1909-1911)
11205 Euclid Avenue
Architects: Cram, Goodhue, and Ferguson, & J. W. Corbusier

Originally called the Euclid Avenue Presbyterian Church, the parish merged with the Second Presbyterian Church and was renamed the Church of the Covenant in 1920. The church, built of Indiana limestone, was dedicated in 1911. Cram, Goodhue, and Ferguson designed the structure, while J. W. Corbusier was the local supervising architect.

The overall aspect of the church is English Gothic. A graceful tower is unusually placed at the corner of the sanctuary and the parish house. The front facade has a great arched entrance with a rose window above flanked by octagonal turrets. Stained glass windows line the side walls. Though the interior is quite elegant, the walls themselves are undecorated. The nave is very high and wide, with no side aisles. There are deep galleries over the transept arms and narthex. The shallow choir is dominated by a richly carved reredos added by Ralph Adams Cram in 1930-1931 when the chancel was redesigned.

St. Martin of Tours Catholic Church (1962-1963)
14600 Turney Road, Maple Heights
Architects: Conrad and Fleischman

Dedicated on August 12, 1963, this octagonal church is noted for its "striking contemporary architecture." The roughly circular form bears comparison to Conrad and Fleischman's Holy Family Catholic Church (1964-1965) in Parma. Above the centrally-located altar of St. Martin's, a large octagonal dome is situated. The dome, featuring colored glass, is topped by a tall spire, which is then topped by cross. The adjacent school building was designed to harmonize with the church and was built at the same time.

St. Martin of Tours parish was established in 1891. The previous church, at East 23rd Street and Scovill avenue (near downtown Cleveland) was built in 1906 and demolished in 1960 for construction of a freeway.

St. Stephen's Roman Catholic Church (1873-1881)
1930 West 54th Street
Architects: Cudell and Richardson

Built of Amherst sandstone, this church was constructed for Cleveland's largest German-speaking Catholic parish. Although cruciform in plan, the absence of a clerestory gives the effect of a hall church. Its massive, permanent appearance on the exterior is contrasted by the delicate wood carvings of the interior, which was decorated over time. The pulpit was created in Germany and won first prize at the 1893 Chicago World's Fair before being sent to St. Stephen's. The pulpit and wood carvings are of exceptional workmanship. The stained glass windows and the statues are also from Germany.

St. Theodosius Russian Orthodox Cathedral

(1911-1913)
733 Starkweather Avenue
Architect: Frederick C. Baird

St. Theodosius was constructed for Cleveland's first Eastern Orthodox parish, which had been established in 1896. The architect worked with Rev. Bail Lisenkovsky, and the plan of the church is said to have been based on that of the Church of Our Savior Jesus Christ in Moscow. The church, dedicated on July 19, 1913, cost $70,000 to build. The central dome, and surrounding 12 domes, signify Christ and his apostles.

St. Theodosius has the traditional features of Russian Orthodox architecture: the Byzantine cross plan, a cruciform shape with four limbs of equal length, the three-barred cross, and the onion-shaped cupola. The exterior is buff-colored brick, and the walls are articulated by flat Tuscan pilasters.

The church was furnished with many items from the Old World including an immense chandelier from Czechoslovakia and an icon screen from Kiev, Russia. In 1953, the church was redecorated. The walls and ceiling of the church were covered with icon murals by artist Andrei Bicenko and his assistants at a cost of over $100,000. The church was then rededicated on October 3, 1954. St. Theodosius continues to be one of the best examples of Russian church architecture in the U.S. It was the site of much of the popular film, *The Deer Hunter*.

The Temple (1923-1924) (1958)
East 105th Street and Ansel Road
Architect: Charles R. Greco

This temple, a Neo-Byzantine design reflective of Hagia Sophia, was built for the Tifereth Israel congregation. It is done in a seven-sided plan, which was dictated by the triangular shape of the property. The exterior is Indiana limestone in subtle banding, and features a circular dome of golden tile. The entrance consists of three arches with columns and capitals, framed by a single large arch which echoes the dome. There is inlaid marble over the entrance arches. On the interior, the circular seating arrangement reflects the shape of the dome overhead.

In 1958, an annex and adjoining Silver Park were dedicated. The annex was designed by Perkins and Will of Chicago, in conjunction with Michael Kane of Cleveland. Faced in limestone like the main building, the annex included a library, schoolrooms, and an auditorium.

St. James Roman Catholic Church (1925-1934)
17514 Detroit Avenue at Granger Road, Lakewood
Architect: Edward T. P. Graham

St. James parish, organized in 1908, built the adjacent school and hall in 1913. The existing church, however, was not constructed until 1925-1934. This stone-faced church features a rose window over the tripartite entrance. There are two towers with open belfries and projecting balconies. Statues and tile work above the main entrance maintain the Mediterranean character. The entrance also contains great bronze doors, a multitude of colored enamels, and rows of variegated marble pillars with intricately carved capitals. Of special interest is the interior which is profusely decorated in mosaic tessarae.

St. Johns's Episcopal Church (1836-1838)
Church Avenue at West 26th Street
Architect: Hezekiah Eldredge

Built by a carpenter and builder who was a native of Connecticut, the church is Cleveland's oldest religious structure. Church member Hezekiah Eldredge constructed this "Gothicized meeting house" church of tan sandstone quarried from the banks of the Cuyahoga River.

After a fire gutted the building in 1866, transepts and a chancel were added, enlarging the church. This also created a cruciform plan on the interior. The pinnacles of the tower were removed in 1965. The chancel was rebuilt after wind damage in 1955.

The parish is a direct descendant of Cleveland's first religious organization. For ten years, from 1850-1860, St. John's served as an underground railroad station, hiding slaves on their way to freedom. During the latter half of the 19th century, when the West Side flourished, many influential Clevelanders were members of this congregation.

East Mount Zion Baptist Church (1905-1908)
(Euclid Avenue Christian Church)
9990 Euclid Avenue
Architect: George W. Kramer

This church is noted for both its unusual green-colored stone exterior and its Romanesque style. The stone, known as serpentinite, was quarried in West Chester, Pennsylvania, and contrasting-colored stone is used for trim. There is a large central octagonal cupola with a peaked roof. On the Euclid Avenue facade there are towers at the corners and two Romanesque entrances. The stained glass windows were done by Frederick Lamb of the Lamb Studios in New York. Sienna marble and hand-carved oak are used to decorate the interior.

Construction of this structure, originally known as the Euclid Avenue Christian Church, began in 1905, and dedication took place on April 12, 1908. When the congregation of the Euclid Avenue Christian Church was formed in 1843, it was known as the Disciple Church at Doan's Corner. An earlier church stood on this Euclid Avenue-East 100th Street site from 1867-1905. The congregation relocated in 1955, and the structure then became East Mt. Zion Baptist Church.

Amasa Stone Chapel (1910)
10940 Euclid Avenue at East Boulevard
Architect: Henry Vaughan

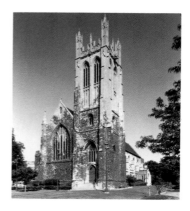

Inspired by St. Cuthbert's Church in Somerset, England, this structure was originally conceived as a college chapel. Mrs. John Hay and Mrs. Samuel Mather, daughters of Amasa Stone, funded construction of this $168,000 structure and donated it to Western Reserve University. Years earlier, Amasa Stone had donated money to Western Reserve University, which enabled it to move from Hudson, Ohio to Cleveland.

The floor plan of this Gothic Revival chapel consists of nave, choir, and narrow side aisles. The interior is lighted by the clerestory and two large windows, one each at the north and south ends. The tower rises 121-feet high, and upon it three angels and a gargoyle are located. Above the east entrance is a likeness of Amasa Stone. It was removed from the old Union Station (built 1866), which Stone had helped to build.

Shiloh Baptist Church (1906)
(B'nai Jeshurun Temple)
East 55th Street and Scovill Avenue
Architect: Harry Cone

This brick and stone temple has a Greek Cross plan and is a domed assembly room church. It features a central dome supported by a windowed drum, and a portico with six Corinthian columns. The golden saucer cupola surmounts a small open lantern. There is an oculus in the pediment and round-arched doors and windows.

The Jewish congregation which built this temple was organized in 1866. Originally Orthodox, it had become Conservative by 1906. In 1924, the temple was purchased by Cleveland's oldest Black Baptist Church, Shiloh, which was formed in 1849.

Victoria George
Drew Rolik

Section 12

Health Facilities

The Cleveland Clinic Complex

Euclid Ave. to Carnegie Ave., E. 90th to E. 102nd Sts.

In 1989 Cleveland's leading private employer was the famed Cleveland Clinic. Founded by Dr. George Crile, the first of what is now a major complex of structures was erected on Euclid Avenue at East 93rd St. in 1922, where the original, white brick structure still stands. Designed by the Ellerbe office of St. Paul, MN, the building once featured an atrium replete with stained glass skylight. It was here that a major disaster struck in 1929 when fumes from an X-ray film fire took over one hundred lives. From this event, building codes were rewritten nationally.

Many buildings now constitute the campus-like cluster of The Clinic. Ellerbe added to the original group but in later years both local and national firms carried out significant additions. Of note are the following:

The Clinic's main building by Cesar Pelli is a commanding mass of granite and glass with a distinctive set-back profile.

The Cleveland Clinic Building, Mall & Skyway (1985)
Architects: Cesar Pelli and Associates and Dalton, van Dijk, Johnson and Partners

An award-winning, 14-story structure with stepped-back profile and sheer walls of granite and glass. A three-story atrium surrounds the entry.

The East 100th St. Parking Garage & Bridge (1985)
Architects: Cesar Pelli and Associates

A 1,500 car facility of penetrated masonry walls featuring a glass stair tower at the main corner.

The Cleveland Clinic Hotel (1975)
Architects: Bialosky and Manders

An 18-story structure where many of the Clinic's patients, including international heads of state, have resided.

The Guest House Hotel & Shopping Center (1989)
Architects: Whitley and Whitley

A residential-type hotel built to satisfy the needs of families attending patients from distant places and for patients on long-term monitoring programs.

The Magnetic Resonance Building (1980)
Architects: Dalton, Dalton, Newport

This was the first structure built for magnetic resonance imaging. There is no iron in the building and the rooms are shielded from radio waves. Wood replaced ferrous metal throughout.

The Clinical Laboratory Building (1920) (1978)
Architects: Albert Kahn; Dalton, van Dijk, Johnson Partners

This modern lab building absorbed an existing Packard Motor Car facility the showroom of which is still expressed at the corner.

As The Clinic's expansion absorbed neighboring blocks, it is noteworthy that two of the city's distinctive churches, which existed in the path, were spared to continue to serve their congregations as well as add architectural texture and relief to the otherwise single-purposed mass of the hospital buildings. These churches are East Mount Zion Baptist Church (Euclid Avenue at E. 100th Street) and The Euclid Avenue Congregational Church (Euclid Avenue at E. 96th Street).

W.O. Walker Industrial Rehabilitation Center (1988)

Euclid Avenue at E. 105th to E. 107th Streets
Architects: Collins, Rimer and Gordon

This facility occupies much of an urban site of 9.2 acres, once the thriving sub-center of East 105th Street and Euclid Avenue. Created for the treatment and rehabilitation of injured workers, the 3-story base contains treatment modules, administration, pool and gym. It also shoulders a 15-story tower housing extended stay quarters for claimants. The building serves as a visual terminus to the bend in Euclid Avenue.

University Hospitals
Euclid Avenue to Circle Drive, between Adelbert and Cornell Roads

The classically-inspired University Hospital's original design elements still dominate the expanded building complex.

University Hospitals originated with a largely voluntary effort to alleviate the plight of numerous local survivors of the Civil War. From humble beginnings on Lake (now Lakeside) Avenue, the hospital affiliated with the Western Reserve University's Medical School in 1897. Subsequent mergers and moves brought the institution to its present site. Now one of Cleveland's largest hospital complexes, the University Hospitals group occupies a large block adjacent to Case Western Reserve University for which teaching and research facilities are provided. Beginning in the 1920s an elegant group of classically-inspired buildings were assembled as the core of a complex which has expanded with a commanding array of contemporary buildings. Of these, the following are noted in particular:

Directly south of the Hospital group is the *School of Medicine of Case Western Reserve University*, (1927) Abram Garfield, Architect. This original building, now referred to as the West Wing, has been extensively remodeled (1980-1990) by Barnes-Neiswander Associates Inc., who also designed the Mechanical Tower addition at the rear (1983).

A major *Health Sciences Complex*, covering approximately five acres, was built just east of the School of Medicine, completed in 1971. The *East Wing of the School of Medicine* was designed by John Williams and Associates, but all other parts of the Center (*School's of Dentistry and Nursing*, student commons, lecture rooms, research labs and two-story garage) were the work of Barnes-Neiswander Associates Inc., working with William Priestly who was then Director of Case Western Reserve University's School of Architecture and Architectural Advisor to the university President. The superstructure of the schools that sit on the podium are of pre-cast exposed aggregate concrete and were delivered to the site full height and complete with fixed glazing. The *Dental and Nursing buildings* reflect a strong Mies van der Rohe influence.

Behind the Health Sciences on Circle Drive is the *Power Plant* serving the university and the hospitals. The addition to that facility, also designed by Barnes-Neiswander Associates Inc., won a First Honor Award from the Architects Society of Ohio in 1969.

Lakeside Hospital and Hanna House (1931)
Adelbert Road
Architects: Coolidge, Shepley, Bulfinch and Abbott (Boston)

This initial structure still commands attention by way of its refinement of design and classical symmetry. A set-back concept allowed several roof decks to be used as outside terraces for patients. The "H"-shaped plan culminates in a large colonnaded penthouse brightly illuminated at night. Two flanking buildings create a courtyard approach to Lakeside Hospital. The left-hand building is Hanna House, largely devoted to patients' rooms, and to the right the Pathology Building, a part of Case Western Reserve University.

Residence Halls (1931)
Euclid Avenue
Architects: Coolidge, Shepley, Bulfinch and Abbott (Boston)

Here also is a refined, symmetrical design complementing adjacent Lakeside and Hanna halls with pale tan brick and limestone.

Rainbow Babies and Childrens Hospital (1972)
Adelbert Road
Architects: John Williams and Associates

A multi-floor building of contemporary design breaks away from the more classical format predecessor buildings.

Southwest General Hospital

18697 Bagley Road, Berea (1973-1975)
Architects: Collins Rimer & Gordon

Southwest General is one of the few contemporary hospital plants constructed as one consistent architectural statement. Several additions have been blended into the original maintaining the unified design. Currently at 500,000 sq. ft. the red brick and pre-cast, 3 and 4 story building is on a 20 acre site.

Malcolm M. Cutting, AIA

Section 13

Industrial Buildings

Industrial growth, starting from about 1850, gave Cleveland much of its present size and shape. Thousands of new jobs were created in the industrial sector leading to rapid growth in the city's population. Barges from Michigan and Minnesota carried iron ore down the Cuyahoga. Shiploads of white pine from the Lake Superior region arrived and contributed to Cleveland's look as a frame city rather than a masonry one. The railways brought petroleum and coal from Pennsylvania. Oil refineries were seen all over town especially along the Cuyahoga River. Ship building prospered. A strategic location, Cleveland became a thriving center for trade.

Towards the end of the nineteenth century, Cleveland's production diversified. The automobile, electrical and textile industries came during this period of growth. Soon came the industry of public transportation. Each broadened Cleveland's skyline. Good industrial architecture is abundant in Cleveland. Many structures have design qualities of high merit. A few have become city landmarks placed on the National Register. They are artifacts reflecting the past as well as clear prototypes guiding the future. The following is a small list of the many industrial facilities close to Cleveland's heart.

Nela Park (1911 with many additions)
(General Electric Lamp Division)
Noble Road, by Terrace Road, East Cleveland

Despite the success of Cleveland's urban industrial facilities in the late 19th Century, some companies wished to escape the cramped and polluted downtown. Therefore, by 1911, Nela Park had been begun in a neighboring suburb of Cleveland. It was America's first industrial park developed in a naturally wooded suburban setting.

Envisioned by Franklin S. Terry, a manager of the National Electric Lamp Association (NELA), new offices with laboratory facilities were placed on the site. These same buildings with many additional facilities are today dispersed throughout a mature, well-maintained landscape, giving the appearance of an inviting college campus.

The park located near Euclid Avenue and Noble Road has several attractions. Most popular is the lighting lab otherwise known as the Lighting Institute Building which is open to those interested in the latest lighting trends. Frank E. Wallis of New York City with his assistant, Frank Goodwillie, designed several of the Georgian-style buildings at Nela Park. Nela Park is now the World Headquarters for General Electric's Lamp Division.

Brown Hoisting Machinery Company Factory (1901)
Hamilton Avenue at E. 45th Street
Architect: J. Milton Dyer

Dyer designed an expansive steel and brick building at the Brown Hoisting Machinery Company in the city's burgeoning near-east side industrial-warehouse district. The structure which measures about five hundred feet in length and three hundred feet in width was built to replace a number of buildings at the plant destroyed by a fire. Its most distinctive element is the facade on Hamilton Avenue composed of a gently-sloped center piece and two flanking wings. Under new ownership, the facility has been used as a warehouse.

Peerless Motor Car Company Administration Building (1906)
Quincy Avenue at E. 93rd Street
Architect: J. Milton Dyer

A number of fine buildings within industrial complexes were designed by Beaux Arts-trained architect J. Milton Dyer, designer of Cleveland City Hall. One of the best of Dyer's structures is the Administration Building of the former Peerless Motor Car Company located at East Ninety-Third Street and Quincy Avenue. Built in 1906, this distinguished structure was designed with modernist, crisp, clean lines as well as curvilinear Art Noveau elements. Details such as the canopy over the main entrance and the refined metal window mullions draw reference from the leading architectural trends at the turn of the century. By 1931, the Peerless Motor Car Company became a brewery, now abandoned. Most of the building, however, remains intact although in a vandalized condition.

Richman Brothers Company (1916)
1600 E. 55th Street
Architects: Christian, Schwarzenberg and Gaede Co.; Dana Clark

In 1916, the Richman Brothers Company relocated from outdated facilities to 1600 East Fifty-Fifth Street. First built at the site was the four-story factory structure of brick and reinforced concrete. With a U-shaped plan, the building is composed of a center piece with two flanking L-shaped wings enclosing a courtyard. The exterior brick exquisitely articulates the vertical with horizontal elements of the building's facade. At the time of its completion, the award-winning structure was heralded as Cleveland's best-designed factory. By 1930, five more buildings designed by the Christian, Schwarzenberg and Gaede Company were built at the site.

Warner and Swasey Company (1905) (1908)
East 55th Street either side of Carnegie Avenue
Architect: Arnold W. Brunner

Located at East Fifty-Fifth Street and Carnegie Avenue, the Warner and Swasey Company has left a facility that includes two machine shops. The first machine shop, sited north of the facing Carnegie, is a four hundred-foot, five-story structure built in 1905. Once housing a maker of precision tools, the Cleveland facility remains a symbol of quality craftsmanship. The building complex is currently being considered for adaptive reuse as a city service center. Extensive renovations were made (1973) by Architect Joseph Ceruti who also did the factory addition on the west.

Fisher Body Company Assembly Plant (1923)
Architect: Albert Kahn

Located on Coit Road and East 140th Street is the Assembly Plant of the Fisher Body Company. Albert Kahn, a Detroit Industrial Architect, designed the huge six-story structure (1150 foot by 70 foot) in 1923. The plant's simple use of the reinforced concrete frame with glass and brick infill remains a model for structures of today and tomorrow. Kahn designed several of the other original buildings around the Assembly Plant.

RTA Central Maintenance Facility (1984)
E. 55th Street overpass of the rail lines
Architects: URS Dalton with Heery-Ramco-Praeger

Built recently is the Central Rail Maintenance Facility for the Greater Cleveland Regional Transit Authority (RTA). Completed in 1984, the facility rests on a narrow eighteen-acre site containing three buildings for the complete maintenance and repair of RTA's train cars. The buildings incorporate RTA's orange and red graphic stripe on a stainless steel skin to maintain uniformity. Technical features such as skylights and underground heat storage conserve energy within the facility. The Central Rail Maintenance Facility is located below the East 55th Street bridge over once extensive railroad yards.

David L. Sturgeon

Section 14

Multi–Family Housing

Winton Place (1963)
12700 Lake Road, Lakewood
Architects: Loebl, Schlossman & Bennett

Located along Cleveland's west side lakefront, the series of boxes as seen from the Downtown area is the most concentrated area of population in the city.

The most elegant of these high-rise buildings is Winton Place. This thirty-story structure was once advertised as the tallest apartment building between New York and Chicago. The building sets on six percent of the eight acre site, 500 feet back from Lake Road and connects to "Pier W", a restaurant which cantilevers over the cliffs above the lake.

Winton Place was designed by the Chicago firm of Loebl, Schlossman & Bennett and built in 1962-1963. It has a reinforced concrete frame with continuous concrete vertical columns emphasizing the building's height.

Lakeview Terrace (1935-1937)
Tower (1975)
Terrace Architects: Weinberg, Conrad & Teare
Tower Architects: Weinberg, Teare & Herman

Lakeview Terrace is located on a 22 acre site at West 28th Street, secluded between the Main Avenue Bridge and the lake. The development has been called "one of the best public housing projects in the country" and "a milestone in the history of American architecture".

It's Architects, Joseph L. Weinberg, William H. Conrad, and Wallace G. Teare, with Frederick Bigger, serving as site planning consultant, positioned the 49 buildings on the hilly site so that each apartment and town house receives daylight and a view towards the lake. The buildings only occupy 23% of the site. The complex is internationally known as a landmark in public housing and was one of the first to be authorized by the federal government. Lewis Mumford uses Lakeview Terrace as an illustration of public housing in his book, *The Culture of Cities,* with the comment: "Good plan, well-adapted to site, with combination of apartments and smaller dwellings. Note the placement of the dwelling at right angles to the roads, the skillful use of contours on the left, the abandonment of useless and costly streets, and ample interior playground."

Construction started in 1935 and was completed in 1937. It included 620 residential units, an auditorium, child day care facility, community building, recreation rooms and playground and administrative offices. At this writing, a convenient food store has been constructed and proposals are currently being considered to redevelop the site to include market rate housing.

Mr. Weinberg's European influenced International Style design incorporates face brick on tile walls with curved corners, poured concrete roof and floor structure, metal lath and plaster interior partitions and horizontally arranged steel casement windows.

A 19 story apartment tower was added in 1975 with 214 suites for senior citizens overlooking the Main Avenue Bridge, on the southerly side of the site.

The Chesterfield (1967)
Chester Avenue at E. 12th Street
Architects: Weinberg, Teare, Fischer, Herman

The Chesterfield Apartments at Chester Avenue and East 12th Street was Cleveland's first luxury apartment house and first housing effort in the Early 60's Erieview Project. The building is 20 stories high and contains 411 apartments, office space and a rooftop swimming pool.

The building features poured concrete column and floor construction with an aluminum operable window-wall set in face brick panels.

Belgian Village (1931)
(Fairhill Road Village)
Fairhill Road at E. 124th Street
Architects: Antonio DiNardo and Harold O. Fullerton

During the development of Shaker Heights a group of artists, architects, designers, musicians and writers decided to build a "village" at the suburb's westerly edge.

The five acre site was located on Fairhill Road, east of Martin Luther King Drive on Ambler Park's deep ravine. This private residential development represented a type of social, financial, and artistic collaboration which would become increasingly rare after the twenties.

The original plan of double homes was designed by architect Antonio Di Nardo in 1928. The final plan was executed in 1931 by architect Harold O. Fullerton with A. Donald Gray's landscape and site designs. Some units are placed directly on Fairhill Road with others served by a private drive and courtyard. The architecture is reminiscent of Cotswold Cottages being constructed of stone and stucco and with steep slate roofs.

Lexington Village (1985) (1989)
Hough Avenue at E. 79th Street
Architects: Hemni Associates, Teare Herman & Gibans

Lexington Village was the first market-rate housing development of its size to be built in Cleveland since 1955. In 1985, 45 buildings with 183 one, two, and three bedroom apartments and townhouses were constructed at East 79th Street and Hough Avenue in what was a severely depressed area of the city.

With its success, a second phase was constructed in 1989 with an additional 94 apartments and townhouses, which were rented before construction completion. The complex includes a community building with administrative services, recreational facilities swimming pool, and laundry building.

Architects for the project were Hemni and Associates, Inc. of St. Louis, Missouri, and Teare, Herman, and Gibans of Cleveland as associate architects. The designs incorporated traditional residential themes of vinyl siding, face brick, and shingle roofs with internal access driveways and parking areas within the confines of the building clusters.

Its residences represent a cross-section of the community attracting those from the suburbs back to the city. At this writing, a Phase 3 is in the planning stage.

Reserve Square (1973) (1990)
(Formerly The Park and Park Centre)
1701 East 12th Street
Architects: Dalton-Dalton-Little-Newport
Renovation: H.O.K.

Once thought to be the most important potential catalyst for
Cleveland's downtown redevelopment, Park Centre was built as
a multi-use center comprising apartments, offices, shopping mall
with restaurants, parking garage and rooftop recreational facilities.
The $42.5 million development received the then largest FHA loan
in the history of the agency and was the second largest financial
investment in Cleveland behind the Terminal group. The building
followed the "Erieview Plan" guidelines of two twenty-three story
towers with a two-story shopping complex at its base.

The building uses exposed, rough textured concrete with
specially formed grooves in the building's columns and portions
of the exterior. This treatment along with slots and reveals in the
surfaces, characteristic of Brutalism, helped create a three-dimen-
sional sense to the wall assembly.

In 1990, a portion of the complex was converted to a 252-suite
Radisson Suite Hotel and office facility and its name changed to
Reserve Square.

Moreland Courts (1923) (1928)
Shaker Boulevard from Shaker Square to Coventry Road
Architects: Alfred W. Harris and Philip L. Small

Prior to the conception of Shaker Square, a thirty million dollar development for a model apartment community was planned for an area on Shaker Blvd. and Moreland Circle, or what is now known as Shaker Square.

In 1922, the Cleveland Discount Company and its president, Josiah Kirby, purchased the land from the Van Sweringens and with Cleveland architect, Alfred W. Harris designed two apartment structures 1,500 feet in length on Shaker Blvd. (between Coventry Road and Moreland Circle), business and retail buildings and a theater on the circle, and terrace homes on South Moreland (Van Aken) Blvd. The complex had its own central heating plant and market house.

The initial construction only included the large apartment block. The building was a conglomerate of several periods of English architecture ranging from Elizabethan, Late Gothic, Tudor, Jacobean to Georgian. One newspaper account stated that the architect will have written the entire history of English Architecture all in one building when the project was completed.

In 1923 the Cleveland Discount Company failed and in 1924 O.P. and M.J. Van Sweringen decided to complete Kirby's development of the Moreland Courts but not carry out the remainder of the Harris plan. The office of Philip L. Small was then retained to plan Shaker Square on the Moreland Circle site. In 1978, the apartment building was transformed into condominium units.

Row Houses on Prospect Avenue (1873) (1876) (1880)
Prospect Avenue east of E. 36th Street

Because of Cleveland's abundance of land, there was very little need to consolidate homes together as was the case in most large east coast cities. Over a period of time, between 1875 and 1880, a miniature illustration of the development of Victorian architecture was constructed at 3645 to 3655 Prospect Avenue by different builders.

The three center homes were built in 1873 in an attempt to copy a dated style. The easterly-most house was built in 1880 by C. H. Bulkley, father of Senator Robert J. Bulkley. The westerly home was built in 1876 by Amasa Stone, a Cleveland philanthropist for his niece, Mrs. S. A. Raymond. Its facade features a three-story bay and parapet details suggestive of the work of Frank Furness of Philadelphia.

Today the building has been subdivided into apartments. The building, and the large elm tree on its treelawn, have been declared local landmarks.

Oppmann Terrace (1905)
West 102nd Place
Between Detroit and Madison Aves.

Another example of a "Row House" exists with unique develop-
ment at West 101st between Madison and Detroit Avenues.
Andrew W. Oppmann, retired president of the Oppmann Brewing
Company built the block in 1905.

The building is a continuous row of sixty-eight, two-story dwelling
units on a gradually sloping site some 1,100 feet long. The
windows, porch, and cornicework detailing reflects the simple,
traditional standard builders' construction methods of the day and
created an economical and thoughtful approach to the site.

A court at the Project's south end divides another row of homes
that is only 1/4 as long as the westerly structure and appears to
have been a part of a block-long plan which never materialized.

Ernest J. Bohn Tower (1971)
Superior Avenue at E. 13th Street
Architects: William Dorsky Associates

This slender concrete slab of
22 stories begins the "wall" of
hi-rise structures along
Superior Avenue from the east.
Its smooth concrete exterior
with linear patterning contrasts
with its neighbor, Reserve
Square's (The Park) broken
vertical rib texture. The CMHA
structure occupies a small site
without green areas but with
two paved terraces.

Willson Housing (1970)
Chester Avenue at E. 55th Street
Architects: Visnapuu & Gaede, Inc.

A combination of low-rise family units grouped in row-house
clusters as a village, in conjunction with a 22-story tower for
elderly units, the CMHA project was to satisfy both residential
needs. The brick and stucco of the two-story houses contrasts with
the severe concrete shaft of the tower shaped as a square
in plan with recessed corners.

James G. Herman, AIA
Robert L. Weygandt

Section 15

Single Family Residential

The Glidden House (above) typifies Cleveland's rich stock of revivalist mansions. Built for the Glidden family in 1910, it has now been expanded into a hotel.

Cuyahoga County, is a 450 square mile area with a population of approximately 1,400,000. In view of the near impossibility of singling out a dozen or two individual residences, free of constraints upon visitation and scattered widely, the *Guide* has been designed to lead the visitor and metropolitanite to several areas where historic or architecturally significant houses abound in proximity. Once located, the architectural buff is urged to explore at will and savor both individual works as well as the ambience of the neighborhood. Now and then, a particularly unique residence is cited.

While Shaker Heights and portions of Cleveland Heights are reviewed under one of the driving tours, it is necessary to reflect in this category of the *Guide* that it is the single-family housing of these areas that lend them such special quality, especially for housing of the period 1910-1940. For equivalent housing of later decades, one is advised to explore the next range of easterly suburbs such as Pepper Pike, Beachwood, Moreland Hills and the Chagrin Valley. Set a visitor down at Lee Road and Woodland in Shaker Heights and the revelation of eclectic houses with well-manicured settings is remarkable. The styles are nearly always Colonial Revival, Georgian Revival, Tudor Revival or French Country Villa, the scale from modest to enormous. On average, these houses date from the 1920s so that, at 70 years of age, the concerns of preservation are paramount. The presence of enlightened community planning, architectural boards of review and landmark commissions together administer to this sensitive challenge.

Clifton Park, an enclave at the western edge of Lakewood (see map of Lakewood/Gold Coast) is a zone of noteworthy residences closely matching those of the "Heights" on the east side of the city. The same styles are favored and the era of construction is parallel.

A typical home within the Clifton Park area.

Heading westward from the City of Cleveland boundary are sporadic zones of singular residences along Edgewater, Lake and Clifton Blvds. embracing the "Gold Coast" (W. 117th to Nicholson Ave. north of Lake). In the neighborhood of Lake at Whippoorwill are a group of distinctly elegant Georgian style houses and a few of French derivation.

This Lakewood Queen Anne survives.

These perfect interpretations of classical themes are the work of Clarence Mack, master builder, developer and interior designer par excellence. Mack duplicated his westside effort in Shaker Heights including some residences of country villa scale. These are centered on South Park Blvd. and Courtland Blvd. His era was 1925-1932, and the perfection of his designs was rarely matched.

A Clarence Mack design respected classical models fastidiously.

During the years 1910-1940, as Cleveland grew rapidly, a core of architects well versed in eclectic design was needed to keep pace with fine residential construction. Among these were Meade and Hamilton, Philip Small, Howell and Thomas, Bloodgood Tuttle, Charles Schneider, Walker & Weeks, and the firm initiated by Abram Garfield. Now and then a major commission fell to the distinguished McKim, Mead and White or other out-of-town office. When the design departed from the standard range of revivals, one might anticipate the influence of Bohnard & Parsson or Albert Oviatt. After the WWII years a whole new generation of practitioners appeared to explore the modern movements.

Another locale replete with houses on the grand scale is the small suburb of Bratenahl, a sliver of land along the shore of Lake Erie. Here the great families developed grand estates with gardens to

Gwinn is a striking blend of white stucco pallazzo and formal garden, all within a walled estate on the Lake Erie shore.

match. Today one may observe and visit Gwinn (1908), the one-time home of William G. Mather and representative of the era. Designed by Charles Platt, Gwinn and its gardens are maintained as a public meeting facility.

A small cluster of fine houses was developed adjacent to the Cultural Center along East Boulevard and Magnolia Drive. In nearly all cases these buildings have been adapted into uses appropriate to the institutions of University Circle. Notable among them are the two classical revival structures on East Boulevard which have been integrated into the Western Reserve Historic Society complex. The John Hay House (1910), Abram Garfield architect, and the Mrs. Leonard Hanna House (1918), Walker and Gillette architects, are typical.

One of the grandest streets exhibiting splendid houses is that of Fairmount Blvd. in Cleveland Hts. (See Section 20E) which travels east from Cedar to the Chagrin Valley. In its first two miles it parades through a virtual handbook of the residential arts of the early 20th Century. Among these is one rather unique to Cleveland, the Tremaine-Gallagher House (1914) by Frederic W. Striebinger. This Italian Pallazzo is of stucco and stone exterior and is surrounded by landscaping in the formal tradition.

Robert C. Gaede, FAIA

Section 16

Architectural Details

Most architectural works, large and small, are enhanced by adjunctive, often intricate, details of many types including masonry, metal, glass and wood work, as well as lighting. Any attempt to cover the broad range of details imaginative architectural designers and skilled artisans have used to adorn Cleveland's buildings would, in a city of this size, be worthy of a small volume in itself.

In this short section of the guide we have only scratched the surface of the wealth of architectural detail to be found gracing Cleveland's many outstanding architectural works both old and new.

An architectural artifact of exceptional design and delight is the corner lamp of Society Bank.

A. LIGHTING

1. *Corner Bracket Fixture*

Society for Savings (1890)
127 Public Square
Architects: Burnham & Root

A decorative, foliated wrought iron post supports an acorn-style basket light fixture hung from it – the entire ensemble being attached to the southwest corner of this Public Square landmark.

2. *Three Arm Candelabra*

Board of Education Building (1930)
1380 East 6th Street
Architects: Walker & Weeks

This pair of graceful fixtures have three curving, drop-stem arms supporting classically styled lanterns. They occur at the East 6th Street entry of the building.

3. *Interior Lighting Standards*

Cuyahoga County Courthouse (1913)
1 Lakeside Avenue
Architects: Lehman & Schmitt

These free-standing bronze standards occur throughout the main lobby and are notable for the unusual detailing of their bases.

4. *Interior Lighting Standards*

Huntington (Union Commerce) Bank Building (1924)
Euclid Avenue at East 9th Street
Architects: Graham, Anderson, Probst & White
Restoration: Dalton, van Dijk,
Johnson & Partners (1975)

These free-standing bronze standards are notable for their large scale and foliated designs. They are also unusual in shape and occur throughout the "L" shaped lobby – primarily near entrances.

5. *Exterior Lighting Standards*

Old Federal Building (East Entry) (1905-1911)
201 Superior Avenue
Architect: Arnold Brunner

At the east (Third Street) entry porch are a pair of free-standing exterior standards of weathered bronze. These are about 6 feet tall, classically styled, and unusual in the downtown area.

6. *Entry Fixtures*

Ameritrust (Pearl Street Savings & Trust) (1929)
West 25th Street and Clark Avenue
Architects: Walker & Weeks

A series of four light fixtures adorn the entrance to this small branch bank. They are notable for integrating a clock, two shields, two eagles, and two urns into the overall Art Deco design of the structure.

This combination of Art Deco and Classical motifs is an extraordinary production of the metal worker's craft.

B. STONE MASONRY

1. *Entry Surround*

Landmark Office Towers (Midland Building) (1930)
Prospect Avenue, west of Ontario Street
Architects: Graham, Anderson, Probst & White

This polished granite entrance surround, Art Deco style,
is one of the most graceful in the City. It is complemented
by an abundance of Art Deco detail executed in stone
throughout the remainder of this office complex.

2. *Industrial Motifs*

Lorain-Carnegie (Hope Memorial) Bridge Pylons (1932)
Architects: Walker & Weeks
Sculptor: Henry Hering

These occur as pairs of massive sandstone piers,
approximately 42 feet tall, at either end of this main access
bridge. While the overall design is stylized Art Deco, the
stone details symbolize transportation and Cleveland's
industrial heritage.

3. *Gargoyle (Face)*

Society for Savings
127 Public Square (1890)
Architects: Burnham & Root
Restoration: van Dijk, Johnson & Partners (1990)

This stone motif is unusual for the "twisted" expression
of the figure's face – a whimsical architectural statement
adorning this rugged sandstone building.

4. *Marble Floor*

Ameritrust (Cleveland Trust) (1908)
Euclid Avenue at East 9th Street
Architects: George B. Post & Sons

Several different types and colors of marble combine with
terrazzo to form a beautifully executed geometric pattern in
the Rotunda floor. The Cleveland Trust seal is executed in
bronze at the center.

5. *Stone Eagles*

Old U.S. Post Office (1934)
M.K. Ferguson Plaza
Prospect Avenue at West 3rd Street
Architects: Walker & Weeks and Philip Small
Restoration: van Dijk, Johnson & Partners (1977) (1990)

These stone motifs are notable for their polished granite
surface and stylized Art Deco design. They occur above
the simple, rectangular stone entries along both Huron and
Prospect Avenues. The "restrained" or "pulled back" nature
of the stone detail overall is evocative of the period.

6. *Window Lintel Tracery*

Jimmel Block (1888)
1223 West 6th Street, Warehouse District
Architect: Unknown

The curving stone tracery of the window heads of the West 6th Street facade of this 19th century commercial building reflects the emerging technology of shaping stone with power tools rather than by hand. Note that each floor is characterized by its own unique design.

7. *Stone Entrance*

Pilgrim Congregational Church (1894)
West 14th Street & Starkweather Avenue (Tremont)
Architect: Sidney R. Badgley

The overall character of this Romanesque style, sandstone entry sequence is exceptional with wide stone steps and a segmented arch, metal grillework and railings, and heavy paneled wood doors. The interior of this historic church is also a spectacular architectural statement.

8. *Stone Stair*

Cuyahoga County Courthouse (1913)
1 Lakeside Avenue
Architects: Lehman & Schmitt

This curving stair, all executed in white marble, is an exceptionally graceful and sculptural concept. It occurs to the east of the main hall. The richness and attention to marble detail, including the newel and balustrade, is remarkable.

9. *Granite Stairs*

BP America Atrium (1985)
200 Public Square
Architects: Hellmuth, Obata, Kassabaum (HOK)

At the northwest and southwest corners of the Atrium are wide stone staircases which double back and allow access to the second floor balcony. The spatial aspects and fine stone detailing of each of these stairs make them excellent *new* additions to Cleveland's stock of architectural details. The design of these staircases was purportedly based on existing models in the famed Arcade.

10. *Mary Chisholm Painter Gate*

CWRU (1904)
11205 Euclid Avenue
Architect: Charles Schweinfurth

This limestone gate is four-square in plan and frames a main pedestrian path within Case Western Reserve University adjacent to the Church of the Covenent. Monumental gateways are not common to Cleveland; thereby this example is the more special.

C. TERRA COTTA MASONRY

1. *May Company Clock*

May Company Store (1912)
158 Euclid Avenue
Architects: Daniel Burnham & Co.;
Graham, Anderson, Probst & White (1931)

One of the most visible and striking architectural details in the city, this terra cotta clock and ornamental parapet adorns the top of the Public Square facade of the May Company Store.

2. *Terra Cotta Parapet Detail*

Dobama Theatre Building (1927)
Southwest corner of Coventry and Lancashire Roads,
Cleveland Heights
Architects: W.S. Ferguson Co.

This lavish terra cotta detail occurs on Coventry Road atop a two story commercial structure. The fluid and molded nature of the design embodies the plasticity of this early 20th century building material. Known originally as the Betty Burke Bldg., its terra cotta skin was fabricated by the South Amboy Terra Cotta Co.

3. *Terra Cotta Starburst*

Standard Building (1924)
1370 Ontario Street
Architects: Knox & Elliot

The rich geometry of these terra cotta details were characteristic of the Knox & Elliot firm and are observed in interesting variations in other terra cotta work by the

firm. The "starburst" design is unique and occurs throughout the 22-story structure from the base to the cornice. The
geometric detailing of the Knox & Elliot firm is suggestive
of the work of the noted architect Louis Sullivan.

D. MISCELLANEOUS

1. *Elevator & Cab, Surround*

Severance Hall (1932)
11001 Euclid Avenue
Architects: Walker & Weeks

This is one of but a series of architectural details which
comprise this spectacular Art Deco interior. The stylized
stone and metalwork of the elevator cab and surround are
a special component of this grand interior space which
belies the staid, Classical exterior design.

2. *Stained Glass*

Ameritrust (Cleveland Trust) Rotunda (1908)
Euclid Avenue at East 9th Street
Architects: George B. Post & Sons

Perhaps one of the finest examples of stained glass in
the City, this stained glass dome is approximately 60 feet
in diameter and is dominated by shades of blue, green
and yellow.

3. *Cast Iron Facade*

Rockefeller Building (1905)
614 Superior Building NW
Architects: Knox & Elliot

The intricate iron surfacing of this turn-of-the-century
skyscraper is reminiscent of the work of famous Chicago

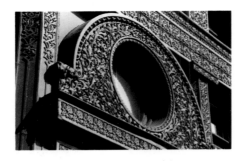

architect, Louis Sullivan. The geometric and foliated designs
are extensively used throughout the first two floors.

4. *Wood Detail*

Old Stone Church, (Interior) (1855) (1884)
91 Public Square
Architects: Heard & Porter
Renovation: Charles and Julius Schweinfurth

The extensive interior oak trim is the result of the later
work of the Schweinfurths, after a disastrous fire in 1884.
The barrel vaulted wooden ceiling and structural trusses
are especially notable – and in the spirit of the original
Romanesque design.

5. *Coffered Ceiling*

National City Bank (1895) (1914)
623 Euclid Avenue
Architects: Shepley, Rutan & Coolidge (Original)
Renovation: Walker & Weeks

The subtle pink coloring and classical detailing of this
patterned ceiling in another of the City's great banking
rooms is a visual delight. The adjacent longated Lobby
is equally impressive if somewhat less elaborate.

6. *Metal Grillwork*

Federal Reserve Bank (1923)
East 6th Street at Superior Avenue
Architects: Walker & Weeks

The large, arched bays of the main interior lobby are
infilled with heavy, black wrought-iron screens in decorative patterns. Each screen wall contains a central shield
representing one of the Federal Reserve districts. The
contrast of the metalwork against the polished Sienna
marble adds to the visual impact of the room.

7. *Front Door*

Schweinfurth House (1894)
1951 E. 75th Street
Architect: Charles Schweinfurth

A heavy wood door with decorative hinges and hardware
is embraced by a stone arch, the entire composition being
the front entrance to this architecturally historic house,
originally the home of the architect. The design of the
house (and door) is an early example of Tudor Revival
in the City.

8. *Murals*

State Theatre Lobby (1921)
Playhouse Square
Architect: Thomas Lamb

These colorful and magnificent murals were painted by
James H. Daugherty in 1920. They are entitled "The Spirit
of Cinema America" and depict movie production scenes.
These examples are considered some of the artist's best and
reflect the influence of movie technology on the American
lifestyle during this period.

9. *Tiffany Window & Mosaic*

Wade Memorial Chapel (1900)
Lake View Cemetery
12316 Euclid Avenue
Architects: Hubbell & Benes

Cleveland's best example of original Tiffany work, occurs
in the interior of this memorial chapel – which was entirely
designed by the Louis C. Tiffany firm. It is significant for
the level of collaboration between architect and artist –
an example of this early 20th century design trend.

10. *Ticket Booth*

Cleveland Convention Center (1922)
(Public Hall lobby, Lakeside Avenue)
Architects: J. Harold MacDowell, City Architect;
Frank Walker, Consulting Architect

A pair of these unique, free-standing marble and brass architectural elements grace the Lakeside Avenue lobby of Public Hall – part of Cleveland's Convention Center. The restrained classicism evident in the design of the ticket booth is typical of the entire structure. The decorative brass in many sculptured forms is also notable.

11. *Water Fountain*

Halle Building (Lobby) (1910)
1228 Euclid Avenue
Architect: Henry Bacon

This early 20th century version of the public water fountain features classical detailing and a recessed design in polished white marble. While typical of the period, it is an unusual architectural element in Cleveland, nonetheless.

12. *Oak Room, Tower City Center* (1930)

Architects: Small and Rowley

This unique dining hall was a striking feature of the Union Terminal development and served Cleveland's business elite from 1930 to its closing in 1975. More accurately the English Oak Room, the walls and columns of the high-ceilinged, 70' x 60' space are paneled in a dark-hued oak of notable graining and inlay work. A restrained Art Deco feeling prevails until the ceiling and cove moldings are reached. These are expressed in plaster in the fullest geometric extravagancies of the era. Today's visitor must try to imagine the space with its high-backed black leather seats, Sheffield silver and the service carts rolling upon the black and white marble floors.

William E. Samstag

This forceful bronze sculpture by Henry Hering (1923) fronts the Superior Avenue side of the Federal Reserve Bank Building.

Cleveland Architectural Firms, 1850-1950

1. **Daniel Burnham** (1846-1912) Though not a Cleveland architect, a historical guide of Cleveland would be incomplete without mention of this great Chicago architect and planner. He was a partner with Burnham & Root in the construction of the Society for Savings Building on Public Square in 1889-1890, but Burnham's major contribution to the development of downtown Cleveland was in his role as Chairman of the Group Plan Committee, appointed by the Governor in 1902. Burnham, along with John Carrere and Arnold W. Brunner, produced The Group Plan of the Public Buildings of the City of Cleveland in 1903 which provided the central focus and impetus for architectural growth in Cleveland for the first three decades of the twentieth century. After Burnham's death the successor firm of Graham, Anderson, Probst & White were named the architects for the Union Terminal Project as well as for the Union Trust Building, now the Huntington Bank. Burnham himself had objected to working with the Van Sweringens on their project for a union railroad station feeling it was a conflict of interest since he was working as a consultant to the city which was also trying to build a union station.

2. **Coburn & Barnum** – Forrest A. Coburn (1848-1897) and Frank Seymour Barnum (1851-1927) practiced together in an architectural firm from 1878-1897, when Coburn passed away unexpectedly. Like the other firms from this period, the firm of Coburn & Barnum produced notable examples of several different types of architectural structures. They built several churches including the Woodland Avenue Presbyterian Church, First Congregational Church on Franklin Avenue, Euclid Avenue Congregational Church, and The Brooklyn Congregational Church. In terms of residential architecture the firm designed residences or additions for such prominent Cleveland residents as William J. Morgan, the lithographer, George Howe, and Jeptha H. Wade II. They also added a library to Lawnfield, James A. Garfield's home, in 1885. The firm was responsible for the construction of the Washington H. Lawrence residence in Bay Village in 1898, which later became Bay View Hospital, now Cashelmara Condominiums. At Western Reserve University they built the Medical School (1885-1887) and Guilford College (1892) and at Case School they built the Electricity Building (1896). The firm also played an important role in the city's cultural life having designed the Olney Art Gallery (1893), and the Western Reserve Historical Society Building in 1898. Both W. Dominick Benes and Benjamin S. Hubbell worked for this firm prior to opening their own firm in 1897. Barnum continued after Coburn's death as consulting architect to The Cleveland Board of Education for which he designed and supervised more than 75 educational buildings until he retired in 1915.

3. **Cudell & Richardson** – Frank (Franz) E. Cudell (1844-1916) and John N. Richardson (1837-1902) formed this partnership in 1870. The two are best known and remembered for their Victorian Gothic-style churches erected in Cleveland during the 1870s. Their

success resulted from Cudell's having been born in Germany, thus his familiarity with German Gothic architecture, and a growing Northern and Eastern European immigrant population of Cleveland who desired their churches built in a familiar style. The firm built the following churches: St. Josephs Catholic Church in 1871, St. Stephens Catholic Church in 1873 and the Franklin Circle Christian Church in 1874. Their commercial buildings include The Root and McBride Warehouse in the Warehouse District, 1884; The George Worthington Company, 1882; and the Perry-Payne Building, (1889). Frank Cudell was also a vocal opponent of the 1903 Group Plan, believing that Cleveland architects were as qualified to plan their own city as the famous outsiders brought in by Mayor Tom L. Johnson and the Chamber of Commerce. He also strongly disagreed with the placement of public structures, like the City Hall and Cuyahoga County Court House, on the Lakeshore; he believed instead that the lakeshore was a place for public parks. Richardson was an engineer as well as an architect and assisted in the construction of large numbers of power plants in Cleveland and other cities.

4. **J. Milton Dyer** (1870-1957) Dyer, who moved to Cleveland from Middletown, Pennsylvania, with his family in 1881, attended Cleveland schools before attending the Ecole des Beaux Arts in Paris at the turn of the century. Upon his return to Cleveland he set up practice in Cleveland and was a prominent architect for the first two decades of the twentieth century, doing the majority of his work between 1900-1911. The collection of his works which are still standing today show an architect who was extremely versatile. These works include: Brooklyn Savings & Loan Association, (1904); The Tavern Club, (1905); First Methodist Church, (1905), Peerless Motor Car Company, (1906); Cleveland Athletic Club, (1911); Cleveland City Hall, (1916) and the U.S. Coast Guard Station at the mouth of the Cuyahoga, (1940). The Tavern Club sports a Northern Renaissance, monumental-gabled facade, an appropriate choice for a private men's club, while, eleven years later, his design for Cleveland's City Hall echoes the Beaux Arts classicism of the other buildings completed in the 1903 Group Plan. Several of his works completed between 1906 and 1909 show the influence of Frank Lloyd Wright, specifically the Peerless Motor Car Company and the Welch Company. Dyer excelled in all types of architecture: residential, ecclesiastical, industrial and public buildings – including temporary structures designed for the Cleveland Industrial Exposition of 1909. His works were considered so important in 1906, only six years after he set up practice in Cleveland, thathe was featured in a nineteen-page article in *The Architectural Record.*

5. **Abram Garfield** (1872-1958) was the son of the 20th President of the United States, James A. Garfield. After studying at Williams College, MIT, and traveling for a year in Europe, Garfield returned to Cleveland to open his own architectural practice in 1897. In 1898 he opened a partnership with Frank Meade and, as Meade & Garfield, the two established a local reputation as residential architects. He practiced as Abram Garfield, architect from 1905-1922 and as his work expanded he added partners becoming Garfield, Stanley-Brown, Harris &

Robinson in 1926. In 1936 the partnership was renamed Garfield, Harris, Robinson & Schafer and in 1957, Garfield, Harris, Schafer, Flynn & Williams (1957-1959). In Cleveland architecture his work is represented in many of the fine homes in Shaker Heights and Bratenahl; Eldred Hall, CWRU (1900), Bratenahl School (1901), Mrs. John Hay residence, 10915 East Boulevard (1910) now part of WRHS; and the original Babies and Childrens Hospital (1923). Garfield founded The Cleveland School of Architecture in 1924, and stayed with the school when it became part of Western Reserve University, becoming the vice-president and vice-chairman of the board (1929-1941), He served as a member of the Cleveland City Plan Commission from 1928-1942. He was appointed to the National Council of Fine Arts in 1909, the National Commission on Fine Arts in 1925, and as Chairman of the Committee on Blighted Areas & Slums in 1932.

6. **Hubbell & Benes** – Benjamin S. Hubbell (1867-1953) and W. Dominick Benes (1857-1935) practiced together under the firm name of Hubbell and Benes from 1897 until Benes death in 1935. The firm continued under the name until 1939. Prior to opening their own partnership both men had worked for the firm of Coburn, Barnum, Benes & Hubbell – Benes since 1876. Benes achieved a reputation as the personal architect to Jeptha Wade whose memorial he designed in Lake View Cemetery. And it was this Wade's grandson who commissioned the firm to create perhaps their best known building in Cleveland, The Cleveland Museum of Art, a classical revival structure meant to serve as Cleveland's "Temple of Art and Culture." The two architects were greatly interested in city planning and tried to create smaller public group plans in different parts of the city. They drew up plans for a cultural center in Wade Park with the Museum as a central focus surrounded by grandiose University buildings. The West Side Market was the only building completed in their plan for a public center in Ohio City which was to have included a bathhouse and gymnasium, among other buildings. The Market itself is built, basilican style, in the tradition of the great European indoor/outdoor markets and features wonderful monumental columns sporting terra-cotta capitals showing fruits, vegetables and animals. Hubbell and Benes were responsible for a number of the important commercial and public structures created in Cleveland between 1905 and 1930. Other works include: The Wade Memorial Chapel in Lake View Cemetery, (1900) with interiors designed by another friend of Jeptha Wade, Louis Comfort Tiffany; Equity Savings & Loan Company, (1905), now demolished; Women's College Gymnasium, Mather College, (1907); Illuminating Building, Public Square, (1915); YMCA Building, (1913); West Side Market, (1912); The Cleveland Museum of Art, (1916); Ohio Bell Telephone Building, (1925-1927); and the Phillis Wheatley Association Building, (1928).

7. **Joseph Ireland** – Ireland was a New York architect who practiced in Cleveland between 1865-1885, but certainly left his mark on Cleveland in a number of structures. Ireland built the first of The Society for Savings Buildings on Public Square in 1867 (now demolished) which became the first home of the Western Reserve Historical Society. He was a favorite architect

of Amasa Stone for whom he constructed the Adelbert College of Western Reserve University in 1882. He had become acquainted with Stone while designing the National Bank Building on Superior Avenue at West Avenue (1867), Stone was one of the bank's trustees. His major claim to fame was his skill at fireproof constructions. Ireland's buildings still standing are the Adelbert College, the Geauga County Courthouse in Chardon (1869), Stager-Beckwith House (1863), and the H. B. Perkins residence in Warren, Ohio.

8. **Charles Schweinfurth** (1856-1919) Schweinfurth was one of the most distinguished residential architects of the late nineteenth century in Cleveland. He constructed homes for Samuel Mather ("Shoreby," 1890) and Marcus Alonzo Hanna (1890), now demolished. He completed at least fifteen of the residences on "Millionaire's Row," the section of Euclid Avenue between E. 12th and E. 40th. The only one of these still standing is the Samuel Mather house (1910) at 2605 Euclid Avenue. He also built residences in the University Circle area (Gordon Morrill residence, 1915). Schweinfurth's own fortress-like home still stands on E. 75th St., between Euclid and Chester. At Case Western Reserve University he built the former Backus Law School (1896), Florence Harkness Chapel (1902), and Haydn Hall (1902). His finest work is thought to be Trinity Cathedral, and its associated Parish House, at East 22nd and Euclid Avenue, completed in 1907. He also had a hand in remodeling the interiors of the Old Stone Church, on Public Square. He designed Calvary Presbyterian Church, E. 79th and Euclid Avenue and he played an important role in determining the interior design of the Cuyahoga County Court House. His structures most often feature the heavily-rusticated exteriors, reminiscent of medieval donjons, favored by historically attuned architects of the late nineteenth century.

9. **Small & Rowley** – Philip Lindsley Small (1890-1963) and Charles Bacon Rowley (1890-1984) practiced together in the partnership of Small and Rowley for only eight years from 1921-1928 before moving on to individual careers. The partnership is important, however, because it was one of the firms chosen by M. J. and O. P. Van Sweringen to design five demonstration homes for the Van Sweringen's Shaker Heights development. Their architectural style is a mix of traditional Colonial and English architecture, and in their time together they completed more than 40 Georgian and Tudor style residences in the Cleveland area. The firm was also responsible for the Van Sweringen's country estate, Daisy Hill Farm in Hunting Valley, the Cleveland Play House (1926-27), Moreland Courts Apts., and Shaker Square (1927-28). Small later planned and designed John Carroll University's initial buildings, while Rowley went on to design public schools, the Mayfield Country Club, buildings for Kenyon College, and the Shaker Heights Public Library.

10. **Walker & Weeks** – Frank Ray Walker (1877-1949) and Harry E. Weeks (1871-1935). Both Walker and Weeks were educated at MIT. Walker studied architecture in France and traveled for a year in Italy. Weeks, the elder of the two, after working for a number of architectural firms in Massachusetts, opened his own firm in Pittsfield, Mass. Both Walker and Weeks moved to Cleveland in 1905 at the suggestion of John M. Carrere, a member of the Group Plan Committee, who advised them of the great building opportunities available here. Both men worked for the firm of J. Milton Dyer, prior to opening their own practice in 1911. The firm became specialists in financial buildings and completed over 60 banking institutions throughout Ohio; in Cleveland the men were also known for their commercial, religious, cultural, and public structures. The better-known works by this firm in Cleveland include: The Bingham Co. Warehouse (1915), renovations of what is now the old National City Bank Building (1915), Public Auditorium (1922); The Federal Reserve Bank (1923); The Cleveland Public Library (1925); Epworth-Euclid Methodist Church, with Bertram Goodhue (1928); Municipal Stadium (1931); and Severance Hall (1931). Frank Walker also worked as a consultant on a number of projects throughout the twenties and thirties.

Dr. Holly Rarick Witchey

Section 18

Architectural Styles

The stone arch embracing the Superior Avenue entrance of the Arcade is one of Cleveland's noblest Romanesque Revival accomplishments.

Cleveland's architectural heritage embraces a wide assortment of buildings built over a period encompassing more than 150 years. These buildings can be identified according to styles of American architecture. These styles are associated with a period in our history and are shaped by the technology, culture and economy of the era. As Cleveland grew from a frontier settlement to a major Midwest industrial and financial center by the late nine-teenth century, the types of buildings also changed, from rude log structures to skyscrapers which were in the forefront of the technology and design innovation of the time. During its earliest period up until perhaps about 1850, Cleveland did tend to import its building styles from available illustrated pattern books and from builders trained on the East Coast. However, by the time of the Civil War, Cleveland was a leading commercial and industrial center which was able to attract professional architects who were fully versed in the latest trends in architecture. By the late nineteenth century architects from larger cities such as Chicago and New York were designing a number of Cleveland buildings, which helped the city to keep abreast of the latest developments in architecture.

While Cleveland owes its present physical appearance to the rich diversity of its architecture, a mixture of old and new, the city never embraced a separate style apart from that of other cities or regions of the country. Cleveland's buildings from before the Civil War have largely been erased by the relentless growth of the city. But since Cleveland achieved major city status earlier than many contemporary Western and Southern American cities, it has been able to attain a broader diversity in terms of its architectural styles. The following styles are fairly broad categories of American architecture and in some cases may embrace a few distinct sub-styles which are refinements of the general category under which they appear. By studying this section and noting the indentifying features and notable Cleveland examples of each style, the reader will become more acquainted with American architecture and may be able to relate other buildings not in this guide to a particular style, thereby gaining some knowledge about the period in which the building was erected.

Federal Style

This is the earliest style to appear in Cleveland and dates from roughly 1790 to 1830. Because Cleveland has undergone so much change from when the Federal style was popular, no major examples exist in the city. Two rare, but altered, brick federal style houses exist in Cleveland neighborhoods and are largely identifiable by their stepped gable roofs. One is at 3015 Bridge Avenue in the Ohio City neighborhood and the other is at 1419 Auburn Avenue in the Tremont neighborhood.

Greek Revival

Perhaps no other style in the history of American architecture was more uniformly embraced than the Greek Revival, which was popular from about 1830 to about 1860.

Particularly in Midwestern towns, such as Cleveland, which lacked many significant buildings before 1830, the Greek Revival style dominated the building industry, appearing in houses, churches and commercial and industrial buildings almost without exception until the late 1850's. Cleveland had many fine examples of the Greek Revival style, including some magnificent mansions on Public Square and out along Euclid Avenue, but these have all disappeared because of the tremendous growth of the city. Perhaps the most noteworthy example of the style in Cleveland is the Dunham Tavern Museum, a frame structure at 6709 Euclid Avenue dating from 1842. Cleveland has some commercial buildings which are Greek Revival in style. The Hilliard Block, at West 9th and Frankfort in the Warehouse District, has massive stone storefront piers. Its stepped gable roof on the side is a holdover from the Federal style, even though the building dates from 1850. The Jobber's Block, the Johnson Block, and the Chamberlain Block are on the west side of West 6th south of St. Clair Avenue. They display the transition in styles from the Greek Revival to the Italianate. Jobber's, the southernmost, dates from 1851-1852 and is the most pure example of Greek Revival, although it has elaborate cast iron storefront columns rather than thick stone piers. The Johnson and Chamberlain blocks date from 1853-1854 and have round-arched, top floor windows and elaborate cornices which are indicative of the Italianate style.

Gothic Revival

This revival of the Medieval Gothic style used throughout Northern Europe in the Middle Ages coincided with the Greek Revival style but was far less popular and examples of this style are quite rare. St. John's Episcopal Church on Church Avenue in Ohio City (1838), Hezekiah Eldredge, builder, is the city's oldest church and is a fine example of this style with its pointed arch windows and steeply pitched roof. This version of the gothic is generally simpler than later revivals. A residential example exists at 1904 Ansel Road in the vicinity of University Circle. Because of the frequent use of elaborate wood trim made with a scrollsaw, this style is sometimes called Carpenter Gothic.

Early Romanesque Revival

This style spans the period from about 1840-1870, coinciding with the Greek Revival and Gothic Revival styles. James Renwick's Smithsonian Institution in Washington, D.C., dating from 1849, is a prominent example of this style. Cleveland is fortunate to have a major example of this relatively rare style. Old Stone Church on Public Square was built in 1856 from designs by Charles Heard and Simeon Porter. The interior was remodeled after a fire in 1884 and the tower was remodeled in 1900, otherwise the exterior retains a high degree of integrity.

Italianate

The Burgess Block anchors an entire street-side of Italianate facades.

From the period just before the Civil War until about 1880, this style of architecture was popular in Cleveland and throughout the country. Featuring elaborate cornices and window hood moldings, often made of pressed metal, the Italianate style was born in the American industrial revolution, when mass production techniques made it possible for even modest buildings to have lavish ornamentation. As its name implies, the style derives from the architecture of the Italian Renaissance. For a time, downtown Cleveland was dominated by rows and rows of three and four-story Italianate commercial blocks. Some survive today, especially in the Warehouse District. The Burgess Block (1874) and the Hoyt Block (1877) are on West 6th Street and are beautifully rehabilitated examples of the style. Many fine residences still exist in Cleveland neighborhoods in this style, including the Merwin House (Rowfant Club), transformed from an earlier Federal style house in 1858 from designs by Charles Heard and located at 3028 Prospect Avenue, the R.R. Rhodes House (1874) at 2905 Franklin Boulevard and the Frank Lynch House (ca. 1870) at 2913 Clinton Avenue, both in Ohio City.

Victorian Gothic

After the Civil War the Gothic was revived again but in a more elaborate form which emphasized use of different materials and different colors together. Many exceptional neighborhood churches were erected in this style such as Franklin Circle Christian Church (1875), Cudell & Richardson architects, located at Franklin and Fulton, and St. Michael the Archangel Roman Catholic Church (1892), Adolf Druiding architect, located at Clark and Scranton. Another outstanding example of this style is St. Ignatius College (now St. Ignatius High School), which dates from 1889 and was designed by Brother Wipfler. It stands on West 30th Street just north of Lorain Avenue in Ohio City. The Garfield Memorial in Lakeview Cemetery (1890), George W. Keller, architect, displays the rich interior decoration often associated with this style.

Second Empire

*The University Club's mansarded attic floor
expresses a favored Second Empire vogue.*

This style, popular from about 1860 to about 1890, is identifiable by a key feature, the steeply pitched mansard roof. Otherwise its elaborate exterior and interior decorations are very similar to the Italianate style. This style appears most frequently in residences. The Stager-Beckwith House (University Club) stands at 3813 Euclid Avenue as the last 19th century mansion remaining from "Millionaires' Row". It dates from about 1863. A number of business blocks were built in this style, and a portion of the Lorenzo Carter Building (ca. 1870) on West 9th between Frankfort and St. Clair has a mansard roof. A neighborhood commercial landmark of this style stands at 9119 Lorain Avenue.

Queen Anne

Named after the English monarch whose reign occurred 150 years before this style became popular in the 1880's through 1900, the Queen Anne style features gables, turrets, dormers, porches and generally an animated exterior punctuated with delicate Classical details. This style was primarily used in residences. McKinley Apartments at Detroit Avenue and West 81st Street dates from 1906 and was designed by Knox & Elliot. Its large corner tower and numerous elaborate porches are hallmarks of the style. The house, which prominent late 19th century architect Levi T. Scofield designed for himself at 2438 Mapleside in 1898, is another good example of this style. Queen Anne houses appear with frequency in older Cleveland neighborhoods, where some quite elaborate examples dominate street corners with their octagonal towers and ornate porches.

Richardsonian Romanesque

Based on the work of one of America's most prominent architects, Henry Hobson Richardson (1838-1885), this style derives from a fresh interpretation of medieval Romanesque forms which was pioneered by Richardson. The style was popular from about 1880 until about 1910. The Arcade (1890), John Eisenmann & George Smith, is best known for its magnificent interior. But its exterior facades along Euclid and Superior, with their massive arches and ranks of windows grouped within multi-story arcades, are in this style. Grays Armory (1893), by Fenimore C. Bate, is a magnificent example with its crenelated corner tower. It stands at 1234 Bolivar Road. Pilgrim Congregational Church (1893), S.R. Badgley, is one of a number of churches standing in Cleveland which are of this style. It is on the corner of Starkweather and West 14th in the Tremont neighborhood.

Neoclassical

The return to a more strict interpretation of classical forms in architecture began shortly before the turn of the century and lasted until the Great Depression. It constitutes one of Cleveland's richest groupings of historic landmarks for within this category fall the Terminal Tower (1930), Graham, Anderson, Probst & White, and the Beaux Arts – inspired buildings of Cleveland's famous Group Plan such as the Federal Building (1911), by Arnold Brunner, and the Cleveland City Hall (1916), by J. Milton Dyer. Many other downtown buildings are in this style, including tall buildings such as the Superior Building (1922), Walker & Weeks, (originally known as the Cleveland Discount Company Building) and institutional buildings such as Severance Hall at University Circle (1930), Walker & Weeks. The Union Club (1903), by Charles Schweinfurth, stands at Euclid and East 12th and is a stylistic variation of Neoclassical known as Second Renaissance Revival.

Neogeorgian

This revival of an American colonial style was popular from about 1900 through about 1940. It uses Georgian details usually in wood which is often painted white to contrast with a red brick background, such as was used often in colonial times. Shaker Square at Shaker Blvd. and Moreland Blvd. (1929), Small & Rowley, is a prominent example of this style. Many residences and churches are in this style. Plymouth Church (1923), by Charles Schneider, Coventry and Weymouth Roads, Shaker Heights, and Archwood United Church of Christ (1929), by George Farnum, 2800 Archwood Avenue, are prominent examples of this style. They feature tall steeples and white wood trim contrasting with red brick walls. In houses, Neogeorgian buildings often featured Palladian windows. The William Coates House (1901), by Frederic Striebinger, at Archwood and West 33rd, is a good example of this style.

Tudor Revival

The Tudor Revival could be baronial; as witness the stone and brick Samuel Mather mansion.

This style was popular from about 1910 to about 1940. It is based on medieval English prototypes from the Jacobean period. The Hermit Club (1928), by Frank B. Meade, stands on Dodge Court behind Playhouse Square and is highly picturesque example of this style. The Samuel Mather House (1910), by Charles Schweinfurth, (now known as University Hall) at Euclid and East 25th, is an impressive example of this style.

Arts and Crafts

At the turn of the century there was much experimentation in architectural design and some buildings of the era were inspired by a new approach to design which emphasized craftsmanship and natural forms over strict adherence to classical principles. Cleveland's heritage from this period is reflected in a number of residences and some outstanding commercial buildings such as the Lindner Company Store (1915), Robert D. Kohn, now the Prescott, Ball & Turben Building, at 1331 Euclid Avenue. In this building terra cotta and iron are joined into unique but visually pleasing forms.

Art Deco

Named after an exhibition in Paris of modern works, this style was popular from the late 1920's until after World War II. Rare in houses, this style was used for a number of downtown buildings. The Republic Building (1930), Graham, Anderson, Probst & White, stands at Prospect and Ontario and uses the flowing, vaguely Mayan-shaped ornament associated with the Art Deco, as well as the stepped profile commonly linked to the style in skyscrapers. The Ohio Bell Telephone Building (1927), by Hubbell & Benes, at 750 Huron Avenue, is a fine example of this style. The U.S. Post Office Building (1934), Walker & Weeks and Philip Small, at Prospect and West 6th, is a more conservative example of the style, with its stripped Neoclassical details.

NeoGothic

This third revival of the Gothic forms in Cleveland is a more academically correct interpretation of medieval forms and was often used in churches. Trinity Cathedral (1904, Charles Schweinfurth) which stands at Euclid and East 22nd is an imposing example of this style, which was popular from about 1900 through about 1940. Epworth Euclid Methodist Church (1928), Bertram Goodhue with Walker & Weeks, is a unique example of this style and stands at 1919 East 107th Street near University Circle.

Art Moderne

Cleveland has some highly significant examples of this style, which was popular from about 1930 until about 1950. Emphasizing streamlined forms and eschewing most ornamentation, this style bridged the gap between historically inspired and contemporary architecture. Cleveland Harbor Station, U.S. Coast Guard (1940), by J. Milton Dyer, stands at the end of a breakwall near the mouth of the Cuyahoga and resembles a streamlined ship. The Greyhound Bus Terminal (1948), by W.S. Arrasmith, stands at 1465 Chester Avenue. Cedar-Central Apartments (1937), by Walter McCornack, are bounded by E. 22nd, E. 30th, Cedar and Central. The Colony Theatre (1937), by John Eberson, stands at Shaker Square and has an interior with streamlined flowing lines all formed with smooth plaster.

The U.S. Coast Guard Station's smooth white exterior and rounded profiles reflect the Art Moderne era.

International

This modern style, which emphasized plain geometric shapes with the structure expressed and an abundance of glass, first appeared in downtown with the Illuminating Company Building (1958), by Carson & Lundin, at 55 Public Square, a plain rectangle elevated above a plaza with a largely glass exterior. Erieview Tower (1963), Harrison & Abramovitz, is a major downtown structure which takes the form of a rectangle with green-tinted glass sheathing. Until a few years ago, it faced a large plaza, now the site of the Galleria. Several other buildings around Erieview Tower were built in this style as part of this urban renewal project.

Modern Movement

This style, popular from the 1950's through the 1970's, explored various ways of decorating buildings in a new idiom. The Society National Bank Building (1969), by Charles Luckman, (formerly Central National Bank Building) at Superior and East 9th and the Ameritrust Tower (1971), by Marcel Breuer & Hamilton Smith, (formerly Cleveland Trust Tower) show two different approaches to articulating the details of contemporary office towers. In the first instance windows are grouped in vertical rows between brick piers with a ponderous cornice above. In the second instance, the windows are recessed within rounded precast panels, giving a sculpted appearance. The Jewish Community Federation (1965), by Weinberg & Teare and Edward Durrell Stone, stands at Euclid and East 18th and achieves a distinctive appearance by virtue of the grand colonnade in front.

Postmodern

This movement had its beginnings in the 1970's and competes with Modern architecture for public favor, with sometimes strong opinions expressed for one style or the other. While some prominent examples of this style are planned for the downtown, the most visible example remains the Cleveland Playhouse additions completed in 1985 from designs by Philip Johnson. Standing on Euclid Avenue near East 80th Street, the forms of the new work compare favorably with the 1920s portions by architects Small & Rowley.

Steven McQuillin

Downtown East Walking Tour

Your walking tour begins at the northeast corner of East 9th Street and Euclid Avenue, in front of the massive Huntington Building (1924, Graham, Anderson, Probst & White; restored 1975, Dalton, van Dijk, Johnson & Partners). Reputed to be the second largest office building in the world at the time of completion, this structure still houses one of the world's largest public banking rooms. The building lobby offers 28 elevators and a marble shopping concourse, on two levels.

Across Euclid is Ameritrust's rather Baroque headquarters (1908, George B. Post & Sons), offering another magnificent banking room – with Tiffany-style skylight atop a glorious four-story rotunda. Ameritrust's adjacent tower (1971, Marcel Breuer with Hamilton P. Smith), facing East 9th Street and originally intended to have a twin tower facing Euclid, is a distinctive skyscraper clad with richly textured, gray Vermont granite.

Proceed eastward down Euclid on the south side. This stretch of the Avenue, graciously appointed, offers some of the ambience of New York's dignified Fifth Avenue in the East 40s and 50s. At 1118 Euclid is the Cleveland Athletic Club building (1911, J. Milton Dyer), an unusual arrangement with men's health club/residence occupying eight floors above a seven-floor office building. The terra cotta facade is of eclectic Gothic design similar to that of New York City's Woolworth Building (1909).

Ameritrust's main office is the classical epitome of the popular image of a bank.

Just to the east of the Athletic Club building is the Halle Building; this was the second-to-be-built section of the prestigious Halle Brothers department store complex (Henry Bacon, 1910, 1914, 1920; Walker & Weeks, 1927, 1948). The terra cotta facades, with delicate Neoclassical motifs and portes cocheres, have been meticulously restored by Forest City Enterprises and the interior successfully transformed into a first-class office building with food court and elegant shops, the work of Cope Linder Associates of Philadelphia.

Across Euclid, at the northeast corner of the intersection with East 12th Street, stands Cleveland's venerable Union Club (1905, Charles F. Schweinfurth), a restrained, Florentine bastion for many of Cleveland's elite and typical of the turn-of-the-century urban men's clubs with sumptuous quarters.

At the northwest corner of this intersection is the enormous bulk of the Statler Office Tower, originally the Hotel Statler (1912, George B. Post & Sons, Charles Schneider) once a grand hotel of 1,000 rooms, now adapted to office and retail uses.

The Prescott Ball & Turben headquarters features a dramatic facade of iron, glass and terra cotta.

Continue down Euclid until you come to the Prescott, Ball & Turben Building (1913, Robert D. Kohn; restoration/renovation 1981, Landmark Design Team). Originally the Lindner Coy clothing retailer, which in the '50s became a Bonwit Teller, this fanciful building has an intricately carved, terra cotta facade with much space devoted to windows and delicate railings – all in the flavor of the works of Victor Horta.

Flanking East 14th Street at Playhouse Square is the Hanna Building and the Renaissance.

At the southwest corner of Euclid and East 14th is the Renaissance at Playhouse Square building (1990, Richard L. Bowen & Associates with Kaczmar Architects), a stepped, Postmodern extravaganza faced with dark pink granite and tinted glass. On the southeast corner of East 14th and Euclid stands the Hanna Building (1921, Charles A. Platt), a most impressive office building of great stateliness – note, for example, the balustrade – with a lavish theater facing E. 14th.

Continuing on Euclid, you will see four theaters on the north side, facing the Hanna Building. Together these theaters form the backbone of Playhouse Square, now a glittering district of theaters, restaurants, and still a few elegant shops. The Allen Theater (1921, C. Howard Crane) is at 1407 Euclid and in the Bulkley Building; the Ohio and State Theaters (both 1921, Thomas W. Lamb) are in the Loews Building; and the Palace Theater (1922, Rapp & Rapp) is in the 21-story highly decorative, terra cotta Keith Building at the corner of East 17th – a majestic sentinel guarding Downtown's eastern gate.

Of these four theaters, the Allen's fate is yet in question, but its sister theaters were painstakingly restored and renovated from 1972 (when they had been threatened with demolition!) through 1988, under the aegis of Dalton, van Dijk, Johnson and Partners. The Palace, originally a stage theater, is the most magnificent, and the Ohio was revived, mainly for opera and ballet, in a somewhat Contemporary mode. All four theaters have lobbies decorated in the grand manner, as well-befitting the early '20s theatrical world of fantasy.

The Jewish Community Federation

Continue east down Euclid, on the south side, to the Jewish Community Federation (1965), Weinberg & Teare Architects and Edward Durrell Stone Associate Architect, just before East 18th – a graceful structure typical of Stone's designs, with arched windows atop slim pilasters and a "lid" roof, all bathed in a light tonality. The Federation's setback offers a welcome landscaped plaza to the Euclid Avenue streetscape.

Following Euclid to East 22nd Street you will come to Trinity Episcopal Cathedral (1901-1907) at the southeast corner, often called Charles F. Schweinfurth's masterpiece. A late Gothic Revival edifice, Trinity is very English in conception, and all interior furnishings were designed in a composition consistent with the Indiana limestone exterior.

Cleveland State University Natatorium

Continue further down Euclid until you are across the street from Fenn College Tower (1930), George B. Post & Sons, built as Art Deco home of the classy, but shortlived, National Town and Country Club – going through several uses until its absorption into campus life at Cleveland State University. Several buildings to the east of Fenn Tower directly before the Innerbelt is University Hall (1910), Charles F. Schweinfurth, formerly the home of mining and steel magnate Samuel Mather and Euclid Avenue's grandest former mansion, extant or lost. Adjacent to University Hall is the Physical Education Building and Natatorium (1973), Dalton, van Dijk, Johnson and Partners, a massive structure of brick and concrete suggesting its huge interior spaces.

Double back on Euclid, walking this time on the north side. You will come to the long Main Classroom Building of CSU (1970), Dalton, Dalton, Dalton & Little, opposite East 22nd Street. Extending from Euclid to Chester and connected with other campus buildings via raised plazas and pedestrian links, this concrete and brick structure, with much of the first floor an open plaza, was the largest classroom building in Ohio when completed.

At E. 22nd Street walk along the west side of this building and then rise up to the plaza in front of the Library and its University Tower (1971), Outcalt, Guenther & Associates, a 23-story shaft of precast concrete housing offices. Between the Library and Euclid Avenue is the University Center (1974), Don Hisaka, most notable for its five-story atrium which fills with sunlight.

Walking around the Center you will return to Euclid Avenue. To your right is Cleveland State's new Music and Communication Building (1990), van Dijk, Johnson & Partners, distinguished by pronounced horizontal bands on its walls and pyramidal skylights, from the basement level, surrounded by raised platforms.

Continue west (back toward Public Square) down Euclid, and you will come to the Cleveland Marshall School of Law (1977), Van Auken, Bridges, Pimm, Poggianti with Ireland and Associates, on the northeast corner of the intersection with East 18th Street. The main entrance of this strip-windowed, brown-brick structure is reached by climbing a flight of steps facing a pleasant planted plaza.

Turn right on East 17th Street, following the side of the Palace Theater with its visually interesting arrangement of fire escapes and stage doors. Turning left on Chester Avenue, you will see behind the theater complex – and, technically, situated on narrow Dodge Court – the Hermit Club (1928), Frank B. Meade. Resembling an authentic English tavern and actually a clubhouse for an organization of amateur thespians, the organization plays a similar role to that of Boston's Tavern Club, also in a theater district. Remain on Chester Avenue, however. To your right will be the Greyhound Bus Terminal (1948) W. S. Arrasmith, one of Greater Cleveland's few remaining Streamline Style structures and what has been called "the quintessential American bus station" in character.

After crossing East 13th Street, look to your right and you will see, at the southeast corner of East 14th and Superior (one block north of Chester), the Ernest J. Bohn Tower (1974), William Dorsky, a slab highrise for the elderly named for the Director of the Cleveland (later, Cuyahoga) Metropolitan Housing Authority from 1933-1968. Staying on Chester, you will pass Reserve Square (1973, Dalton, Dalton, Little & Newport). Originally called Park Centre, it is composed of two apartment towers with parking garage and two-level shopping/eatery concourse. The Brutalist complex was in 1989-1990 fashioned into the Radisson Suite Hotel, new shops, and offices and with one tower remaining apartments.

Turning right on East 12th Street, now a divided parkway, you will see on your left Chester Commons Park (1972), City of Cleveland, a popular, urban mini-park with the typical man-made mounds of earth plus playful concrete sculptural forms associated with the landscaping language of the 1970s. Facing the Commons, at the southwest corner of East 12th and Superior Avenue, is the Diamond Building (1971), Skidmore, Owings & Merrill, a dark metal and glass tower related to the International Style and pristine in its slick, solid form.

At the northeast corner of East 12th and Superior Avenue is First Federal Savings Bank (1988), Richard L. Bowen & Associates, a dark blue, mirrored glass and marble structure accented with bold, zigzag wall sections on its facade.

Eaton Center

Turn left on Superior. To you right, on the northwest corner, is Eaton Center (1983), Skidmore, Owings & Merrill, a shimmering, black reflective-glass tower with the Madison Avenue corporate look. Note the chamfered corners and slight setback near the top. Continue west down Superior to East 9th Street – the heart of Cleveland's financial district the past two decades.

On the southeast corner of the intersection is the East Ohio Building (1959), Emery Roth & Sons, a no-nonsense corporate tower of black glass and aluminum expressing an early local example of curtain-wall construction. On the northeast corner is St. John's Cathedral (1852), Patrick C. Keely; (1946-1948), Stickle & Associates, a hybrid created by the redesigning of a Gothic Revival brick church, with central steeple, into a sandstone-clad complex of a more monumental church character, along with academic and other Diocese-related structures. If you have a chance, visit the sanctuary, where a fine Victorian church interior can be experienced.

The Galleria at Erieview

Head north up East 9th Street. On the east side of the block, between Rockwell and St. Clair Avenues, is One Cleveland Center (1983), Hugh Stubbins & Associates – a smaller version of New York's Citicorp Center (1977) and designed by the same firm. The six-sided tower, which is connected to a large parking garage and health club, is clad in gleaming aluminum and its glass-roofed atrium lobby is dramatically situated.

Crossing St. Clair you come to the Galleria at Erieview (1987), Kober/Belluschi Associates, a block-long, upscale shopping mall connecting Cleveland's premier International Style skyscraper, the Tower at Erieview (1964), Harrison & Abramovitz, with the busy 9th Street corridor. The mall replaced an oversized, windswept plaza with little-used fountains and skating rink. The Galleria is at once monumental, urban, ultra-trendy, and steeped with the Postmodern color scheme of pinks and aquas, arches galore, and columns inspired from ancient civilizations. The glass roof, formed by several series of barrel arches, is breathtaking.

The building to the Galleria's left is the new Ohio Bell headquarters (1984), Dalton, Dalton & Newport – granite clad and most notable for its sweeping, curved wall of offices overlooking Lake Erie. Walk through the Galleria and Tower at Erieview to East 12th Street and turn left. If the Galleria is closed, walk instead to East 12th via either St. Clair Avenue or the plaza between the Galleria and the Ohio Bell buildings.

Go up East 12th to Lakeside Avenue; you will see the broad expanse of Lake Erie in the distance. On Lakeside, to the right and just to the East of Cardinal Mindszenty Plaza, is Cleveland's Public Utilities Building (1971), Thomas T. K. Zung, a polished marble structure with cantilevered fifth floor and offering the visitor one of Cleveland's earliest "modern" atriums.

Turn left on Lakeside Avenue. You will be passing the Holiday Inn-Lakeside (1974), William W. Bond & Associates to the right, a fairly standard, 1970s highrise chain hotel which has a second-floor projecting deck vaguely echoing the Utility Building's fifth floor.

Just past the hotel is a complex of two new luxury office facilities – the North Point Building (1986) Dalton, Dalton, Newport (Jerry Payto, designer) and North Point Tower (1990), Payto Architects. Both offer reflective glass and distinctive angular forms; the Tower is stepped and is an almost overpowering, climactic backdrop to the view from the East 9th-Lakeside vicinity.

Your walking tour ends at the corner of Lakeside and East 9th, with a view of the exciting, newly developed North Coast Harbor down East 9th and the vast Lake beyond. A short stroll up East 9th to Euclid will take you to where your walk commenced.

Kenneth Goldberg

Section 19B

Downtown West Walking Tour

Begin your walking tour at the Bond Court Building (1971), Skidmore, Owings & Merrill, stationed at St. Clair Avenue and East 9th Street – Cleveland's homage to the curtain-walled, slab highrises of 1960s and '70s corporate America. Bond Court and its neighboring hotel were built on land cleared in the massive Erieview renewal project. Walk north on East 9th and you will pass the newest of Cleveland's Federal Buildings (1967), Dalton, Dalton with Outcalt, Guenther, Rode & Bonebrake, a 32-story skyscraper with stainless steel facing and plazas from both East 9th and East 6th Streets.

Turn left on Lakeside Avenue, where the Lake Erie expanse and Cleveland's new North Coast Harbor development are to your right. You will pass Cleveland's staid City Hall (1916), J. Milton Dyer, a Neo-Classical edifice well befitting the "City Beautiful" image Daniel Burnham envisioned in his Group Plan of 1903. The building stands as an impressive terminus to East 6th. On your left is Public Auditorium (1922), by Frederick H. Betz & J. Harold MacDowell; Music Hall (1927), by Herman Kregelius; (1964), Outcalt, Guenther, Rode & Bonebrake; (1988), URS Consultants and City of Cleveland Division of Architecture, largest convention hall in the U.S. in the early 1920s. With a lavish Music Hall added in 1927, and still later extensive additions, refurbishing and restoration work, this behemoth rivals the far newer facilities of many a city.

You may turn left onto the walk that goes before the Auditorium's 1964 Mall Entrance and follow the auto drive-through to St. Clair Avenue, or you may go slightly farther on Lakeside and turn left onto the attractively landscaped Hanna Plaza with pool and fountains, well shaded terraces and benches. This replaced a former parking lot and, indeed, covers an underground garage.

The new Federal Building

Proceed left down St. Clair Avenue and turn right on East 6th. To your right is Cleveland's Board of Education Headquarters Building (1930), Walker & Weeks, the final Group Plan structure, Neo-Classical but

Public Auditorium

with more Baroque flourishes – note the front entrance lanterns – than have its neighbors along the Mall. Turn right on Rockwell Avenue and then left through the ornate iron gates brought from a Euclid Avenue mansion for Cleveland Public Library's Eastman Reading Garden (1959), George Creed, should the Garden be open. The Library's main building (1925), Walker & Weeks, to your right, is a Beaux Arts monument – housing one of the world's largest collections – and known architecturally for its grand foyer and General Reference Room and for its interior light court. In 1989 an architectural competition for expansion of the Library was won by Hardy Holzman Pfeiffer Associates and URS Consultants.

Considerable public discussion ensued over the disposition of the garden, but the plans were put on hold in 1990. If you are unable to enter the Garden, continue past the gates and turn left on East 3rd Street.

Across Superior from the Library's main entrance is The Arcade (1890), John Eisenmann & George H. Smith, Cleveland's most notable single landmark. A Late Victorian masterwork of bold, uncompromising design, The Arcade possesses surely the most breathtaking interior space in Greater Cleveland and is now a successful, restored commercial/office development in a most enviable of locations. This was the first of Cleveland's four downtown arcades and was worlds ahead of the others in ambitiousness.

You will exit the Garden, or East 3rd, to Superior Avenue and turn left. Upon crossing East 6th, you will encounter the Federal Reserve Bank (1923), Walker & Weeks. This pink granite-and-marble Renaissance palace symbolizes security and stability. Note the allegorical sculptures at the two entrances, by Cleveland's Fischer-Jirouch Company and Henry Hering. At the southwest corner of Superior and E. 6th Street is the Leader Building, a 15-story limestone-faced office structure (1912), Charles A. Platt, of refined classical form featuring an imposing double-entry Lobby. To your right across Superior from the Federal Reserve Bank, is Bank One Center (1990), RTKL Ohio Corp., a granite-cladded highrise with Postmodern setbacks and window treatment and a marble lobby – built on the site of two consecutive Hollenden hotels.

At the southwest corner of East 9th and Superior, to your right, is the Society Building (previously, The Central National Bank Building) (1968), Charles Luckman. This handsome brick highrise stands upon a paved podium and has deeply recessed windows set in strongly vertical slots.

The Society Building

Turn right on the East 9th corridor and you are in the heart of Cleveland's financial district. At the corner with Euclid Avenue stands the travertine-faced National City Center (1978), Skidmore, Owings & Merrill, the fourth substantial structure on that site since the 1850s.

If you cross Euclid and venture further south down East 9th you will see the terra-cotta faced Rose Building (1900), George H. Smith, and the Ohio Bell Telephone Building (1926), by Hubbell & Benes on Huron Road, a set-back style tower with early Art Deco overtones. Back at East 9th and Euclid, turn left onto Euclid and you will immediately approach, to your right, two more buildings now owned by National City Bank. Number 623 Euclid, the National City Bank Building (1895), by Shepley, Rutan & Coolidge; (1914), Walker & Weeks, was originally the New England Building and had a Richardsonian arched entrance. The building's banking interior is known for an extraordinary coffered ceiling. The building's neighbor, at East 6th (1893), Henry Ives Cobb, was formerly the Garfield Building. The first steel-framed commercial building on Euclid, the Garfield Building is considerably remodeled on its lower stories.

Continue west down Euclid and turn left on East 4th Street – downtown Cleveland's congested, honky-tonk side street of small shops situated in mostly turn-of-the-century structures; these form both a local and an Historic District on the National Register. The Euclid Avenue Opera House stood on the southeast corner of Euclid and East 4th (formerly, Sheriff Street), in a district housing several theaters.

Turn right on Prospect Avenue and cross Ontario Street. You are now amid Tower City, originally the Van Sweringen brothers' enormous Union Terminal Group when completed in 1934 a mixed-use complex as extensive as New York's Rockefeller Center. You sense you are within a special district when

Ohio Bell, Huron Road

East 4th Street from Prospect Avenue.

you notice the streetlights – new, but resembling those found in sections of Cleveland in the early years of this century. To your left is the Landmark Office Towers, originally the Republic, Guildhall, and Midland Buildings (1930-1932), by Graham, Anderson, Probst & White. Decorated in the Art Deco mode, these structures now offer a consolidated lobby of the 1980s and house the national headquarters of several corporations. An underground passage connects this complex to the shops and theaters of Tower City's immense complex. Turn left on West 2nd and walk around the new Tower City shopping mall/RTA station entrance.

Across Huron is the site of the future Rock and Roll Hall of Fame (I.M. Pei). Coming up West 3rd and back toward Prospect, to your left will be the M-K Ferguson Plaza, formerly Cleveland's main Post Office (1934), Walker & Weeks with Philip Small, a typical large urban Post Office of its era. Some of its sandstone was replaced in 1978 with a facsimile facing.

Turning right on Prospect, double back to Ontario Street, and turn left. On your left is Higbee's department store (1931), Graham, Anderson, Probst & White, whose low-key exterior is matched by a quietly elegant atmosphere within. To the west is the main thrust of the Tower City complex – Terminal Tower (1928), Graham, Anderson, Probst & White (1990), RTKL Ohio Corp., a 52-story office tower now with multistoried shopping mall and Rapid Transit station below. Originally the complex housed Cleveland's massive Union Terminal, along with an array of shops and restaurants on one level. Terminal Tower, upon completion, was the second tallest structure in the U.S. (and tallest outside of

Landmark Office Tower's uniquely Art Deco ornamental exterior.

New York City until 1965) – a glamorous symbol for Cleveland for decades. It rises in stages and was probably modeled after the New York Municipal Building in Manhattan (1911-1913) by McKim, Mead & White. Perhaps you will have a chance to venture to its Observation Deck for marvelous views of the city and Lake Erie.

Proceeding on Ontario Street to the north you will walk through the center of Public Square, first staked out by Moses Cleaveland and his surveyors in 1796.

Where Euclid Avenue branches off the Square's southeast corner stands the May Company building (1912), Daniel H. Burnham & Co., a fanciful terra-cotta structure with Chicago School windows; the top two stories were added (the clock tower was actually raised) and the marquee area modernized in 1931. Facing the east side of Public Square is the BP America Building (1984), Hellmuth, Obata & Kassabaum, a pink granite structure with a glorious nine-story public atrium. This building replaced Burnham's Cuyahoga Building of 1894, the Williamson Building, and several other structures. The Cuyahoga Building was Cleveland's first building with complete steel frame.

Coming to the north side of the Square, you will see two of Cleveland's oldest and most venerable landmarks – Old Stone Church (1855), Heard & Porter to the left, and Society National Bank (1889), Burnham & Root; these bring a comfortable, 19th-century presence to the heart of downtown. The church-the last 19th century religious structure in the central business district-is Early Victorian Romanesque and once boasted a tall east spire. The bank, recently saved to be incorporated into the Society Center (1991), by Cesar Pelli Associates with restoration of the 1889 building by van Dijk, Johnson & Partners, is a Romanesque and Gothic sandstone structure known for its turn-of-the-century banking lobby as well as housing Cleveland's oldest incandescent lighting fixture. The Society Tower will be Cleveland's tallest skyscraper, but only until the Ameritrust Center, to face Public Square's northwest quadrant, is completed. Toward the northwest corner of the Square can be seen the Illuminating Building (1958), Carson & Lundin, the first tall building in Cleveland to display a glass curtain wall.

Proceeding up Ontario Street you will come to the Standard Building (1924), Knox & Elliot, a terra-cotta confection built as the Brotherhood of Locomotive Engineers Bank Building. The lobby matches the exterior in patterns of ornament, and both slightly predate, but show a relationship with, Art Deco styling. Continue north on Ontario to Lakeside Avenue, where you will face the handsome Beaux Arts Cuyahoga County Courthouse (1912), Lehman & Schmitt. Closely

The Standard Building

The Justice Center's granite surfaces and sharp edges are its recognizable features.

resembling City Hall, the Courthouse has a more showy interior, with a featured marble stairway lighted with impressive stained glass windows.

On the southwest corner of Ontario and Lakeside is the Justice Center complex (1973-1976), Prindle & Patrick with Pietro Belluschi, an entire block of pink granite structures, of varying heights, amid raised plazas; these house City and County offices and offer vast public interior spaces. A Noguchi sculpture, "Portal," guards the Ontario Street entrance, and other artwork visually enhances the complex's otherwise rather cold demeanor.

Turn west on Lakeside Avenue and proceed to West 3rd Street, where two renewed loft buildings signal the revitalization under-way. On the northwest corner, the Crown (now Courthouse Square) Bldg. (1915) by the Forest City Engineering Co. faces the steel-windowed L.N. Gross (now Lakeside Place) Bldg. (1917) by Christian, Schwarzenberg & Gaede Co., remodeled (1990) by Planning Resources Inc. Continue on Lakeside Avenue to West 6th Street, again turning left. This stretch of West 6th is the hub of Cleveland's Warehouse District, a mainly 19th-century district bordering the Flats and now a trendy locale for restaurants, lofts, galleries, boutiques, offices, and apartment complexes. Note the distinctive streetscaping along West 6th – colorful pavement and concrete slabs resembling packing crates and thus reminiscent of the types of commercial activity preoccupying the district in the 19th century. At the northwest corner of West 6th and St. Clair Avenue, to your right, is the Hoyt Block (1875), Walter Blythe and (1987), van Dijk, Johnson & Partners, an imaginatively renovated and restored, Italianate commercial block. This is the only remaining stone commercial block downtown; originally the walls were stained red to match the brick of neighboring buildings.

The Hoyt Block

On the southwest corner of West 6th and St. Clair stands a series of connected commercial structures, together called the Johnson Blocks (1851-1854). Recently rehabilitated and restored, these buildings display colorful Victorian storefronts and an interesting interplay of contrasting cornices and window treatments. Continuing southwest you will come to the Rockefeller Building (1903, 1911), Knox & Elliot, at Superior Avenue. Here is an early highrise closely resembling Louis Sullivan's Wainwright Building of St. Louis (1890-1891) and Guaranty Building of Buffalo (1894-1895).

Turn right on Superior and you will pass on your right the venerable, but unrestored, Perry-Payne Building. (1889), Cudell & Richardson, a redstone structure once with an atrium now covered over. Adjacent thereto is the ten-story limestone-faced office building now called the 820 Building, but built (1922), by Charles Schneider, for the Brotherhood of Railroad Trainmen. The structure was both restored and remodeled in 1985 by Gaede, Serne, Zofcin Architects Inc. Across West 9th Street you will come to the Western Reserve Building (1891, 1903), Daniel H. Burnham & Co. This was the third of Burnham's Chicagoesque commercial buildings in Cleveland – cleverly molded to a difficult site, irregularly shaped and sloping toward the river. Restoration/renovation was undertaken in 1975-1976 by Hoag-Wismar Partnership with Lawrence Halprin Associates; the addition to the north, with facade of terra-cotta-like material, was designed by Keeva J. Kekst Architects and completed in 1990. Your tour ends here, where you can savor a spectacular view of the Cuyahoga River and Cleveland's Flats development along its banks.

The 820 Building

Kenneth Goldberg

Ohio City Walking Tour

Ohio City, once a competitor to the early 19th Century burgeoning community of Cleveland, was amalgamated into its larger partner in 1854. The historic distinction persists today with the district's unique mix of small-scaled residences and churches as well as a kind of "Main Street" quality of its principal commercial thoroughfare, W. 25th Street. A testing ground of gentrification versus affordable housing by newer arrivals to Cleveland's ethnic mix, Ohio City has experienced considerable rehabilitation in its effort to maintain its character into the future.

Begin the tour at the recently-completed Market Plaza Shopping Center (1990), architects Jeffrey H. Bogart & Associates. Note the dominant surrounding structures, the United Office Building (1926), Walker & Weeks, a late classically inspired bank and office structure clad in limestone and the West Side Market (1912), Hubbell and Benes, Architects. The Market, a Cleveland favorite, has both indoor and outdoor stalls. Its Beaux Arts era tower and barrel-vaulted market hall are unique landmark features. The complex was extensively restored in 1988-1989 by City of Cleveland, Division of Architecture and HWH Architects and Engineers.

Walk north past tiny Market Square on the west side of W. 25th along the busy shopping street featuring a thoroughly American display of commercial architecture, some restored, from the 1880-1930 era. (Among the more notable: the Merrill Block (ca. 1895), attributed to F.S. Barnum on the NW corner of W. 25th at Carroll Avenue, and the Metzner Block (ca. 1890), Cudell & Richardson, 1901 W. 25th Street.) Turn left on Bridge Avenue to W. 28th Street, thence right (north) past Jay and Vestry Avenues to Franklin Circle. A brief detour onto Jay Avenue will introduce visitors to one of the most completely rehabbed streets in the district.

At Franklin Circle little remains of the once clearly stated circle, but its image in walkways and building setbacks still is revealed. The block-large cluster of Lutheran Medical Center dominates on the southeast. The seven-story brick and pre-cast structure (1972), Visnapuu & Gaede, was expanded and modified (1989) by Braun & Spice Architects. On the south edge of the Circle is the Heyse Building (1898) restored to commercial uses (1982), and on the southwest corner, the lively Gothic-revival Franklin Circle

The Lutheran Medical Center at Franklin Circle.

Christian Church (1875), Cudell and Richardson. On the west edge of the Circle stands a wholly different architectural statement, the pristine neo-classical Franklin Circle Masonic Temple (1932), Charles Hopkinson, Architect.

Travel north on W. 28th Street to Church Avenue. Turn right to the (1836) St. John's Episcopal Church, Hezekiah Eldridge, Architect. This rugged stone church with a delightful wood-clad Parish Hall is Cleveland's earliest remaining church building. Minus its tower finials, the early Gothic revival character still prevails.

Walk around the block bounded by Church, W. 25th, Detroit and W. 26th Street. At the northeast corner is the restored Forest City Bank Building (1903-1905), designed by Searles & Hirsh. Suffering a devastating fire in 1985, this highly visible structure was returned to use in 1990. The once active subway entry to the city's streetcar system is the circular corner feature of the building.

Walk west along Detroit Avenue to W. 28th Street, thence south to Church and west to Dexter. At the southeast corner note the rehabilitated Firehouse No. 4 (1874). Continue south on Dexter to Franklin Circle, thence west on Franklin Blvd. to W. 32nd Street you will pass several restored Italianate houses, notably the (1862) Sanford House, 2843 Franklin and the (1874) Rhodes House, 2905 Franklin, recently home to the Cuyahoga County archives.

Turn south on W. 32nd Street to Woodbine Avenue, west to W. 38th Street and south to Bridge Avenue. This pathway will offer a penetrating view of residences in the process of discovery, renewal and restoration. Moving east on Bridge Avenue, the single-towered St. Patrick Roman Catholic Church (1871), by

Carnegie West Branch Library in Ohio City.

Market Square neighborhood, Ohio City.

Alfred Green, dominates the street. Its rough-faced Sandusky sandstone walls embrace a tall nave all in a Victorian Gothic style. Opposite to the church is the richly articulated, Beaux Arts-styled Carnegie West Branch of the Cleveland Public Library (1910), Edward L. Tilton, architect. This landmark building, saved from demolition by the Cleveland Landmarks Commission in the 1970's, was extensively restored and remodeled internally (1979) by Koster & Associates, Architects.

Continue east on Bridge to W. 30th Street, then to the right and past Carroll Avenue to St. Ignatius High School (1888-1891), a towered, High Victorian Gothic structure of Germanic influence. Once St. Ignatius College, it was to have had a balancing south wing. Beyond the building is bustling Lorain Avenue. Turn east (left) on Lorain and come once again to Market Square, the Market and the United Bank Building at which point the tour commenced.

Robert C. Gaede, FAIA

University Circle Walking Tour

Cleveland's University Circle is one of the nation's largest and richest concentrations of institutions and cultural monuments to be found. Its sixty-member group of organizations established University Circle Inc. (UCI) as institutional consortium with special concern for land use in the district. Visitors and citizens of Cleveland are welcomed to obtain more general information and a more complete map by contacting UCI at its headquarters at 10831 Magnolia Drive, Cleveland, OH 44106, telephone 791-3900.

The tour begins at Adelbert Hall (1882, Joseph Ireland, architect), which was the "Old Main" of the Western Reserve campus of the federated Case Western Reserve University. Across Adelbert Road and to the right are the central buildings of University Hospitals described in the Health Facilities Section. Walk north on Adelbert to Euclid Avenue, Cleveland's best-remembered avenue. On the corner is the dignified Allen Memorial Medical Library (1926), by Walker & Weeks, architects, a chaste marble palazzo. Across the street rises famed Severance Hall, 1930, also Walker & Weeks, described in the Theaters & Auditoria Section. The classical exterior wraps around a spectacular Art Deco interior. Try to have a look. Move east on Euclid past Thwing Hall (1913) (see Clubs and Societies Section). Across the street at the corner of Abington is the Cleveland Hearing and Speech Center (1966), by Ward and Schneider, unique for its three-story bay windows. Presently you reach the Mary Chisholm Painter Memorial Arch on the left. Pass

Severance Hall's classical portico.

through this delightful arch, built 1904 and designed by Charles F. Schweinfurth, and observe the very commanding Church of the Covenant (1909-1911), Cram, Goodhue & Ferguson, architects, to your right. This elegantly detailed Neo Gothic structure is worth your time to enter.

Pass behind the Church along the lane which borders the center of the Mather College campus of the original Western Reserve University. See the Educational and Historic District Sections for more comment. As the lane meets Ford Drive, look across the street and down Hessler Road, a short block of turn-of-the-century houses and apartments in close, compact grouping. A wooden paved street (Hessler Court) lies beyond if you wish to explore. This enclave was the first historic district designated by Cleveland's Landmarks Commission.

The Triangle development mixes high-rise housing with retail and decked parking.

A short distance south on Ford Drive at Euclid presents the viewer with a major urban complex, The Triangle, in construction 1987-1990 and designed by Monroe Schwartz in an overall consistent theme emphasizing masonry construction from shopping plaza to high-rise apartments.

Just beyond this development is a unique re-use of an abandoned Ford Motor Car Factory (1914), Albert Kahn, architect, now an extension of the Cleveland Institute of Art, remodeled (1980-1984), Christian & Klopper Architects.

Turn north on Ford and cross Bellflower Drive where the Mandel School of Social Sciences is in the construction stage. A James Stewart Polshek and Partners design the building will be completed in late 1990. Just beyond it is one of Cleveland's most interesting adaptive uses – Glidden House, a bed and breakfast combining a (1910) city mansion with a new hotel wing of compatible design by Keeva Kekst & Associates, completed 1989. Note the reconstructed porte-cochere in the garden, now a gazebo.

To your left is the striking hulk of the Gund School of Law (1972), Skidmore Owings and Merrill, architects. This non-classical structure of strongly articulated windows and recessed openings holds down an important visual bastion on the curving East Boulevard you have entered. To the left and within the large Wade Oval park is the low-key Garden Center of Cleveland (1965) by Geoffrey Platt, a quietly contemporary structure faced with rustic stone and surrounded by noteworthy landscaping.

The Gund School of Law at Case Western Reserve University.

Walking north around the park on East Blvd. to Hazel Drive, you will pass the Cleveland Institute of Music on the right. Built (1961) and designed by Garfield, Harris, Robinson & Schafer, the Brasilia-like structure also dominates the roadway. Turn east on Hazel and pass by (on the left) the elegant stone and stucco townhouse of Mrs. John Hay (1910), architect Abram Garfield. This marks the east end of the sprawling Western Reserve Historical Society. Walk on to Magnolia Drive and make a short turn to the right to observe the one-time Edward Burke Residence (1910), J. Milton Dyer, architect, now Cleveland Music School Settlement. Double back on Magnolia Drive and note the combination of residential and institutional uses each of the street's notable set of original city villas has become. Interrupting them is the new (1984) library wing of the Western Reserve Historical Society by Kaplan/Curtis, Architects. The surprisingly ornamental window of the otherwise stark masonry mass of the building is the former entrance of the Cuyahoga Building, an 1893 architectural feature by D. H. Burnham & Company, salvaged from the site of today's BP America Tower at Public Square. Continue around the block on E. 108th Street back to East Blvd. and return to the main entrance of the prestigious Historical Society, a gathering of buildings comprising one of the nation's oldest private historical institutions. The Mrs. Leonard C. Hanna mansion (1918), by Walker and Gillette is the centerpiece of the whole and offers distinguished interiors, as does the Hay mansion mentioned earlier.

Turn back to E. 108th Street and look right to the huge Veterans Hospital whose original bulk (1961), by Dalton-Dalton & Associates with Smith, Hinchman & Grylls Associates, Inc., has been recently (1989) expanded streetward by van Dijk, Johnson & Partners in a continuing contemporary mode. Walking along the Oval, one arrives at the Cleveland Museum of Natural History, a substantial structure initially erected in 1955 to the design of Garfield, Harris, Robinson & Schafer and added to in 1970, Flynn, Dalton, van Dijk & Associates, and in 1990, Richard H. Kaplan, architects.

*The Museum of
Natural History*

Continuing around the Oval, walk to the main north entrance
of the Cleveland Museum of Art, passing by the stoical stone
sculpture of Isamu Noguchi and under the dramatic canopy of the
Museum's 1971 addition by Marcel Breuer and Hamilton P. Smith.
The original building (1916) was the white marble, Neo Classical
temple facing the lagoon. This elegant beginning has had three
distinct additions (see Section 1). If possible pass on through the
Museum and appreciate its great size and auspicious content. If
closed, move around to the south side and view the Wade Park
Lagoon as a centerpiece of the picturesque park designed by the
Olmsted Brothers, at its peak in April. Walk around the west side
of the pond and glance through the trees across Martin Luther
King Drive at the Chinese Cultural Garden, an oriental temple
platform in white masonry. Looming above is the large, one-time
Wade Park Manor (now Judson Manor), a 1923 residential
apartment by George B. Post & Sons, and now a retirement home.
And, visible beyond is the striking dome of the Temple (1924),
Charles R. Greco, architect.

Closer to the Lagoon is the towering spire of the Epworth-Euclid
United Methodist Church (1928), a dominating piece designed by
Bertram Goodhue and completed by Walker & Weeks, culminating in a copper dome and spire. The granite-clad structure is a
modernized version of late 1920's gothic revivalism.

Walk around the south end of the Lagoon and back up to the
front of Severance Hall, which faces the corner of Euclid Avenue
and East Blvd. Across the street on the Case campus is one of the
city's most exquisite churches, Amasa Stone Chapel, a 1911 piece
by Henry Vaughan, done in the perpendicular Gothic mode (See
Churches). Around the corner on Adelbert is the starting point; the
tour is complete.

Robert C. Gaede, FAIA

*Chinese Cultural
Gardens*

Heights Driving Tour

Shaker Square

Cleveland's unique topography is dominated by rivers and streams running south to north into Lake Erie, each with distinct and steep-sided valleys, and an escarpment of land to the east and southeast representing the edge of the Appalachian plateau. This rise gave land developers a ready cause to name a number of suburbs with additive modifier "heights". Several of the communities so named came to be laid out imaginatively and attracted superior housing and institutions. To some extent the term "heights" became synonymous with an idealized living environment. Shaker Heights and its neighbor, Cleveland Heights may be the chief examples of this phenomenon. Thus, this driving tour is organized to reveal the special qualities of these major suburbs, largely laid out and built up in the period 1910-1940 with some post World War II infill to complete the land usage.

Most visitors to Cleveland will be confronted early-on with some mention of the "Heights". Most Clevelanders acknowledge that our version of the romantic dormitory suburb has few equals in the U.S. for extent, scale and quality of the architecture and landscaping. Largely an East Side happening, the "Heights" has its parallel in Lakewood and Rocky River, west side residential bastions for which a second driving tour is incorporated in this volume.

Starting the Heights Tour at celebrated Shaker Square (which is actually within Cleveland's boundaries), the Colony Theatre, notable for its Art Moderne interior may be considered as point zero. Moving east around the Square (actually, an octagonal plan), pick up Shaker Blvd. and travel east a long block to Coventry Road. This distinctive block has an assemblage of large apartment houses on both sides, that on the left being the handsomely conceived Moreland Courts group (1923-1928). By turning south on Coventry, a large and finely-detailed Neo-Georgian church, Plymouth Congregational (1924), Charles Schneider, Architect, appears on the right. Moving south on Warrington Road, turn left on South Woodland. In a short distance Woodbury School (1919), appears over a great lawn, facing a portion of the City of Shaker Heights Southerly Park. Turn right at the next intersection (Parkland) and pass the Shaker Board of Education Building on the right. Completing a campus of educational buildings are the High School and Onaway Elementary School, (1923),

A Shaker Heights vista.

Charles W. Bates, Architect. The whole ensemble is carried out in a Georgian Revival format, one of the favored Shaker Heights traditional forms.

Following Parkland eastward, observe the variety of historic derivatives expressed by the residences. Turn right on Lee Road (south) and proceed three blocks to find the Shaker Heights City Hall (1930), Charles Schneider, Architect, on your right. As you cross Van Aken Blvd. which straddles the "Rapid" tracks, note the Kingsbury Building (1926), by Walker & Weeks, a medieval revival commercial and residential structure in stone, brick and stucco with lively half-timbering. Proceed another block to Chagrin Blvd. Then turn left (east) and proceed through the city's main shopping area undergoing a massive reshaping on the north side of the street. Proceed east on Chagrin Blvd. until the busy intersection of Warrensville Center Road and Northfield Road is reached. Cross the intersection and proceed one block to Helen Road to make a left turn. Note before the turn the tall, modern office building on the right. This is Tower East (1968) by the TAC group and Walter Gropius and expresses the International Style with wall surfacing clearly detailed to mitigate direct sunlight. Proceed north on Helen one block to Farnsleigh Road and turn left proceeding through Warrensville Center Road. The imposing Wren-like tower on your left is Christ Church Episcopal (1959), Copper, Wade and Associates, Architects.

Continue to Van Aken Blvd. and move west between a phalanx of mid-rise apartment houses, largely built in the 1950's and 60's and expressed in a safe Neo-Georgian mode. Beyond the charming remnant of a Van Sweringen Rapid stop shelter, turn right back onto Parkland and follow a gentle curve to the intersection with Torrington Road. Turn onto Torrington, which briefly divides the prestigious Shaker Heights Country Club, and rise up to South Woodland. Take South Woodland past a selection of its notable residential examples to the first cross street, Courtland Blvd. Turn left on Courtland and proceed a long block to Shaker Blvd. Typical Shaker Heights romantic villas line up in what seems, at times, to be an endless demonstration of the romantic stylistic revivals. Turn right on to Shaker Blvd.

Tower East

At Warrensville Center turn left across the "Rapid" bridge, but look ahead on Shaker before the turn to note the sprawling Byron Junior High (now Middle School), (1960) Perkins & Will with Michael Kane, Architects. This building helped to break the resistance in Shaker Heights to "modern".

Over the bridge, a half-right turn onto Claythorne focuses your attention on the soaring spire of University School (1926), Walker & Weeks, Architects. This Georgian campanile identifies one of Shaker's several prep schools each with a small campus of its own. Driving north on Claythorne past the school dog-leg back to Fairmount Circle, one of a number of traffic roundabouts identifying major intersections in the "Heights". As you pass the small shopping group on the right, look to the distance and observe the main building cluster of John Carroll University, dominated by its Neo-Gothic Grasselli Tower (1935), by Philip L. Small, Architect. Drive around the Circle until Fairmount Blvd. (going west) is reached. Drive to the Eaton Road crossing and as you turn left, note the enormous limestone structure and soaring Gothic tower of First Baptist Church (1929), Walker & Weeks, Architects.

Continue on Eaton to Shelburne. At Shelburne turn left (east) to Courtland Boulevard. Drive south on Courtland Blvd, past another of Shaker's private schools, Hathaway Brown, which appears on the left. This large Tudor Revival structure with broad play fields was con- structed 1927 from the designs by Walker & Weeks. An addition of a Gallery (1970) and Gymnasium (1980) by Dyer and Watson is a contemporary interpretation of the major building.

University School Tower

Turning west at South Park Blvd., one passes through an area of exceptional residences of the period 1915-1960. In the first block are several by Clarence Mack, Cleveland's noted builder, designer and furnisher. The largest of the group, the one-time Van Sweringen residence (1924) an elongated Tudor Revival by Philip L. Small, Architect, occurs where South Park begins to border Horseshoe Lake. At 16740 is the Shaker Historical Society and Museum, a converted residence. Turn north onto Lee Road and enter Cleveland Heights. Proceed several blocks to come upon the Church of the Saviour on the right at 2531 Lee. This large and visually striking stone-faced building was built (1929), John W. C. Corbusier, Architect, with additions in 1950 and 1958 by Travis Gower Walsh.

Continue north on Lee Road through the Cedar-Lee Shopping Center to Superior Road where you turn right and follow the curving street bounding the Cain Park outdoor park and theater, revised and enhanced by van Dijk, Johnson & Partners in 1988.

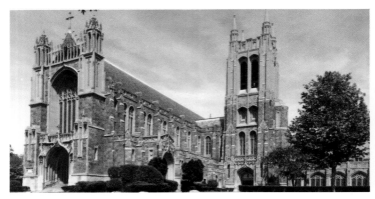

Church of the Saviour

At the end of the Park at Taylor Road, turn left and drive north to the first of several openings into Severance Center, a large shopping mall built (1963) upon the grounds of the John L. Severance estate, which featured a grand residence, now gone. The area was acquired in the early 1960's for development and a long discussion ensued as to the best use. Ultimately, the shopping mall and a ring road connecting a variety of commercial-residential uses was the choice. The new city hall built (1986), Dickson & Dickson, Architects, was also fitted to the ring road.

Leave the Severance Center site on the north (Mayfield Road) and turn left toward Taylor Road. On the right are two structures of note: The Jewish Community Center (1960) designed by Braverman & Halperin with George B. Mayer. This structure houses an active cultural program for the Heights area. At the corner is a noteworthy fire station (1982), architects, Koster & Holzheimer. Continuing west on Mayfield one observes Sts. Constantine and Helen Greek Orthodox Cathedral (1957), (See Section on Churches). Along the way, one passes the site of Park Synagogue (1950) just out of sight. This unique design by the internationally recognized Eric Mendelsohn was both modern and traditional. As the intersection of Mayfield with Lee Road approaches, the substantial masonry edifice of the one-time Temple on the Heights (1928), architect Charles Greco, now adapted to office and cultural center uses, appears on the left under its new name, the CIVIC.

Cain Park's open air theater.

At the northeast corner of the Lee Road intersection is one of Cleveland's most richly textured and articulated low-rise office buildings, the Heights Rockefeller Building (1930) by architect Andrew Jackson Thomas. Within the structure is a notable interior, that of the Ameritrust Bank, one of a number of distinctive branches put in place by the (then) Cleveland Trust Co. during the late 1920's. This interior was renewed and restored (1977) by Barnes-Neiswander.

Progressing westward on Mayfield Road one crosses Superior Road. Directly on the north side is an architectural anomaly – an historic building fragment (the entrance to the earlier City Hall) surrounded by a contemporary glazed auto showroom. This unique conjunction was built in 1986 to the designs of Orvis-Pentilla, architects. Continue westward on Mayfield to Coventry Road, an intensively active neighborhood of shops and apartments. Turn left on Coventry and drive south past such architecturally rich residential streets as Edgehill, East Overlook and Berkshire to Cedar Road. On the left is the commanding facade of the very classical St. Ann's Roman Catholic Church (1945-1952), architects Walker & Weeks and Horn & Rhinehart. A few blocks further south at Fairmount Blvd. is the Gothic Revival cluster of St. Paul's Church (1927-1929) by Walker & Weeks, with additions (1951) by J. Byers Hays and (1990) by Collins, Rimer and Gordon. Both churches provide landmark towers above the tree line of the Heights.

On the northeast corner of the inter-section is Fairmount Presbyterian Church, a three-component group of very different styling yet all within an English Tudor Revival calling. The Nave structure (1941) by Walker & Weeks, expanded on the original stucco and wood building (1924) by Bloodgood Tuttle.

St. Paul's Church tower is a familiar Heights landmark.

At this point Fairmount Boulevard extends both east and west and presents the visitor with as monumental an assemblage of fine eclectic houses as anywhere in the city. The park-like center strip once contained an inter-urban rail line in the manner of nearby Shaker Boulevard. Continue south on Coventry Road to North Park Blvd. and turn right following the quietly curving avenue to Harcourt Drive where a right turn into the Chestnut Hills residential quarter (see Neighborhoods) will offer several blocks of outstanding early 20th century residences. Exit the area on the north and turn right on Cedar Road. Within the architecturally lively shopping area (Cedar-Fairmount) turn left on Surrey Road crossing Euclid Heights Blvd. and continuing as Kenilworth Road.

This residential area matches that of Chestnut Hills in many respects. Kenilworth terminates at Mayfield at the upper entrance to Lake View Cemetery which is here accessible until closing time. Just within the gate is the new Mausoleum (1990) Harley, Ellington, Pierce & Yee of Southfield, Michigan, a dramatic design in rough-faced granite and glass of non-classical nature yet supremely symmetrical in plan. The tour ends here, but with the visitor at the top of magnificent Lake View Cemetery as a choice for continuation.

Robert C. Gaede, FAIA

Mausoleum at Lake View Cemetery.

Lakewood–Gold Coast Driving Tour

Downtown Lakewood

As the swiftly developing industrial city of Cleveland spilled outward into the grid of original townships which surrounded it, smaller communities became the loci from which major suburbs would materialize. To the west was Lakewood, founded in 1819, but not incorporated as a village until 1903 and a city in 1911. In a surge of development 1900-1930, Lakewood rose to 70,000 in population, largest in Cleveland's metropolitan area until surpassed in 1960 by Parma. Now, among the inner ring of mature suburbs, Lakewood's population has subsided but has maintained a considerable assemblage of comfortable houses, numerous apartment buildings, and a seasoning of public buildings and churches. Lakewood's business properties almost exclusively front on Detroit and Madison Avenues. Linear as these are, there is a reasonably "downtown" district in the vicinity of Detroit Avenue and Warren Road.

Lakewood's other urban feature is the "Gold Coast". The development along the lakefront from W. 117th Street on the east to Nicholson Avenue on the west, a narrow zone of high rise apartments fronting Edgewater Drive and a portion of Lake Avenue. At the far west end, above the curving course of Rocky River, is the city's most prestigious residential quarter with curved streets and large romantic revivals of the familiar eclectic tastes of the early 20th Century.

The tour will try to offer the architectural buff a taste of Lakewood's several characteristic faces. Beginning at the parking lot where West Blvd. meets the lakeshore (yet in Cleveland), the path leads west along Edgewater Drive past substantial houses and vacant parcels suggesting some recent losses of one-time villas. A short loop around Harborview Drive passes (at 11320) an all-terra cotta residence, (1915), William S. Lougee, Architect, one of only two in the Metro area. Shortly the city's boundary is reached and the lake side of the street is solidly filled up with 10 to 20-story balconied apartments from the Post World War II era except the Lake Shore Apartment Hotel (1929) (now Lake Shore Towers) 12506 Edgewater Drive, Frank W. Bail, architect. Tallest of the group is Winton Place, a 30-story gray and white brick tower (1963) by Loebl, Schlossman & Bennett.

High rises along the Gold Coast.

At the corner of Lake and Nicholson Avenue are two of the most unique houses in Lakewood. A frame Victorian occupies the northeast corner while a stuccoed Beaux Art design (1910) built by George Morse and surrounded by a richly-detailed iron fence, occupies the southwest. Just west of Whippoorwill are grouped several fine residences by Clarence Mack, noted for their refined classic proportions and detailing.

Move west on Lake Avenue and notice at 13900 one of the nation's most unique service stations, designed to vanish from the sight of passersby and neighbors. An earlier station, fully visible, was deemed too incompatible with the strictly residential setting, so that its successor was obliged to shift rearward and below natural grade to remain in place but not break the continuity of landscaped front yards. Only a discreet sign announces its presence.

The work of Clarence Mack is typically a precise Georgian Revival.

At Lakewood Park may be found the city's Oldest Stone House Museum, relocated to this site in 1952. Built in 1838 it is the home and museum of the Lakewood Historical Society. Beyond the Park 1920's low-rise apartments mingle with residences in comfortable conjunction, typical of other areas of the city. Farther west Lake Avenue curves into Clifton Park, an enclave of larger suburban residences of the Georgian and Tudor Revival styles of the early 20th Century. A looping path is indicated which returns eastward to the junction of Clifton Blvd. and West Clifton Blvd., actually a north-south street.

A Clifton Park vista.

Drive south on West Clifton to its intersection with Detroit Avenue. Here are two of Lakewood's many churches of distinction. Lakewood Congregational (1913), W.H. Nicklas, architect, with 1954 additions by Carr and Cunningham, is on the northeast corner and St. Peter's Episcopal (1926), J.W. Chrisford, architect, is on the southeast. The former is a large frame building with Georgian Portico; the latter a stone structure with strong resemblance to an English village parish church. The visual contrast is another testimonial to our diversity of form via our diversity of heritage.

Moving south on West Clifton to its terminus at Riverside, one sees the steep declivity of the Rocky River valley – the West Side's most distinctive natural feature. Take Riverside to Indianola Avenue and turn left onto Hilliard Road and continue east to Madison Avenue. The mix of commercial, residential and institutional is here very typical of Lakewood's rapid growth in the 'teens and 'twenties.

Take Madison east to Warren Road, a major north-south avenue, and turn left (north). Proceed to Detroit Avenue where the symbolic center of Lakewood is located. Observe the excellence of signage and building facades in the commercial area along the Detroit and Madison Avenues, the product of the city's aggressive Storefront Renovation Program begun in 1979.

Move east on Detroit to Lakewood Center North, a 15-story precast concrete structure serving as a beacon at night by way of its illuminated side walls. Built in 1974, the architect was Theodore Badowski. On the right are the buildings comprising Lakewood Hospital, whose central atrium was part of a major renovation (1985) by Braun & Spice, Inc. Moving further east past the multi-building Westerly Apartment cluster, the work of Weinberg and Teare, Detroit Avenue passes a variety of churches and commercial structures typical of the American strip. In about a mile, one will reach Garfield Elementary School (1895), the city's oldest, with City Hall following on the left. To its south are three parallel streets (Clarence, Grace and Cohassett) of distinctive 1890-1910 residences. Of special note is 1558 Grace, a well-preserved Queen Anne house built by the Hackenberg family.

Proceed two blocks and turn left onto Cove Avenue and continue up to Clifton Avenue. Just ahead on the left, is the steeply-pitched roof of the Cove Methodist Church (1970), by John VonGunten, a striking study of the "A"-frame, set on a rustic ashlar base of Berea sandstone. Turn east on Clifton Avenue which offers drivers an unusual width (8-lanes) accounted for by the split, tree-lawn-located car tracks which once dominated the street. Turn left (north) on W. 117th St. one block to Edgewater Drive and then right, observing the delightfully proportioned Fifth Church of Christ Scientist on the corner. This (1926) structure by Frank W. Bail, is dominated by an octagonal hall and is clad in vari-colored sandstone.

Continue east on Edgewater to W. 104th Street. Turn left and go to Cliff Terrace, a short street set on a cliff's edge. From here the view east across the water is often spectacular. Continue a short distance to the starting point of the tour.

Robert C. Gaede, FAIA

A Lakewood Queen Anne on Grace Avenue.

Glossary of Terms

ASHLAR Stone that has been cut and squared and laid in regular courses on a building facade; generally rough-hewn as opposed to smooth-dressed.

BALUSTER One of a series of short vertical members used to support a rail.

BALUSTRADE A railing running along the edge of a porch, stairway, etc., consisting of balusters and a top rail.

BARREL VAULT An arch projected three-dimensionally; a ceiling or roof consisting of a semi-cylindrical form. (aka **tunnel vault**)

CHURCH (GOTHIC)
    APSE A semi-circular or polygonal projection at the rear of a church, containing the chancel.
    CHANCEL The sanctuary area.
    FLECHE A spire, usually found at the intersection of nave and transept.
    LANCET WINDOW A very narrow window with a pointed arch.
    NARTHEX The central interior entrance portico.
    NAVE The central aisle section.
    REREDOS An ornamental panel or screen behind an altar.
    TRANSEPT In a cruciform plan, the section which crosses the nave at a right angle.

CLERESTORY The windowed upper walls of a building above the aisle roofs; windows set high in a high-ceilinged room.

COLONNADE A series of columns.

CORNICE The projecting molding or crowning decoration at the top of a wall or at the roof line; the uppermost part of a Classical entablature.

CURTAIN WALL In steel frame construction, the exterior, non-load bearing "skin" of a building hung from the skeleton frame, referred to especially when glass and metal or stone elements create a continuous surface plane.

DENTIL A small, square, tooth-like block which appears in a tightly-spaced row beneath a cornice or an eave.

DORMER WINDOW A small window projecting from a sloping attic roof.

EAVE The outer and lower edges of an overhanging roof.

ENTABLATURE In Classical architecture, the horizontal elements (architrave, frieze, and cornice) supported by columns.

FACADE The exterior surface of a building; generally the front, finished, or main side or sides.

Glossary of Terms *continued*

FRIEZE The horizontal panel, often decorated, running below the eaves of a building; in Classical architecture, the part of the entablature below the cornice.

GABLE The triangular portion at the end of a building formed by the slope of the roof.

HIPPED ROOF A roof that slopes to a common ridge on all sides.

KEYSTONE The central wedge-shaped member of a masonry arch.

MANSARD A roof with an extremely steep slope and a flat top, usually clad with slate and pierced by dormers.

ORDER In Classical architecture, the three forms of column and entablature: Doric, Ionic, and Corinthian.

PALLADIAN WINDOW An arched window opening within twin pilasters, flanked by flat-headed openings.

PEDIMENT The space within the triangular gable above a door, window, or portico.

PILASTER A [flat,] non-supporting, ornamental column.

PORTICO A colonnaded entrance to a building.

QUOINS Alternating long and short blocks of masonry forming and accentuating the outside corner of a building.

RUSTICATED Cut stones with strongly emphasized recessed joints and roughly textured faces, usually found on the ground story of a building.

SPANDREL The panel between the window lintels of one story and the sills of the story above.

TERRA COTTA A hard, baked clay often used for commercial facades, noted for its expressive decorative qualities.

WINDOW
    LINTEL The horizontal structural element above the window, often given ornamentation.
    MULLION A vertical, structural member between two or more windows.
    MUNTIN The thin member that separates the panes of the window.
    SASH The framework of a window.
    SILL The horizontal, often projecting, element at the bottom of the window.

Elizabeth L. Waters

Index of Subjects

C continued

D

E

E continued

F

21.6

Index to Architects, Artists, Firms, and Persons

C continued

Cuyahoga Co. Commissioners, 4.1

D

Daley, Leo A., 2.10
Dalton & Dalton, 2.5, 19.9, 19.23
Dalton, Dalton & Little, 10.7, 19.4
Dalton-Dalton-Little-Newport, 14.4
Dalton-Dalton-Newport, 8.9, 8.12, 12.2, 19.7, 19.9
Dalton, vanDijk, Johnson, 1.3, 6.4, 8.9, 10.5, 12.2, 12.3, 16.2, 19.1, 19.3, 19.4
Daniels, Howard, 3.6
Daugherty, James, 4.2, 16.8
Davis, David E., 1.6, 3.11
Dercum & Beer, 14
Dewald, Ernest L., 10.9
Diaquila, Samuel V., 20
Dickson & Dickson, 20.4
diNardo, Antonio, 14/ 14.3
Dorsky, William, 14.6, 19.5
Doyle, Alexander, 3.1
Druiding, Adolph, 11.6, 18.4
Dunham, Rufus and Jane, 1.5
Dunn, D., 10.10
Dunn, William, 26/ 11.7
Dyer, J. Milton, 26, 32/ 2.4, 7.1, 7.2, 9.7, 11.2, 13.2, 13.3, 17.2, 17.5, 18.5, 18.7, 19.1, 19.9, 19.23
Dyer & Watson, 20.3

E

Eberson, John, 4.2, 18.7
Eisenmann, John, 31/ 5.1, 9.2, 18.5, 19.10
Eldredge, Hezekiah, 11.11, 19.18
Ellerbe Co., 12.1

F

Farnum, George, 18.6
F.C.L. Assoc., 9.8
Ferguson, W.S., 16.5
Ferro Corp., 11.4
Fischer-Jirouch, 19.10
Fish, F. Stillman, 11.5
Fleischman, Richard, 2.13, 10.9
Flynn, Dalton & vanDijk, 15/ 8.6, 19.23
Forest City Engineering, 19.14
Fredericks, Marshall, 24/ 3.4
French, Daniel Chester, 24/ 2.3, 3.8, 3.12
Friedlander, Leo, 11.2
Fugman, Godfrey, 10.7
Fuller, Sadao & Zung, 2.10
Fullerton, Harold O., 14.3

G

Gaede, Robert C., 1.5, 1.6
Gaede Serne Zofcin, 1.4, 3.2, 9.7, 19.15

G continued

Gaines, Ervin J., 1.5
Galbreath, John, 8.14, 8.17
Garfield, Abram, 1.2, 12.4, 15.2, 15.3, 17.2, 19.23
Garfield, Harris, Robinson & Schafer, 17.3, 19.23
Garfield, Harris, Schafer, Flynn & Williams, 4.5, 17.3
Garfield, James A. (Pres.), 3.1, 17.1, 17.2
Garfield, Stanley-Brown, Harris & Robinson, 17.2
Georgescu, Haralamb, 11.4
Ginther, William P., 28
Glover, Smith, Bode Inc., 8.18
Goodhue, Bertram, 11.1, 17.5, 18.7, 19.24
Goodwillie, Frank, 13.1
Gould Associates, 2.2
Graham, Anderson, Probst & White, 18, 23, 31/ 5.2, 6.4, 8.1, 8.8, 16.2, 16.3, 16.5, 17.1, 18.7, 19.1, 19.12
Graham, Burnham & Co., 23/ 9.8
Graham, Edward T.P., 11.5, 11.11
Graham, J., 10.10
Gray, A. Donald, 2.13, 3.5, 14.3
Greco, Charles R., 11.10, 19.24, 20.4
Green, Alfred, 19.19
Griffith, F.M., 2.8
Gropius, Walter, 8.12, 20.2
Group Plan Commission (Committee), 24/ 3.4, 17.1, 17.5
Gudin, I. 10.5
Guerin, Jules, 6.4

H

Hackenberg (Harvey) Family, 20.9
Halprin, Lawrence, 19.15
Hamilton, James G.C., 24/ 3.9
Hammond, George, 13
Hanna, Dan, Sr., 25
Hanna, Marcus A., 3.7, 3.11, 17.4
Hardy, Holzman, Pfeiffer, 19.10
Harley, Ellington, Pierce & Yee, 20.6
Harris, Alfred W., 14.5
Harrison & Abramowitz, 8.14, 18.7, 19.7
Hay, Mrs. John, 11.12
Hays, J. Byers, 20.5
Hays & Ruth, 1.3
Heard, Charles, 7.3, 11.8, 18.3, 18.4
Heard & Porter, 16.6, 19.13
Heery-Ramco-Praeger, 13.4
Hemni Associates, 14.3
Hering, Henry, 3.7, 16.3, 19.10
Hisaka, Don M., 15/ 7.5, 10.1, 10.6, 10.10, 19.4
H.O.K. Architects (Hellmuth, Obata & Kassabaum), 5.2, 8.3, 14.4, 19.13
Hopkinson, Charles, 3.2, 3.7, 19.18

Photographers' Credits

Jennie Jones: 11 (Cleveland skyline), 12 (Dunham Tavern), 19 (Shaker Heights), 30 (The Arcade), 31 (Society National Bank), 34 (Engineer's Building), 1.4 (Dunham Tavern – interior), 2.5 (City Hall – interior), 2.7 (Old Main Post Office), 6.2 (Society National Bank), 6.2 (Society National Bank – interior), 6.4 (Huntington Bank – interior), 8.1 (Terminal Tower complex), 9.2 (The Arcade – interior), 9.4 (Halle Bros. – interior), 11.8 (Old Stone Church), 14.3 (Belgian Village), 14.5 (Row Houses – Prospect), 16.1 (Society Bank Lamp), 16.2 (Ameritrust lighting fixtures), 16.5 (May Co. Clock), 16.6 (terra cotta starburst), 16.7 (cast-iron facade, Rockefeller Bldg.), 16.8 (front door – Schweinfurth House), 16.9 (Energy in Repose), 19.18 (Carnegie West Library), 20.2 (Shaker Heights).

David Thum: 11 (Terminal Tower), 16 (East Blvd. Apts.), 1.1 (Cleveland Public Library), 1.3 (Cleveland Museum of Art), 2.1 (Cuyahoga County Courthouse), 2.3 (Old Federal Building), 2.6 (Cleveland Board of Education), 3.3 (Soldiers & Sailors Monument), 3.5 (Wade Memorial Chapel), 3.7 (Lake View Cemetery), 3.8 (Hope Memorial Bridge Pylon), 3.9 (Portal – Justice Center), 3.12 (standing cornice sculptures), 5.1 (Galleria), 6.1 (National City Bank – interior), 6.3 (Ameritrust), 6.3 (Ameritrust – interior), 7.2 (Tavern Club), 7.4 (Cleveland Club), 7.5 (Fenn Tower), 9.5 (Western Reserve Bldg.), 10.4 (Mather Mansion), 11.1 (Epworth-Euclid United Methodist), 11.2 (First Church of Christ Scientist), 11.3 (Trinity Cathedral), 11.4 (Park Synagogue), 11.10 (St. Theodosius – exterior), 11.10 (The Temple), 11.12 (Amasa Stone Chapel), 13.2 (Brown Hoisting Machinery Co.), 13.3 (Richman Bros.), 13.4 (Warner & Swasey), 18.1 (Arcade entrance), 18.3 (Burgess Block), 18.7 (U.S. Coast Guard Station), 19.1 (Ameritrust), 19.4 (CSU Natatorium), 19.6 (Galleria), 19.9 (New Federal Bldg.), 19.12 (East 4th Street), 20.5 (St. Paul's Church), 20.7 (Downtown Lakewood).

William Schuemann: 35 (BP America Bldg.), 36 (One Cleveland Center), 37 (Ohio Bell Erieview), 2.4 (Justice Center), 3.1 (Garfield Monument), 3.2 (Garfield Monument – interior), 3.4 (Hanna Fountains), 5.2 (Landmark Office Towers), 7.1 (University Club), 7.3 (Hermit Club), 7.4 (Union Club), 8.3 (BP America Building), 8.4 (BP America – atrium), 8.5 (National City Center), 8.6 (Ameritrust Tower), 8.7 (Eaton Center), 8.8 (Huntington Bldg.), 8.9 (Ohio Bell – Erieview), 8.10 (Hanna Bldg.), 8.11 (Standard Bldg.), 8.12 (Tower East), 9.4 (Rose Bldg.), 9.6 (First Federal), 11.6 (St. Joseph's), 12.1 (Cleveland Clinic complex), 12.2 (Clinic Mall & Skyway), 14.1 (Winton Place), 18.4 (University Club), 19.6 (Eaton Center), 19.11 (Ohio Bell – Huron), 19.12 (Landmark Office Towers), 19.13 (Standard Building), 19.14 (Justice Center).

Photographers' Credits *continued*

Eric Hanson: 13 (Gold Coast), 28 (Little Italy), 1.2 (Western Reserve Historical Society Museum complex), 3.6 (Woodland Cemetery), 3.9 (Triple "L" Excentric Gyratory III), 4.1 (State Theater Lobby), 4.2 (Palace Theater stage), 8.13 (North Point Tower), 8.17 (One Cleveland Center), 9.1 (Galleria at Erieview), 9.3 (Colonial Arcade – interior), 14.4 (Reserve Square), 19.15 (Hoyt Block), 19.15 (820 Bldg.), 19.18 (Franklin Circle), 19.19 (Market Sq. Ohio City), 19.24 (Chinese Cultural Gardens), 20.2 (Tower East), 20.4 (Church of the Saviour), 20.4 (Cain Park Theater).

Al Teufen: 1.6 (Fleet Branch Library), 2.11 (Cleveland Convention Center), 4.3 (Public Auditorium), 4.4 (Cleveland Playhouse Group), 7.5 (Thwing Hall), 10.2 (Adelbert Hall), 10.6 (Rhodes Tower), 10.6 (University Center), 10.7 (Marting Hall), 12.5 (Southwest General), 13.1 (Nela Park), 15.1 (Glidden House), 15.2 (Clifton Park), 15.2 (Victorian House – Lakewood), 15.2 (Clarence Mack House), 18.6 (Mather Mansion), 19.1 (Skyline Downtown East), 19.2 (Prescott Ball & Turben), 19.9 (Skyline Downtown West), 19.10 (Public Auditorium), 19.22 (Triangle), 19.23 (Gund School of Law), 20.8 (Gold Coast), 20.8 (Clarence Mack Houses), 20.9 (Clifton Park), 20.10 (Lakewood Queen Anne).

Thomas Eiben: Cover, 32 (Powerhouse in the Flats), 4.5 (Severance Hall), 6.5 (Federal Reserve Bank – exterior), 10.1 (Thwing Hall), 12.3 (University Hospitals), 15.3 (Gwinn), 19.3 (Jewish Community Federation), 19.5 (Greyhound Bus Station), 19.21 (Severance Hall).

Western Reserve Historical Society Archives:
33 (Central Armory).

Charles Hudson: 2.8 (Fire Station #20), 2.10 (West Side Market).

Case Western Reserve University:
10.3 (John D. Rockefeller Physics Building).

Cleveland Museum of Natural History:
19.24 (Cleveland Museum of Natural History).

Harley, Ellington, Pierce & Yee:
20.6 (Mausoleum).

Section 22

Maps

Walking Tours

Driving Tours

Historic Districts

City of Cleveland

Cuyahoga County

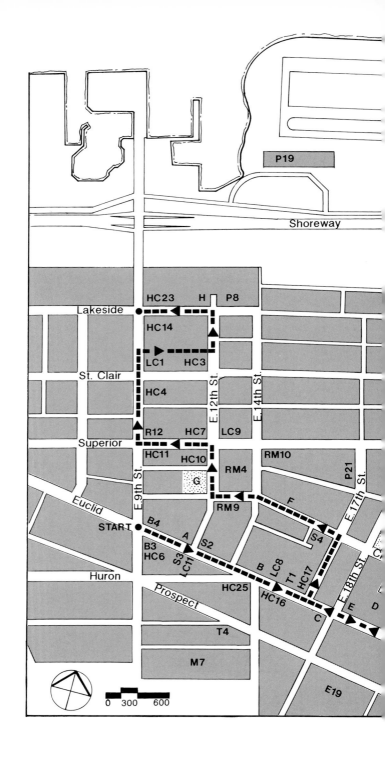

Downtown East

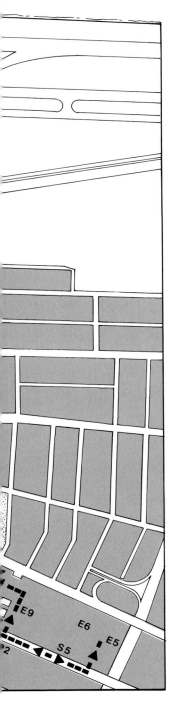

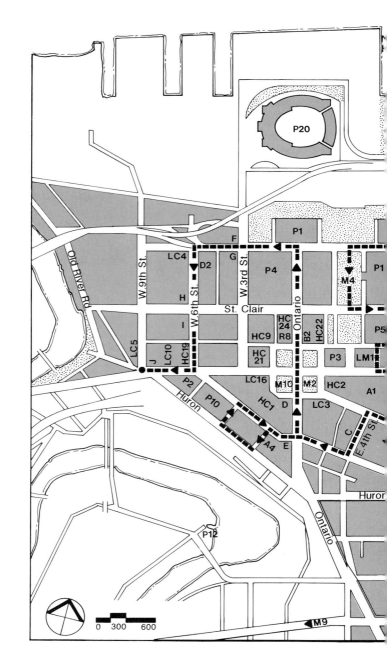

Downtown West

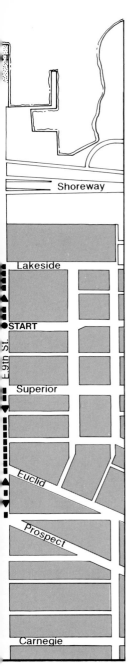

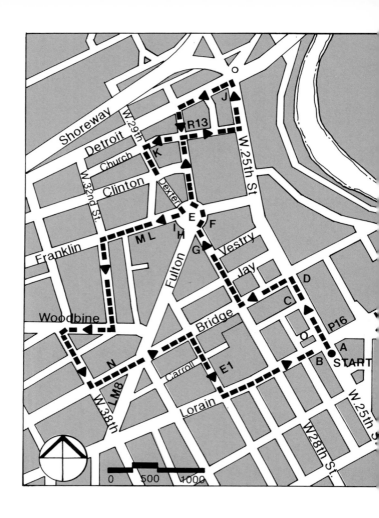

Ohio City Walking Tour

P16	WEST SIDE MARKET
R13	ST. JOHN EPISCOPAL CHURCH
LM8	CARNEGIE WEST BRANCH LIBRARY
E14	ST. IGNATIUS HIGH SCHOOL
M9	LORAIN-CARNEGIE BRIDGE PYLONS
A	MARKET PLAZA SHOPPING CENTER
B	UNITED OFFICE BUILDING
C	MERRILL BLOCK
D	METZNER BLOCK
E	FRANKLIN CIRCLE
F	LUTHERAN MEDICAL CENTER
G	HEYSE BUILDING
H	FRANKLIN CIRCLE CHRISTIAN CHURCH
I	FRANKLIN CIRCLE MASONIC TEMPLE
J	FOREST CITY BANK BUILDING
K	FIREHOUSE #4
L	SANFORD HOUSE
M	RHODES HOUSE
N	ST. PATRICK ROMAN CATHOLIC CHURCH
O	MARKET SQUARE

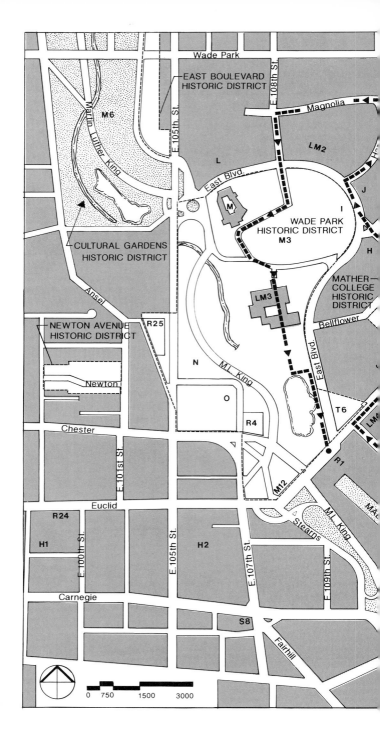

University Circle
Walking Tour

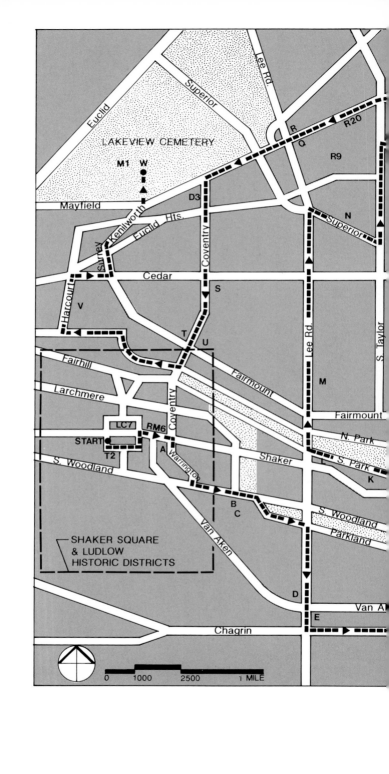

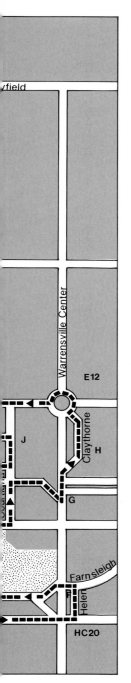

Heights Driving Tour

LC7	SHAKER SQUARE SHOPPING DISTRICT
T2	COLONY THEATRE
RM6	MORELAND COURTS
HC20	TOWER EAST
E12	GRASSELLI TOWER, JOHN CARROLL UNIVERSITY
LC2	SEVERANCE TOWN CENTER
R9	PARK SYNAGOGUE
R20	ST.CONSTANTINE AND HELEN GREEK ORTHODOX CATHEDRAL
M1	JAMES A. GARFIELD MONUMENT, WADE MEMORIAL CHAPEL
M13	DAVID BERGER MEMORIAL MONUMENT
D3	DOBAMA THEATRE
A	PLYMOUTH CHURCH
B	WOODBURY SCHOOL
C	ONAWAY ELEMENTARY SCHOOL
D	SHAKER HEIGHTS CITY HALL
E	KINGSBURY BUILDING
F	CHRIST CHURCH EPISCOPAL
G	MIDDLE SCHOOL
H	UNIVERSITY SCHOOL
I	FIRST BAPTIST CHURCH
J	HATHAWAY BROWN SCHOOL
K	VAN SWERINGEN RESIDENCE
L	SHAKER HISTORICAL SOCIETY MUSEUM
M	CHURCH OF THE SAVIOUR
N	CAIN PARK THEATRE
O	CLEVELAND HEIGHTS CITY HALL
P	JEWISH COMMUNITY CENTER
Q	TEMPLE ON THE HEIGHTS (The Civic)
R	HEIGHTS ROCKEFELLER BUILDING
S	ST. ANN ROMAN CATHOLIC CHURCH
T	ST. PAUL CHURCH
U	FAIRMOUNT PRESBYTERIAN CHURCH
V	CHESTNUT HILLS
W	LAKEVIEW CEMETERY

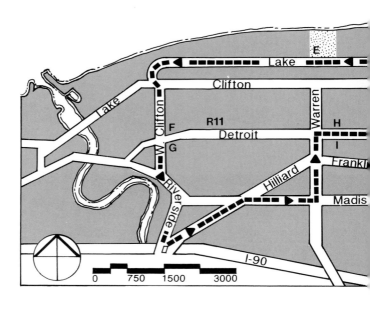

Lakewood/Gold Coast Driving Tour

RM5   WINTON PLACE

LM11 LORAIN LIBRARY
R11   ST. JAMES ROMAN CATHOLIC CHURCH
RM8   OPPMANN TERRACE

A   TERRA COTTA RESIDENCE
B   LAKESHORE TOWERS
C   CLARENCE MACK HOUSES
D   SERVICE STATION
E   OLDEST STONE HOUSE MUSEUM
F   LAKEWOOD CONGREGATIONAL CHURCH
G   ST. PETER EPISCOPAL CHURCH
H   LAKEWOOD CENTER NORTH
I   LAKEWOOD HOSPITAL
J   GARFIELD SCHOOL
K   1558 GRACE
L   COVE METHODIST CHURCH
M   FIFTH CHURCH OF CHRIST SCIENTIST

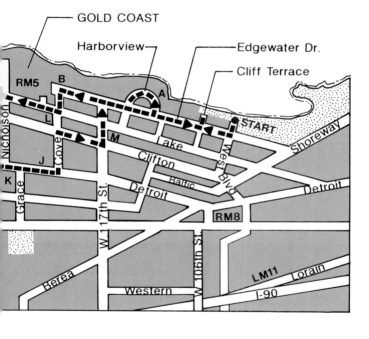

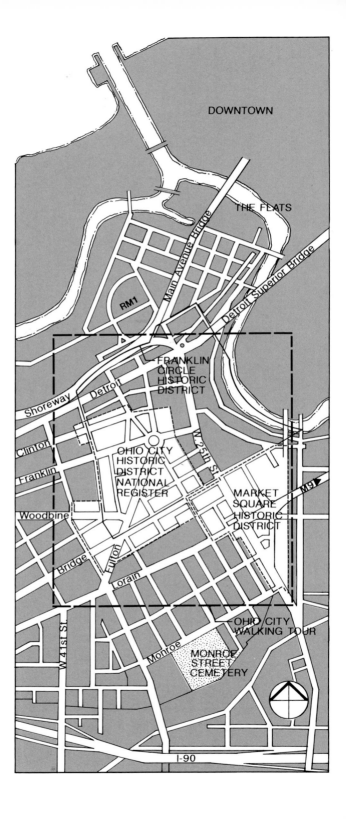

Ohio City Historic Districts

RM1   LAKEVIEW TERRACE & TOWER

MARKET SQUARE HISTORIC DISTRICT
FRANKLIN CIRCLE HISTORIC DISTRICT
OHIO CITY HISTORIC DISTRICT NATIONAL REGISTER

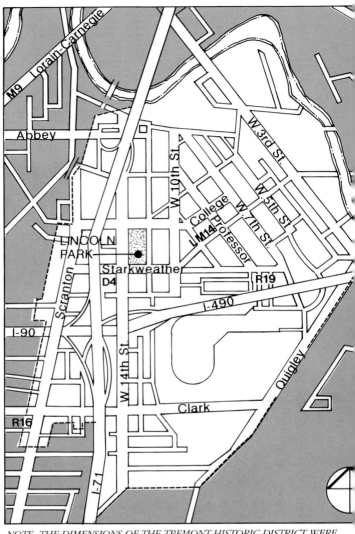

NOTE: THE DIMENSIONS OF THE TREMONT HISTORIC DISTRICT WERE
REDUCED DECEMBER 1990 TO THE AREA AROUND LINCOLN PARK

Tremont Historic District

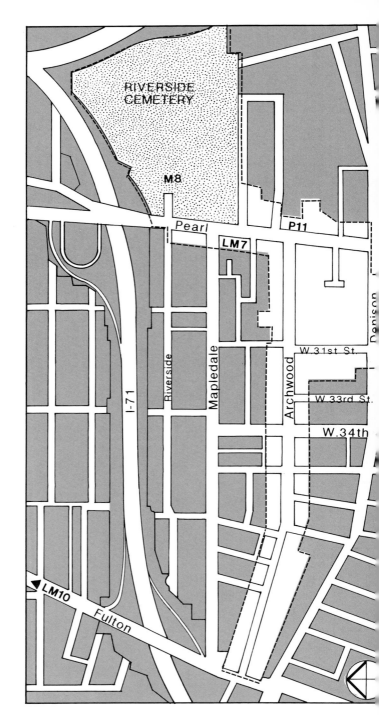

Brooklyn Center Historic District

LM7   BROOKLYN LIBRARY
LM10 FULTON LIBRARY
P11   FIRE STATION #20
M8   RIVERSIDE CEMETERY ADMINISTRATION BUILDING

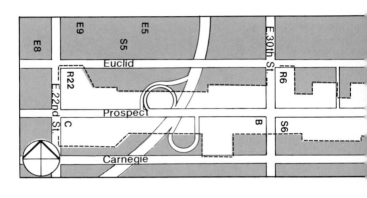

Upper Prospect Historic District

T7	MASONIC TEMPLE AUDITORIUM
S1	TAVERN CLUB
S6	ROWFANT CLUB
S7	UNIVERSITY CLUB
LC13	AMERICAN RED CROSS HEADQUARTERS
LC14	R.TA. COMMUNITY RESPONSIVE CENTER
LC15	PREMIER INDUSTRIAL BUILDING
E8	UNIVERSITY CENTER C.S.U.
E9	MAIN CLASSROOM BUILDING C.S.U.
S5	FENN TOWER
E5	UNIVERSITY HALL C.S.U.
R22	TRINITY CATHEDRAL EPISCOPAL
R6	FIRST UNITED METHODIST CHURCH
RM11	WILLSON HOUSING TOWER
RM7	ROW HOUSES ON PROSPECT AVENUE
A	ST. PAUL'S SHRINE
B	ZION LUTHERAN CHURCH
C	CENTRAL YMCA
D	PROSPECT PARK (Cook Building)
E	FILMLAB SERVICES BUILDING

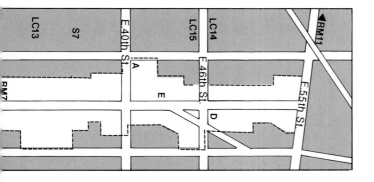

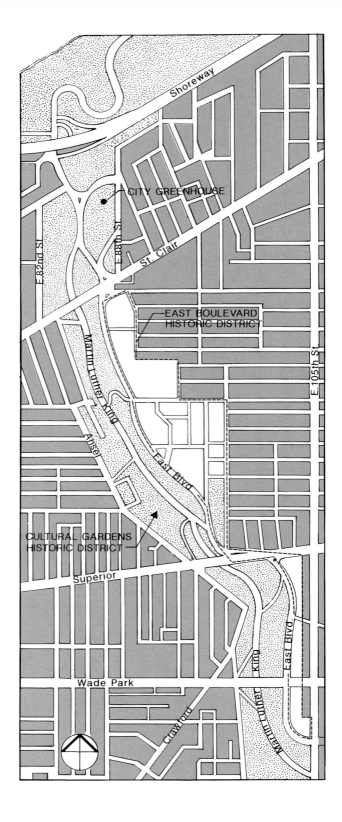

CITY GREENHOUSE

Shoreway

E. 82nd St

E. 88th St

St. Clair

Martin Luther King

Ansel

East Blvd

EAST BOULEVARD
HISTORIC DISTRICT

E. 105th St

CULTURAL GARDENS
HISTORIC DISTRICT

Superior

King

East Blvd

Martin Luther King

Wade Park

Crawford

East Boulevard/Cultural Gardens Historic Districts

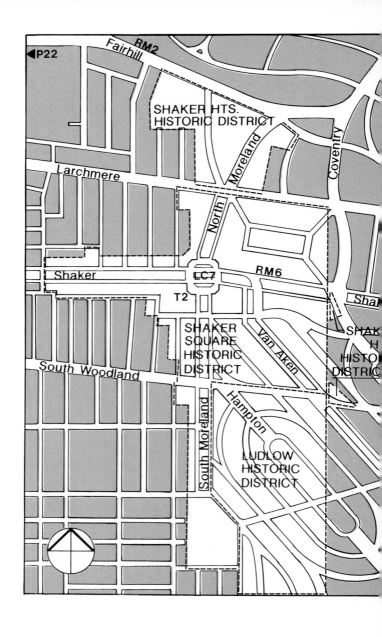